*Joseph Veale a few weeks before his death*

# MANIFOLD GIFTS

## Ignatian Essays on Spirituality

*Joseph Veale SJ*

*Way Books*
*Campion Hall, Oxford*

First published 2006
by Way Books, Campion Hall,
Oxford, OX1 1QS
www.theway.org.uk

*Cover Design: Peter Brook SJ*

*British Library Cataloguing-in-Publication Data*
A catalogue record for this book is available
from the British Library

*ISBN 0 904717 27 5*

Printed and bound by CPI Antony Rowe, Eastbourne

# CONTENTS

# Joseph Veale (1921-2002)

JOSEPH VEALE WAS BORN IN DUBLIN in 1921, the younger of two children. His sister predeceased him. He was brought up in Drumcondra and then in Ranelagh, prophetically just outside the back gate of what was to become Gonzaga College. He said that his parents, devout daily Mass-goers, never seemed to have wanted anything for themselves, and were never elsewhere. He went to the Christian Brothers' School in Synge Street where he was happy, performed well, made lifelong friends and left with a high regard for the Brothers and their teaching.

He entered the Jesuit novitiate in September 1938. When he spoke of his years as a Jesuit student, it was clear that they were not particularly happy. He was an introvert, shy and extremely sensitive; he did not relish the rough and tumble of community life, and was never the easiest person to live or work with in the community. He had little appreciation of the camaraderie that so many of his contemporaries relished. Throughout his life he obtained his social sustenance not from unselected colleagues but from his chosen friends, with many of whom he formed the strongest of bonds and with whom his finest qualities flourished. Academically, he was excellent. While some may have been superior in intellectual sharpness, in high seriousness he was without equal.

He taught at Belvedere College, a Jesuit School on the north side of Dublin, from 1946 to 1949, and was a magnificent teacher. Even eleven-year-olds sensed something special about him. Those of us whom he taught can now see that he was not just a teacher doing his task competently and diligently. It was important for him that we should write well, enjoy poetry, grapple with the demands of English grammar: for him these were not mere tasks for schoolboys, but rather the foundations of a humane life. The impact he made on us in those distant days is shown by the number that kept contact with him to the end. We all carry something of him with us. I am still unable to use the word 'very' without a tremor of guilt as I hear him say, '"Very" does not strengthen, it weakens the proposition'.

After completing his Jesuit training, Joe was sent to Gonzaga College in 1954, where he taught for 18 years. It was young, small and, perhaps, a little precious. The school was a pioneering venture in Irish education, and was relatively free of the exam system. As a teacher of English and Religion, Joe Veale honed his pedagogical skills, sharpened his vision and developed his philosophy of education. His commitment to excellence in thought and expression, his insistence on the highest standards, and the breadth and depth of his intellectual interests made him not just a memorable teacher but also a profound educator. In those years he won many lifelong admirers and friends. In the interest of honesty it must be said that his style alienated some and left a casualty or two on the sideline. I had the good fortune to teach under him for three years. I deeply appreciate what he taught me, and have been ever grateful for his encouragement.

During those years, Joe founded the Gonzaga Debating Society. The standard of debating was remarkably high, and participation in the society was an education in itself. Characteristically, he took the activities of the society most seriously. On one occasion, I attended a debate against Belvedere on the right to join or not to join a trade union. The Gonzaga team was superb; the Belvedere team, which did not approach the debate with Veale-like seriousness, was poor. However from the house there rose a young man who made a witty, irreverent and debunking speech that dragged the debate down to a Belvederian level and almost swung it in Belvedere's favour. Next morning I asked the great man himself what he thought of the debate. A pained look conveyed that my question was inappropriate. Then he said that 'the brat who had ruined the debate' was going to become a Jesuit. The brat, Bruce Bradley, did become a Jesuit and a distinguished one at that.

Joe Veale exercised a national influence on the teaching of English in Ireland, and was largely responsible for reshaping the English curriculum in secondary schools. His widely influential 1957 article, 'Men Speechless', in *Studies,* a quarterly review published by the Irish Jesuits, was a masterpiece, in which he made the moral case for rhetoric and distilled his philosophy and vision of education.

In 1972 he left teaching to study spirituality, seemingly trading adolescents leaning towards agnosticism for devout religious. He applied his ability, commitment and seriousness to spirituality just as he had applied them to his school teaching. He became an authority on the *Spiritual Exercises* of St Ignatius, on the *Constitutions* of the Jesuits, and on Ignatian spirituality. He was a highly successful director of Jesuits in their tertianship; he gave conferences and retreats all over the world; he was a treasured spiritual director. Above all, as a master wordsmith, he produced beautifully written learned articles. He brought to his writing a detailed knowledge gleaned from meticulously scholarly research and from his experience in directing Jesuits and other religious. His study and experience enabled him to illuminate what had been obscured and correct what had been distorted. The result was a presentation of Ignatian spirituality that is at once fresh and rich.

Through his writings and conferences, Joe Veale played a central role in forming directors who applied his understanding of Ignatian spirituality in their own direction, particularly of the full process of the Spiritual Exercises. Within the Jesuits he was one of those who rescued the Jesuit *Constitutions* from oblivion, and so formed a new perspective on Jesuit religious life. Furthermore, he saw that the *Constitutions* of the Jesuits are an integral part of Ignatian, not just of Jesuit, spirituality, and that to understand Ignatian spirituality one has to study the *Constitutions* just as much as the *Spiritual Exercises.* So, while it remains the case that the *Spiritual Exercises* are addressed to a public far wider than the Society of Jesus, nevertheless the Jesuit *Constitutions*, the product of Ignatius' mature years, illuminate and at times qualify the *Spiritual Exercises.* Furthermore, while the *Spiritual Exercises* deal with personal spirituality, the *Constitutions* move towards a communal spirituality.

Along with others, Joe Veale reclaimed the mystical strand in Ignatian spirituality. He argued that from 1600 to about 1965, an ascetical approach dominated and impoverished the tradition. As one can read in the third section of this book, his writings on this issue were intensely personal, and his own unhappiness during his early years in the Jesuits comes across loud and clear. His palpable joy when writing about the emergence of the mystical tradition reminds one sadly that he seldom managed to capture that joy in his life, and that he found consolation, which for him was the normal state of the Jesuit, so elusive.

As a director and counsellor Joe so cultivated his talent for listening that it became, with his teaching, a defining characteristic. Many found that listening enormously helpful. As his rector at the end of his life, I received this from a religious:

> Fr Veale's contribution to the apostolate of the Spiritual Exercises within my own congregation was immense. His many articles and presentations to audiences around the world bear witness to his wisdom and insight. I am more grateful than I can state for his friendship, perception, wisdom and encouragement over many years. His interest in the development of my own work in spirituality and theology was a great support. His belief in the work of the Spirit of God within was always life giving.

In his latter years Joe became more interested in cultural issues and his reflective ruminations mixed with trenchant comments were always arresting. His essay on the sexual abuse of children by priests and religious, reproduced in this volume, is fiercely critical of the Church. He believed that the abuse, hideous in itself, was symptomatic of other serious ecclesiastical deficiencies. In this piece there is an undertow of anger that conceals all his affection for the Church, and gives one a glimpse of an inner cauldron of emotion below the measured exterior.

At 81 Joe Veale was robust and active in writing and directing. I can think of at least two significant articles from his final year. A year before his death he visited Malaysia, India and Kenya and came back convinced that Islam could play a role in the re-evangelization of Europe and greatly encouraged by the Christianity he found in all its varieties, especially in Africa.

Six weeks before he died he walked along the seashore at Brittas Bay, Wicklow, on a beautiful morning with a friend from his Belvedere days. There is a photograph of him taken about an hour before he collapsed, which is reproduced as the frontispiece to this volume. He looks splendid, so young for his years, and with no sign of the approaching attack. After his operation, there were times when a recovery seemed possible. Then came the stroke that swept him away in two days, but not without a furious struggle.

The essays collected in this book reflect Joseph Veale's erudition, scholarship and experience, and will give the reader a unique opportunity to study his pivotal insights into Ignatian spirituality.

*Noel Barber SJ*

# Editorial Foreword

JOSEPH VEALE WAS A CREATIVE, PROPHETIC VOICE in the renewal of Ignatian ministry following Vatican II. His influence was felt chiefly in his native Ireland, but he also had an impact throughout the English-speaking world. *Manifold Gifts* brings together Joe's seminal ideas on the *Spiritual Exercises*, on the Ignatian *Constitutions*, on how the Ignatian tradition has developed over its history, and on contemporary pastoral questions. The collection seeks to include all Joe's significant published ideas, as well as two lectures that have never been published before. More information about the sources can be found in the bibliography at the end, and in the introductions to each section. Many of the articles originally appeared in *The Way Supplement*, and it is particularly fitting, therefore, that this collection appears as one of the first in the series, *Way Books*. We also acknowledge gratefully the other original copyright holders, and their kind permission to reprint in this volume the material which they first published.

Sadly, this collection has been made posthumously, and editing it has involved choices that Joe himself might have made differently. In general, we have not sought to modernise essays which are in some ways dated (notably as regards gender-specific language), nor have we standardised Joe's eclectic use of published Ignatian translations. However, we have updated some of the references, though not the quotations themselves, when he quotes major texts, such as Pierre Favre's spiritual diary, or the journal kept by Luis Gonçalves da Câmara, or the Directories for the *Spiritual Exercises*, for which good English translations have appeared since Joe was writing. We have also quoted from the Ignatian *Constitutions* by the older numbering in terms of parts and chapters, as well by the easier, if misleading, continuous numbering that has more recently become common.

A more difficult issue has been Joe's tendency to publish the same thought on several occasions. Where we have judged him to have been simply recycling material, we have opted not to reprint the piece, or else we have tacitly made some cuts. But often with Joe, as with the writings of Ignatius, the repetition of a similar idea in a different context conveys a subtle point about growth and change, and in such cases we have let the repetition stand. There is something striking about how Joe's tone became more direct as he got older.

*Way Books* has been greatly helped in the production of this volume by a group of Irish Jesuits whose idea the collection initially was and who did a great deal of the initial editorial work: Noel Barber, Dermot Mansfield, Laurence Murphy and Brian O'Leary. In particular, it was Fr O'Leary who did most of the work on Joe's unpublished lecture about the Exercises in an ecumenical setting. *Way Books* also gratefully acknowledges the financial support of the Irish Jesuit province.

*Philip Endean SJ*

# Part 1

## *The Spiritual Exercises*

# Introduction

THE FOUR PIECES REPRODUCED HERE contain the principal ideas on the Spiritual Exercises worked out by Joe Veale in published form over a period of eighteen years. Obviously, throughout his Jesuit life he had been familiar with the Exercises, making them in their entirety during both his novitiate in 1938 and his tertianship in 1953, and also revisiting them during all or most of his annual eight-day retreats. But it was as he moved from his work in education to the field of spirituality that he embarked upon his serious investigation of the Exercises and the study of their contents and the giving of them, alongside his interest in the Ignatian *Constitutions*, remained his passion for the rest of his life.

In 'Manifold Gifts', published in *The Way Supplement* in the spring of 1995, we have arguably the richest piece of all, one that can serve as a title piece for the whole collection. The questions surrounding Ignatian prayer are addressed in an open-ended, and yet authoritative, way. There is perhaps some repetition of statements from earlier essays, and yet even so they seem somehow to carry here their full meaning and nuance. Although Joe Veale had not read widely in spiritual traditions apart from the Ignatian one, he had listened long and well to many people from other backgrounds who spoke to him of their experience. As a result he comprehended more easily the varied approaches to prayer, and ventured beyond any schemata proposed by the other traditions to point to that freedom and growth which God's leading, and authentic human experience, will entail.

The second piece in the collection, 'Ignatian Contemplation', is much older, and appeared in *The Furrow* in February 1977. It may have been intended originally for priests. Its aim is to outline for a wider readership the form of prayer presented in the Exercises, and to place it within the mainstream of the Christian tradition. Though Joe's thought developed in later years, this piece remains a gem in its own right. The interplay of prayer and discernment is emphasized, as is the central role of the personal and imaginative contemplation of Christ. There is a wealth of insight and learning in these brief pages, presented without many notes or references in an easy and non-technical way which makes the piece all the more valuable.

The other two pieces in the collection come from the 1980s. 'The Dynamic of the Spiritual Exercises' was published in 1985, and was addressed to the relatively small circle of those who intend giving the Exercises. It was written during a period of sustained co-operative study of the Exercises by members of the Irish and British Jesuit provinces alongside other retreat-givers sharing in Ignatian spirituality. Papers on various aspects of the Exercises were presented at the annual New Year conferences on the Spiritual Exercises which were held during this time at St Beuno's, in North Wales; and many of the papers were subsequently published in *The Way* or *The Way Supplement*. Despite its title, the paper's concern is not so much with an overview of the different parts of the Exercises as with an articulation of what can happen personally in anyone who responds to their invitation and enters as deeply as possible into their unfolding movement. The style seems to reflect something of that which had evolved at the Centre for Religious Development at Boston, under the aegis of William Barry SJ and William Connolly SJ, in which the psychological and affective aspects of an individual's spiritual journey were being emphasized. Nevertheless, the approach is very much Joe Veale's own and, even with the concentration on aspects of personal growth, we can see his characteristically unwavering attention to the text of the *Spiritual Exercises*. At the heart of this article, after an elaboration of the experience of prayer in the Exercises, is the issue of 'sound and good' choice, entailing God-given growth in personal freedom. And a tantalizing but all too brief glimpse is provided of what may happen beyond the experience of the Exercises. They are said to be 'a point of departure', providing seeds which are expected to flourish in the onward living of daily life.

'The First Week: Practical Questions' is a more specialised piece. Here we see an author speaking to his peers and drawing upon what was by now his own considerable experience. He had thought out intensely the many questions that arise for any director who is conscientiously grappling with St Ignatius' difficult material on sin and with the susceptibilities of contemporary retreatants.

'Manifold Gifts' was later revised and reprinted in a booklet entitled 'St Ignatius Speaks about "Ignatian Prayer"', in *Studies in the Spirituality of Jesuits*. This piece followed an earlier example set by Karl Rahner, by which the author adopted the persona of Ignatius speaking to contemporary Jesuits. Although there is a certain vividness about this approach, it does not seem necessary to republish that 1996 work here, or to provide excerpts from it. What matters here is to present the authentic voice of Joe Veale himself, and the immediate working out of his thought. It is reasonable to consider that these are at their clearest in 'Manifold Gifts'.

# 1

# MANIFOLD GIFTS

IT IS NOT AT ALL CERTAIN that St Ignatius would recognise himself in the term 'Ignatian prayer'. What he tried to make clear was that the only teacher of prayer is the Holy Spirit. This is evident to anyone who has often accompanied people through the full Spiritual Exercises and reflected on the experience. It is not necessarily so clear to those who are unfamiliar with his letters, his *Constitutions* and what was recorded of his conversation. The text of the *Spiritual Exercises* on its own has misled many.

His principle is clear. That level and kind of prayer is best for each one where God communicates Himself more:

> God sees and knows what is best for each one and, as He knows all, He shows each the road to take. On our part we can with His grace seek and test the way forward in many different fashions, so that a person goes forward by that way which for them is the clearest and happiest and most blessed in this life.[1]

St Ignatius always preferred to proceed empirically. He was less at home with generalisations or with rigid nostrums. He preferred the concrete to the abstract. He said there could be no greater error in spiritual things than to direct others 'according to one's own way' (*por si mismo*). This was very harmful, and the work of people,

> ... who neither knew nor understood the manifold gifts of the Holy Spirit and the variety of graces through which He distributes His loving kindness, giving each person their own special and particular graces, to some in one way and to others in another.[2]

---

[1] Ignatius to Francis Borja, 20 September 1548, MHSJ EI 2, 233-237; ET most easily available in Saint Ignatius of Loyola, *Personal Writings*, translated and edited by Joseph A. Munitiz and Philip Endean (London: Penguin, 1996), 204-207.
[2] Luis Gonçalves da Câmara, *Memoriale* n. 256; ET in *Remembering Iñigo: Glimpses of the Life of St Ignatius of Loyola: The Memoriale of Luis Gonçalves da Câmara*, translated by Alexander Eaglestone and Joseph A. Munitiz (London: Gracewing, 2004); Pedro de Ribadeneira, *Vita Ignatii Loyolae,*

That does not look like 'Ignatian prayer'. Yet there has been a way of speaking of '*the* Ignatian method of prayer' and more recently of 'Ignatian contemplation'. It has come partly from an understandable tendency of writers to claim more originality for a saint or a school than the facts warrant. Ignatius borrowed from the living tradition as it was available to him in his time. When it came to trying to put words on the 'understandings' he was given in Manresa or to recommending what his reflection taught him from his guidance of others, he had to work within the limits of the language and the forms of the spiritual culture of his time.

**The Methods**

In more recent years we have heard less frequently about 'the Ignatian method of meditation'. The phrase referred as a rule to the method he commended in the First Week of the Exercises, of using the memory, the understanding and the will. Blood was shed early in the twentieth century in controversies between those who were hostile to methods of any kind and uncritical admirers of method. The argument often ignored the many ways of prayer that are recommended in the *Spiritual Exercises* as well as the many exercises that no one would normally call prayer.[3]

More recently, the term 'Ignatian contemplation' has been used to refer to the simple way of being present with the whole self to events in the gospel, to 'mysteries of the life of Our Lord' (Exx 261). Ignatius introduces the exercitant to this way of prayer in the Second Week of the Exercises. In that context he used the term 'contemplation' to mean something different from what it has normally meant in the tradition. What he desired was that someone making the Exercises should become absorbed in the reality of the deeds and words of Jesus, that they should look and listen and wonder, behold the persons, what they did and said, would assimilate and be assimilated to the 'mystery'. The one contemplating might be drawn through the icon of the scene

MHSJ FN 4, 854-855. The Latin version of the Ribadeneira text ends with what appears an allusion to 1 Corinthians 7:7 (Vulgate).
[3] For example, the practices commended in the various Rules, or the more detailed techniques for examination of conscience (Exx 24-42).

or happening and beyond it into the mystery beyond the 'mystery'. The grace desired was to be given an 'interior knowledge' of Jesus, St Paul's *sensus Christi*, the 'mind' of Christ (Philippians 2:5).

What Ignatius presupposed in all this was that a person setting out on the road to a serious life of faith was being guided by someone experienced in 'the manifold gifts of the Holy Spirit and the variety of graces through which He distributes His loving kindnesses'. The director, if we must use the term, would be aware that 'it is not much knowledge that fills and satisfies the soul but to savour and to taste the reality interiorly' (Exx 2). The one making the Exercises would, in the day-by-day exchange with the director, be shown that 'where I find what I desire, there I remain quietly in repose …' (Exx 76).

That was Ignatius' simple pedagogy by which he opened the door upon the possibility of contemplation and the uniquely personal action of the Holy Spirit. The kind of prayer which ended each day of the Exercises, conventionally called Application of the Senses, is an occasion for a further deepening of a contemplative grace.

What is probably original in Ignatius is that in the Exercises he commends a person who is praying an event in the gospel to hear what the persons in the scene 'say *or might say*' (Exx 123). The movement is from looking on at what is happening to participating in it, from what could be impersonal to what is personal and intimate. Ignatius was concerned to bring the gospel reality into intimate and personal encounter with the contemporary reality of the exercitant's own experience and history. How otherwise was Christ to become incarnate in the world, in greatly different times and cultures, in the faith and life of the believing community?

However subtly Ignatius gave these ways of prayer his own colouring, he picked them up from the many teachers of prayer in his time. The 'contemplation' of the gospel is Franciscan; Ignatius found it in Ludolph the Carthusian's *Life of Christ*, which, as we now know, Ludolph borrowed from the pseudo-Bonaventure and which therefore belongs to the Franciscan tradition. But in those days, happily, the different families within the Church gladly borrowed from each other. Frontiers were open.

What is implied in all that is that these methods of prayer were ways of helping beginners to pray. It opens the question as to how those ways of prayer may or may not be helpful to people who are experienced in prayer. Our terminology is strange. It seems to suggest that we are able to know who is not a beginner, as though any of us ceases to be one. Our language is clumsy. It can be useful to make a distinction between those who are setting out on a serious life of faith and those who have been on the road for some time. Those of us who have been on the road for many a year are likely to feel that perhaps we were able to pray in those early days but that we no longer know whether we pray or not.[4]

The books speak of beginners and of the advanced. It is true that after some time prayer can tend to become simpler, more quiet, more wordlessly attentive; images and ideas seem to get in the way. Prayer becomes darker. Certainly Ignatius expected in the course of a day during the Exercises that one's prayer would become quieter, simpler and more focused. Can we say, as seems often to be suggested, that that kind of prayer is 'better'? Is it common? Is it universal? Is it the way prayer always develops? If we were honest, I think we should say we do not know. We do not have the evidence. At most, from our experience in accompanying others on the journey, we can surmise. Beyond that, it is good to be happy with an educated ignorance.[5]

It is in this connection that some people ask whether the way of contemplating the gospel mysteries is only for beginners. As one 'advances' in prayer, does one leave it behind? St Ignatius would be wary of large statements that tended to be dogmatic or general. For him the only way to judge is 'by their fruits'.[6]

He would explore with a particular person in what direction their spirit was being moved. In what way does God communicate Himself

---

[4] Karl Rahner said of himself: 'One does not know about a relationship to God, whether one has it, how one has it, what is decisive in it …. It is a wise, educated ignorance about oneself, which must be entrusted to God without knowing how it is': *Karl Rahner in Dialogue, Conversations and Interviews 1965-1982*, edited by Hubert Biallowons and Paul Imhof, translated by Harvey D. Egan (New York: Crossroad, 1986), 297.

[5] Augustine, Letter to Proba, Ep 131.15 (28): *Est ergo in nobis quaedam, ut ita dicam, docta ignorantia, sed docta Spiritu Dei.* (There is in us, so to speak, a kind of learned ignorance, but taught by the Spirit of God.)

[6] The best treatment of the question I know of is Dermot Mansfield, 'The Prayer of Faith, Spiritual Direction, and the Exercises,' *The Way*, 25/4 (October 1985), 315-324, especially 320 onwards. The essay was reprinted, under the title 'The Exercises and Contemplative Prayer', in *The Way of Ignatius Loyola*, edited by Philip Sheldrake (St Louis: Institute of Jesuit Sources, 1991).

more? Or, in another of his idioms, where does a person more easily 'find God', find 'devotion'? A sign would be a certain quality of 'consolation', not necessarily sensibly experienced or easily recognisable on the surface. His concern would be to see whether a particular way of praying (or seeming not to pray at all) opened the spirit more to the action of God. Was a person more open to God? Less self-preoccupied? More selfless in service? More unpretentious? Less rigid? More true? Showing effective signs of living the gospel more truly? More authentic in relating with others? Less subject to illusion? Growing in hope and love?

Ignatius would be less inclined to ask whether a person's prayer was more advanced than to explore whether it was more authentic, more suited to this individual's capacity and grace, disposing towards a more authentic way of living, a more selfless service 'in the Lord', as he would say.

## The Historical Inheritance

Of course Ignatius, with his instinctive sense of history, would expect us to have enriched and enlarged his insights, not to say corrected some of them, with the experience of the intervening centuries and the resources of our contemporary culture and theologies. Properly to understand the heritage he left us, to give some true meaning to 'Ignatian prayer' or 'Ignatian spirituality', we need to know something of what happened to his teaching in the intervening time. How did it come about that, within a short time after his death, there were Jesuits who taught a narrow and confining doctrine on prayer?

Within his own lifetime the Exercises came under attack for being too mystical. The Spanish inquisitor Tomás Pedroche, in his desire to identify the Exercises with the errors of the *alumbrados*, was exact in pinpointing those parts of the Exercises that, if we must use the term, can be called mystical. He and Melchor Cano, one of the most learned, distinguished and influential theologians of the time, feared the Exercises because they gave too much place to subjective experience, to affectivity; Pedroche and Cano saw them as being insufficiently ascetical and rational, as seeming to bypass the objective teaching of sound doctrine, and as giving a dangerous prominence to the interior leading of the Holy Spirit.[7] They feared particularly what was the central underlying assumption of the Exercises:

> It is far better that the Creator and Lord Himself should communicate Himself to the devout soul, embracing it to His love and praise ... to allow the Creator to deal directly with the creature and the creature with its Creator and Lord. (Exx 15)

They suspected what Karl Rahner has said was Ignatius' chief concern, 'to help others to experience God'.[8]

The style of theology represented by Cano and Pedroche became a dominant orthodoxy in the Church for more than four hundred years. Jesuits subscribed to it and interpreted the Exercises in its light. It disallowed the central insights of the Exercises, that God deals directly with the soul sincerely seeking Him and that the way forward in a living faith, in prayer as in service, is the way shown to each by the Holy Spirit. The Church was fearful of mysticism. The Spanish theologians who wanted to have the Exercises placed on the Index feared mysticism because they feared illuminism. Later the fear was reinforced after the condemnation of quietism (1687) and after the condemnation of modernism (1907). During all this time, Jesuits experienced in helping others on the way quietly taught the sound Christian contemplative tradition, though not always without being told to stop. It is only with Vatican II that there has been a great flowering in the understanding of the authentic tradition. This has given us the freedom to understand Ignatius better now than, for the most part, he has been in the intervening centuries.

### Finding God's Will

What was original in Ignatius is that he took the contemporary teaching on 'contemplating' the gospel and transposed it to the context of *discretio*, to the Christian search for the circumstances and dispositions that open people to be made free with the freedom of the Spirit

---

[7] Ignacio Iparraguirre, *Práctica de los Ejercicios de San Ignacio de Loyola en vida de su autor* (1522-1556) (Rome: Jesuit Historical Institute, 1946), 98-100.

[8] Karl Rahner, 'Ignatius of Loyola Speaks to a Modern Jesuit', translated by Rosaleen Ockenden, in *Ignatius of Loyola* (London: Collins, 1978), 11, 16, 13.

(Galatians 5: 1, 5: 16, 5: 25). He was concerned with finding God's will for his Kingdom. For him the chief criterion for finding God's will was the *sensus Christi*, a spiritual sensibility that is in tune with the mind of Jesus in the gospel and with the Spirit of Jesus giving life and direction to his Church.

Such an attitude—sometimes called 'indifference'—is presupposed in anything that Ignatius said or wrote about prayer:

> ... the calm readiness for every command of God, the equanimity which ... continually detaches itself from every determinate thing which man is tempted to regard as *the* point in which alone God meets him .... An ultimate attitude towards all thoughts, practices and ways: an ultimate reserve and coolness towards all particular ways, because all possession of God must leave God as greater beyond all possession of Him .... The perpetual readiness to hear a new call from God to tasks [and obviously to ways of prayer] other than those previously engaged in, continually to decamp from those fields where one wanted to find God and to serve Him .... The courage to regard no way to Him as being *the* way, but rather to seek Him in all ways.[9]

What matters, therefore, is neither this or that way of service, nor this or that way of prayer, but rather a readiness to let go of whatever seemed to be the only way to find God in order to give oneself to that way alone in which God *now* desires to be found.

For Ignatius 'prayer' was 'to have God always before one's eyes'. In his *Constitutions* he came back again and again to the need for 'a thoroughly right and pure intention'. He refers to a condition of purified desire that is, as he would say, *de arriba*, from above.

> The love that moves and causes one to choose must descend from above, that is, from the love of God, so that, before one chooses, one should sense that the greater or less attachment for the object of one's choice is solely because of one's Creator and Lord (Exx 184).

---

[9] Karl Rahner, 'The Ignatian Mysticism of Joy in the World' (1937), in *Theological Investigations* volume 3, translated by Karl-H. Krüger (London: Darton, Longman and Todd, 1974), here 290-291.

**Prayer and Illusion**

The other point in Ignatius' teaching that bears on his understanding of prayer is that place in the *Spiritual Exercises* which we know as the Two Standards.

The whole central section of the *Spiritual Exercises*, the part that gives them their specific character and makes them original, is the process of discernment that St Ignatius calls 'election'. It begins with 'a meditation on Two Standards' (Exx 135): the standard of Satan and the standard of Jesus. There is no question here, of course, of choosing between them. Rather a person prays that his or her spirit be clarified in order to be made sensitive to the ways by which the 'enemy of our human nature' deceives the good under the appearance of good in seeking the good. One begs, in the daily repetition of the triple colloquy, to be given an interior knowledge of the contrary ways which are the ways of Jesus in the gospel. Those ways involve a desire to share his experience of poverty, rejection and humility.[10]

Both the *Spiritual Exercises* and the *Constitutions* have to do with godly decision, decision as a mode of prayer. That is what is implied in his two chosen ways of speaking of these things: 'to have God always before one's eyes' and 'to seek and to find God in everything'.

How, in a life of outward fret and stress, in the demands and responsibilities and enjoyments of life, of family, of public life, of kitchen or office or field or classroom or workbench, in the inexorable demands or delights or pains of relationship, is a person genuinely to find God? We all know that in the fret and the stress God often is not found, nor for that matter sought. How is one to grow through these familiar experiences (not in spite of them) into union with God?

It is evident that there are lives of zeal and activity in which God is absent. There are ways of being busy in which people hide themselves from themselves and hide themselves from God. They run from that reality. Prayer itself can be the idol that more comfortably substitutes for the living God. The holiest and most prayerful people can be beguiled by the attraction of power or influence, of learning, of work, of prayer itself or of particular ways of prayer. These are all good things.

[10] Exx 147; Examen, 4. 44 [101].

But the reality that lies behind the Two Standards is that the noblest aspirations can disguise the protean forms of self-seeking. It is easy to build one's own kingdom.

It was his experience of such realities in the Church and in individuals that led Ignatius to speak often of illusion. He knew well how the deceit of the father of lies contaminates action. He spoke in the same terms of prayer. He used to say that of a hundred people given to extensive prayer and penances, ninety were subject to illusion.[11] He had experienced how people given to prayer could be opinionated, rigid, obstinate in judgment and unbiddable.

In the area of prayer as in the area of labour, St Ignatius would look to the graced dispositions and the graces of the Two Standards and of its accompanying Third Degree of Humility. It was by such high graces, *de arriba*, continually sought and begged for in prayer, that one's desire would be purified. Meanwhile both prayer and action could be false. But given those graces and dispositions, both prayer and the activity that completes God's work on earth could be purgative, illuminative and unitive. As Blessed Pierre Favre discovered,

> ... one who seeks God in helping others will later find Him more easily in prayer than one who seeks Him first in prayer and afterwards in action, as we often do.[12]

St Ignatius had said much the same in a letter to Francis Borja,

> ... certainly there is more virtue in being able to rejoice in the Lord in a variety of duties and places than in only one.[13]

### The Need for a New Word

Ignatius spoke and wrote little of prayer as we understand it. He used a variety of terms that gave a great latitude for a great variety of things: '*cosas spirituales*', 'spiritual exercises of devotion', 'piety', 'exercises of

---

[11] Gonçalves da Câmara, *Memoriale*, n.195. See also nn.196 and 256; *Constitutions*, I. 3. 12 [182].

[12] Pierre Favre, *Memoriale*, n.126. ET now available in *The Spiritual Writings of Pierre Favre*, edited and translated by Edmond C. Murphy, John W. Padberg and Martin E. Palmer (St Louis: Institute of Jesuit Sources, 1996), 141.

[13] Ignatius to Borja, 20 September 1548; Ignatius, *Personal Writings*, 205.

piety', 'devotion', 'familiarity with God'. With us the word 'prayer' still obstinately continues to mean what we do when we leave affairs aside and close the door and enter into that inner room. Let us be content with that usage.

We need a new word, one we have not yet discovered. It would encompass not only the prayer that opens the spirit to God and leads towards union with Him but, besides, all those other things which open the spirit to the action of God, just as much as prayer (and sometimes better).

What is indisputable is that under certain conditions of desire and disposition, if you like, in a certain climate of faith, the workaday tasks and responsibilities and delights and frets that draw us out of ourselves towards the needs of others, have been especially blessed, and, as it were, given the likeness of a sacrament, through Jesus' words about washing one another's feet. Whatever brings faith to life, whatever brings faith to bear on everything else we experience, whatever draws the focus away from ourselves, whatever beauty or goodness so absorbs us that we entirely forget ourselves, whatever strengthens hope and makes us more loving, all these can be purgative and illuminative and unitive just as much as prayer can. A sign of authenticity in prayer as in service is that a person grows more godly. To be God-like is entirely to forget oneself. Whether that comes about by a call to become absorbed simply in God or by the circumstances of life that engage a person wholly in others' needs is not for us to say.

It gives us an insight into Ignatius' mind about prayer to ponder the things he lists that unite the human instrument with the divine craftsman. He does not use the word 'prayer', but writes instead of 'familiarity with God in spiritual exercises of devotion'. Moreover this word does not come in the first place.

> The means which unite the human instrument with God and so dispose it that it may be wielded dexterously by His divine hand ... are, for example, goodness and virtue, and especially love, and a pure intention of the divine service, and familiarity with God our Lord in spiritual exercises of devotion, and

sincere zeal for souls for the sake of glory to Him who created and redeemed them and not for any other benefit. (X. 2 [813]) [14]

It is significant that Ignatius never wrote, as Jerónimo Nadal did, of being a contemplative in action. He had the terminology but did not use it. The wording suggests what it intended to rule out, a disjunction between action and contemplation. Ignatius preferred synthesis to separation; he was a reconciler of opposites. He was confident that God's goodness would accomplish with his free gift, *de arriba*, not an alternation of one and the other but a compenetration of the two.

People pray in a thousand different ways. Some are led by a way that is dark and dry and unrewarding, like Karl Rahner's 'winter faith'. Some are called by a way of prayer that seems full of light. There is good reason to believe, as Nadal seems to have done, that for the apostolic contemplative the purifying darkness is there not so much in prayer as in the labour of service itself and in the frequent obscurities and irrationality of obedience. [15]

If prayer is authentic at all, it will be marked, even in situations of distress and pain, by a constant accompaniment of consolation. It is an error to write or speak in a way that convinces people that there is only one way in which the Holy Spirit draws us towards union with God. There are more languages than one, more images than those of one school of thinking, that can be used to attempt to describe the incomprehensible mystery of God's way of giving Himself to this person or to that. Beyond that it is good to fall silent before the mystery.

If we take the Contemplation for Attaining Love to be in some sense a culmination of the Exercises, or if we may take it that there Ignatius was pointing to the way in which a hard-working person might 'keep God always before one's eyes', then it is striking that the final word is *etcetera*. That opens up for one who has been given the Exercises an entry upon unmapped territory, uncharted regions of being drawn into the mystery of God in ways only God knows. What happens later in such a person's prayer? Who knows? That is not our business.

---

[14] All references in this form hereafter are to the Ignatian *Constitutions*.

[15] Maurice Giuliani, 'Nuit et lumière de l'obéissance', *Christus*, 2 (1955), 349-368; ET in *Finding God in All Things*, edited and translated by William J. Young (Chicago: Henry Regnery, 1958).

It is enough that the human instruments in God's service, making available to God all their God-given gifts of ingenuity and initiative, of imagination and intelligence, desire to be used so that God may be God in His world. The instrument is united with God in being used. It is in being used that the person is sanctified.

Or God may build His kingdom by leaving His gifts unused. The possibility that one may not be used at all is entailed in the freedom that Ignatius calls being 'indifferent'. It can be bitter and puzzling to discover that God builds His kingdom also through the impotence of illness, the diminishments of ageing, or the dark ways of obedience. By one path or the other, by achievement or by the frustration of achievement, and always in either by the way of the cross, the instrument is sanctified.

That is God's business, not ours. All that we hand over to Him. Let us think little of it. Meanwhile there are tasks to hand that are our business. Our goal is not to become holy but to be spent.

# 2

# IGNATIAN
# CONTEMPLATION

'GO ON GROWING in the grace and in the knowledge of our Lord and saviour Jesus Christ.' (2 Peter 3:18) In the pastoral ministry nothing else, in the end, is seen to be of any value. We come back to where we began when, in the years of preparation for the priesthood, we were so often told of the importance of private and personal prayer. It is a grace to be brought to our knees when we realise that we can accomplish nothing in the apostolate by our own power. Experience eventually brings home to us that 'without me you can do nothing' (John 15:5). More and more it becomes clear that what people want from us is the reality of Christ:

> What we have seen and heard we are telling you so that you too may be in union with us, as we are in union with the Father and with his Son Jesus Christ (1 John 1:3).

It is in the believing community that the *memoria Christi* is communicated to us and becomes more and more an effective reality in our lives. Christ lives. The faith of the Church has a true instinct that he is not remote, but is powerfully present to us, enabling us to grasp his reality and his presence.

> Something that has existed since the beginning, that we have heard, and we have seen with our own eyes; that we have watched and touched with our hands ... (1 John 1:1).

The Christian response of faith has never been content with an abstract knowledge. Faith needs and desires to see and to hear and to touch. The Spirit of Jesus gives us the desire to know Christ with an intimate and familiar knowledge. It is that desire and the conviction that it is possible that makes us want to contemplate Christ in the days of his flesh and as he is given to us in the gospel.

As to how we may set about this, the living tradition of the Church is rich in many ways of helping us. In these days we are less likely to fall into the trap of crying 'I am for Paul. I am for Apollos.' If we speak out of one family tradition in the Church, it is in the awareness that all Christians belong to the same family and that different ways to the Father nourish and illuminate each other. It is in that conviction that I want to attempt to respond to the invitation to say something that may be helpful about the kind of prayer associated with St Ignatius' *Spiritual Exercises*.

## A Way of Lived Experience

We do not learn to pray from books. It is the Holy Spirit who teaches us to pray, to enter into a real and personal relationship with God in the particular way that God wants of each of us. It is He who takes the initiative in that relationship and retains it throughout. There are as many ways of growing in that friendship as there are fingerprints or scripts. And like all relationships, the friendship, if it is real, is always changing. If many of us fail to grow in prayer, or lose heart and give up, or become frozen in a way that is not helpful, or fail to find our own way, it is usually because we try to go it alone. We are not left without resources in the community. We can be helped to find the way God wants each of us to pray in a kind of apprenticeship. In it, out of our own weak experience, the Holy Spirit helps us to help each other find God. The Ignatian Exercises are partly that.

In his Exercises, St Ignatius suggests a great variety of different ways of praying. He does not commend any one method. It is for the one who makes the Exercises, with the help of the one who gives them, to find a way that helps him to find God, or to be found by Him. One of the chief pieces of advice that St Ignatius gave was that there can be no greater mistake, in things of the spirit, than to want to lead others in one's own way. He wanted us, as far as possible, to be free, at ease in ourselves, and obedient to the light given particularly to each one.

It was very far from his mind, then, to recommend only one method of meditation. At the same time, because we can so easily fall into slipshod and slovenly ways, he believed in going about our prayer in an orderly and disciplined way when that is necessary. To do otherwise would be to be lacking in reverence before the Majesty of God.

Ignatius' whole teaching on prayer begins from a sense of the immense goodness and majesty of our Creator and Lord, who is Christ, the way to the Father. Always, in his own prayer, he was filled with reverence before the Three Persons. The mystical experience from which all his teaching comes was a vision of the Three Persons and of all created things. He saw the Three Persons as themselves apostolic, in the sending of the Son to save humanity. That is why he urges us to approach prayer with great reverence. He recommends that we begin by standing for a time and become aware of 'how God my Lord is beholding me', and then to make an act of profound reverence. And then, before every hour of prayer in the course of the Exercises, to beg for the grace that my whole being be directed purely to the service and praise of the Divine Majesty. Nothing could more clearly signal his conviction that from beginning to end prayer is something we do not do ourselves. What we do, even when our poverty shows us that our 'effort' is needed, is to allow Him to enable us to dispose ourselves to receive His gift.

The Exercises are one of the many schools of prayer in the Catholic tradition. They are also a school of discernment. Scripture tells us that God manifests His particular will to us (Colossians 1:9; Romans 12:2). St Thomas Aquinas teaches that the primary law of the New Covenant is the Spirit who dwells in each of us and shows us God's will in the concrete situation; the gift of discernment is to be expected in the ordinary Christian life (*Summa theologiae*, 1-2.106.1-2). The Spiritual Exercises are a way of disposing ourselves in prayer to be freed from the things that confine and mislead us and, after God has freed us, 'to find and do the will of God'. It is a prayer that is both apostolic and contemplative. It disposes us to receive the gift of sensitivity to the Spirit in all the events and happenings of every day. It is a means of growing towards a familiarity with God in which contemplation enters into the heart of action. St Ignatius' own way of expressing this was the phrase, 'to find God in all things'.

### To Contemplate the Living Christ

The many different ways of praying that St Ignatius suggests need to be seen in that context if they are to be properly understood. Generations of meditation manuals and poor spiritual direction have had people trying to follow a 'method of meditation' when it was no longer helpful to them. For want of some simple guidance many gave up the struggle to pray when they began to fear that it was doing them harm, leading perhaps to unhealthy self-preoccupation. I suppose what most people mean by 'Ignatian meditation' is the way of praying the mysteries of the life of Christ that he outlines in the Exercises from the beginning of the Second Week: that is, once the exercitant has received the grace of a deep conversion of heart. The First Week is given to prayer that seeks for the gift of grief for one's sins, *compunctio*; during that time he speaks of 'meditating'. But then, when the heart has been moved to a deep sense of gratitude and wonder at the goodness of God, he no longer uses the term 'meditation', but speaks of 'contemplating' the human life of the Eternal Word.

The contemplation of the humanity of Christ is the prayer in which the Spirit teaches the apostle to discern the Father's will. It disposes us to receive the grace of familiarity with Christ. 'In your minds you must be the same as Christ Jesus' (Philippians 2:5). It is not a question of an external imitation of Jesus, but of being interiorly formed by the Spirit and conformed with the sentiments and ideas of Christ in his love for the Father and in his dealing with humankind. It is, particularly, the grace needed by those who are sent by the Father to serve Him in continuing the apostolic mission of Christ among men and women.

In this prayer, petition has an important place. We are 'to ask for what we want', confident in our Lord's words at the beginning of Luke 11:

> Persistence will be enough to make him give his friend all he wants .... The one who searches always finds .... How much more will the heavenly Father give the Holy Spirit to those who ask Him?

We need to ask. It is taken that the Holy Spirit has given us a desire to know Christ with a deeper knowledge than the head gives us; and that our faith and prayer have given us intimations of what that knowledge of friendship is like. We have to learn from experience that it is not something to be acquired cheaply or quickly. It takes time. And so, each day in the Spiritual Exercises, one returns again and again to the same event, always begging for the gift of a deep 'interior knowledge of the Lord who is made human for me, that I may love him and follow him more'.

This simple form of contemplation is a way of prayer that St Ignatius absorbed from the monastic tradition of *lectio divina* and transposed to the context of ongoing apostolic discernment. It is less 'busy' than meditation and less likely to be an obstacle to the Creator and Lord when He wishes to treat, Himself, directly with the soul. It is not for those who are in a hurry, who are impatient or demand quick results. It engages not just the brain, but the senses, the sensibility, the imagination, the intelligence, the whole person. It asks that we take seriously two of the most important things St Ignatius said about prayer. The first is: 'Where I find what I want, there I will rest, without anxiety to go further'. We need to learn to know when to be still. The second is: 'It is not much knowledge that fills and satisfies the soul but to taste and savour the reality interiorly'. To taste, to savour, to relish, to take a lingering delight in the company of Christ—it is with such words that the tradition tries to convey what this prayer is like. It is prayer of the heart. It wants to be wholly present to Christ, knowing in faith that he desires to be wholly present to us. This is how Ludolph the Carthusian describes it in his *Vita Christi*, where St Ignatius learned it:

> If you want to draw fruit from these scenes, you must offer yourself as present to what was said or done through our Lord Jesus Christ with the whole affective power of your mind, with loving care, with lingering delight; thus laying aside all other worries and cares. Hear and see as though you were hearing with your own ears and seeing with your own eyes, for these things are most sweet to him who thinks on them with desire, and even more to him who tastes them. You must meditate them all as though they were happening in the present moment; because in this way you will certainly taste a greater sweetness. Then you will feel how full of wisdom and delight they are.

Perhaps it tells us something about our recent culture that one is afraid of sounding flippant or smart in observing that the great medieval writers often describe prayer as *delectatio morosa*. One goes to prayer to enjoy, to delight in, to savour; and they link that savour, *sapor*, with the gift of wisdom, *sapientia*.

## Being Present to the One Who Is Present to Us

St Ignatius asks us simply to be prepared to spend time with Jesus, desiring to enter into his experience, as we might want to recall and go over the experience of a friend with a friend. Like all Christian prayer, it is a prayer of faith, confident that the risen Christ of glory is present to us and powerfully at work in us and through us. 'Jesus Christ is the same today as he was yesterday and as he will be for ever.' (Hebrews 13:8)

There is no question, then, of anything fanciful or false or imaginary. Rather, the imagination is engaged to marshal and centre the whole person, the heart, in entering more deeply into the reality. The reality is the risen Christ, who continues to possess all his human experience. We can come to know him intimately in the continuing loving memory of the eucharistic community, in the whole Christ, through the deeds and words lovingly recorded for us by those who knew him in the days of his flesh. *Ut dum visibiliter Deum cognoscimus, per hunc in invisibilium amorem rapiamur* (As we know God visibly, through him [Jesus] we are caught up in the love of the invisible).

> That life was made visible: we saw it and we are giving our testimony, telling you of the eternal life which was with the Father and has been made visible to us (1 John 1:2).

'Happy are those who have not seen and yet believe.' (John 20:29) We do not see with the eyes of the flesh. The imagination and the interior senses are also graced with faith, inwardly healed and transformed and enabled; and faith desires by means of them to savour and taste the reality of Christ. He is reached through all the acts that the Church preserves for us in its living possession of him.

That is why we can simply place ourselves with Christ and be present to him. We allow him, with all his human experience, to be present to us, and we make his life part of us. The world of action and the world of contemplation are not, in principle, at odds. The needs of God's people are not in rivalry with God for our attention. We bring our world, our concrete and particular experience, to Christ and allow him to enter it, to illuminate it and to give it his meaning. He inwardly transforms our day-to-day experience in his service and enables us to find him at its heart.

To contemplate is simply to take time to look, to behold, to gaze, to wonder, to hear, to listen, to attend, to be present, to enter into the event, because we know in faith that it is 'for us and for our salvation' and is meant to become our experience too. Everything Jesus did and said is sacramental. The Word is present to us in the word. Therefore we quietly place ourselves before the reality, wanting to absorb it and to be absorbed in it, to assimilate it and to be assimilated to it. Baptized into union with Christ, we have taken upon ourselves the qualities of Christ himself.

That grace is deepened and appropriated in the contemplation of Christ's humanity—or, perhaps more accurately, in the contemplation of Christ in his human actions and through them. The Word is continuingly being made flesh in his Church. To want to know him in all the details of his incarnate experience is, in faith, effectively and gradually to be assimilated to him, with all our sin and weakness and inability to pray. This is the new human being spoken of by St Paul in Colossians, which God, its creator, is constantly renewing in His own image, to bring us to a full knowledge of Himself.

Books about prayer can sometimes make us feel discouraged and oppressed with a sense of their unreality. It all seems too easy and remote from our own dry, modest struggles. Or else they make it all seem too hard, only for moral giants and heroes. Prayer is destroyed by anything false in us or unrealistic. We need to learn how to be entirely ourselves with God. But it seems to me that our training left many of us with small expectations of much growth in prayer.

**Receiving the Gift of Wisdom**

God's power, working in us, can do infinitely more than we can ask or imagine (Ephesians 3:20). In these days many are finding a greater hope and freedom when they are able to talk with someone about their prayer and receive some encouragement and guidance. It helps us to be at the same time realistic about ourselves and not over-timid in our hopes of what God works in us when we learn to let Him. If this is true of all the faithful, it is more true of the apostolic priest. It is particularly true when our mission brings us up against the question that more and more people are asking: 'How can I find God's will?' It is a great pity that St Thomas' teaching on discernment is not better known. He does not look on it as something extraordinary or unusual in the ordinary Christian life. When he writes of the gift of discerning wisdom, he explains it by means of the analogy of healthy and unhealthy taste. He is aware of the tradition that connects *sapientia* with a savoured knowledge, *cognitio sapida*, the knowledge that prayer gives. A healthy taste is able to distinguish what is bitter or sweet.

> Similarly the Christian whose mind is renewed by the grace of the Holy Spirit can 'prove', or know by experiencing it, what God's will is and what is good, because such a one already possesses a taste for it and can recognise it by its sweetness.[1]

The apostolic contemplative prayer that St Ignatius taught is a way of disposing a person to receive the gift of discerning wisdom and of learning how to use it. That is what he meant by 'finding God in all things'.

We can be encouraged to pray for this gift in hope and confidence by the thought that St Paul was not addressing anyone very extraordinary when he wrote to the Colossians. His prayer for them is a prayer of the pastoral priest:

> … we have not ceased praying for you and asking that you may be filled with the knowledge of God's will in all spiritual wisdom and understanding, so that you may lead lives worthy of the Lord, fully pleasing to him, as you bear fruit in every good work and as you grow in the knowledge of God. (Colossians 1:9-10)

---

[1] John Mahoney, 'The Spirit and Moral Discernment in Aquinas', *Heythrop Journal*, 13 (1972), 282-297, here 285.

# 3

# THE DYNAMIC OF THE SPIRITUAL EXERCISES

THERE WAS A TIME WHEN PEOPLE SPOKE of the logic of the Exercises. That way of speaking was even then, I think, felt to be defective, as though a submissive subject who gave himself over to them must be persuaded to capitulate to their argument. It is more common now to speak of their dynamic. The term, borrowed from mechanics and physics, has been found useful in many other disciplines, from medicine and law to psychology and biology. The metaphor is used here to suggest organic growth. I take it to mean the way in which the factors or parts in their relationship and interaction make for movement and growth.

It is true that there is some power in the way St Ignatius put the Exercises together. But they are less like a machine or a logical construction than a living organism. It is interesting to submit the text of the *Spiritual Exercises* to a verbal analysis, to show the textual interconnections, the repetition of key words and especially of the characteristic Ignatian doublets (like *sentir y gustar* and so many others), the same themes recurring in different contexts, the way one part prepares for a later one, the way a later part was anticipated in an earlier. That is fairly easily done with a little time and diligence and, in the spirit of the second Annotation, it is all the better for one's having done it for oneself. It is a necessary exercise for anyone who wants to master the Exercises. But somehow, valuable as that is, it does not elicit the dynamic inherent in the process and experience.

Let us suppose, instead, that we were to look less at objective factors, at their sequence and relationship, and look more at the person and his experience. That in no way takes from the fact that St Ignatius considered it to be important to submit one's mind and heart to the Christian truths, to truth or, better, to the Christian mysteries, to begin with humility by using the understanding in order to penetrate the gospel reality, to assimilate and appropriate it. But that is not the whole story.

## Levels of Desire

The Exercises are a way to find God and, in finding Him, to find His will. St Ignatius states plainly from the outset that to find God's will one must first be free (Exx 21, 1). The full Exercises are for those who 'desire to progress as much as possible' (Exx 20). Adaptations or selections of different Exercises are to be given to those whose desire falls short of that (Exx 18, 19, 17). Spiritual Exercises of whatever kind presuppose the presence of desire.

This condition of desire can exist at many levels. It may already be deep and explicit: 'I want God, but I don't know how'; 'I've tried and been frustrated and cannot find the way'. It can be present in a thousand guises, even in a merely implicit longing expressed in words like: 'I am uneasy, restless and unsatisfied'; 'I wish I could find peace of mind and peace of soul'; 'I don't really know what I want, but it may have something to do with religion'. It may simply be a barely expressed longing to find meaning. And all this masks a real desire for God.

If you like, you could say that all St Ignatius is doing is taking a person where he finds them, patiently staying with them, and listening to them, even when they may as yet be some way from being ready to begin. He is trying slowly to uncover the layers of debris that are choking the frail shoots of desire, and to disclose (or better, to enable the person to disclose to themselves) the underlying desire. The underlying desire for what? For God? For Christ? Perhaps for something they would call only goodness?

Then, when they are ready, Ignatius invites them to make 'some exercises in accordance with the degree of progress made and adapted to the needs of a soul so moved' (Exx 18). He goes on to focus, one by one, on the moments or articulations of the 'natural' growth of faith and grace. He suggests the exterior conditions and the interior climate that he has found from experience to favour that growth (Exx 73-90). And as the desire begins to grow, he harnesses it to further growth, always with a view to the end.

So, one element of the dynamic of the Exercises is to bring into a fruitful and powerful conjunction the obscurely desired and as yet unknown finality, and the person's desire for it. To say all this is to name the human side of a process of growth that is entirely the work of the Spirit. What we can do is 'to make some suggestions', and 'entirely to trust' in 'the gentle arrangement of Divine Providence' who 'requires cooperation from His creatures'.[1]

### Magis

St Ignatius would recognise as the reality at the heart of the Exercises the statement of St Thomas Aquinas:

> The greater the love the greater the desire. And desire in some sort prepares and opens the one who desires to receive the one who is desired.[2]

This desire is implanted by the Holy Spirit; it is the Holy Spirit desiring in us. It is part of the basic gift of faith. It is good to remind ourselves that the desire is, somehow and somewhere and however distorted in its expression, present in all men and women.[3]

'The greater the love the greater the desire.' Those comparatives, *maior, maius, magis*, are everywhere present in St Ignatius. St Thomas' statement calls to mind at once the twentieth Annotation (Exx 20). Here, as in so many places in St Ignatius' letters and *Constitutions*, you have an expression of the dynamic of faith; of the interplay of the human and the divine that gives force and propulsion, movement and growth; of the spontaneous need of the human heart to reach forward and to be moved beyond itself to God.

> It will be very profitable for one who is to make the Exercises to enter upon them with magnanimity and generosity towards his Creator and Lord and to offer Him his entire will and freedom, so that his Divine Majesty may dispose of him and all he has according to His most holy will. (Exx 5)

The fifth Annotation is one of the small number of preliminary notes that St Ignatius wished to be given to someone before embarking on the Exercises (Exx 15). It says less about an act of the cold will than about a disposition of the whole person, a level of desire.

---

[1] IV.8.8 [414]; Preamble, 1 [134].

[2] *Summa theologiae*, 1.12.6.

[3] Interested readers might like to consult Harvey D. Egan, 'Christian Apophatic and Kataphatic Mysticisms', *Theological Studies*, 39 (1978), 329-426, especially 418 onwards.

**Principle and Foundation**

When the exercitant is given the Principle and Foundation and asked to ruminate on it for a day or two, the one who is giving the Exercises will be wondering about the exercitant's response to it. It is a kind of touchstone that reveals in some way how far the retreatant is likely to go or to grow. The dry and laconic text is wholly free from emotional resonance and, I think, intentionally so. It contains in its brevity and dryness all that later unfolds. It is less like the foundation of a building than a seed of life, a principle of force, of movement and growth.

This principle of growth is not, of course, in the text or in the words but in the reality that the text expresses. If you like, the Principle and Foundation is like an X-ray that discloses to the exercitant the desire that is already present, perhaps explicitly, perhaps latently, perhaps strongly and consciously, perhaps obscurely and delicately. Naturally, too, it begins to disclose to an exercitant who has some fairly mature experience of life and some realistic sense of himself the ambiguity of his desires, the darkness in his heart, his moral impotence, the feelings that can surge in revolt or revulsion. He is not free. He can desire to be. God wants him to be.

**First Week**

So we may expect to find him moved by the Spirit to desire to be free, to be purified, to be healed, to repent. It is the same dynamic as that of the gospel, of those who encounter Christ: 'Repent and believe the gospel'. The exercitant is invited to enter into a prayer that is an intimate conversation with Christ on the cross, who is present from the first words of the Exercises, and who will be their Way to the end of the Exercises and beyond. Christ is at once the object of the exercitant's desire and the only way to satisfy it. In the triple colloquy of the First Week, exercitants beg for light to see all that has been a burden in the past and a hindrance to their freedom, all that has clogged and distorted the relationship of love between them and Christ, all that constrains or inhibits their freedom to love. They beg to be enabled to see the particular disorder that is the root of their sins, that will accompany them in their living, and that no power of their own will eradicate. The more someone knows about human nature and about themselves, the more they will be made aware that there are undiagnosed imprisonments, unfreedoms of which they do not know; they will have to learn to wait for the time when God sees that he or she is able to be aware of them, to face them and, perhaps, to be obedient to God's will that they remain. There will never be a time when they will not need to surrender their weakness to the weakness and power of Christ, who took all our illnesses upon himself and by whose wounds we are healed.

The gift of such graces as these contains within itself a force that moves the person onward in desire. When it is given, it is an experience of relief and release, of consolation in the presence of goodness and mercy. It begins to disclose a little the true God, the Father of Jesus, who loves unconditionally. It begins to destroy all the false images of God, the broken reflections of a person's egoism, all those attractive or dismaying masks that we construct for God so that we may hide Him and hide ourselves from Him.

The gift of consolation that is the fruit of the First Week of the Exercises is also an enlivening discovery of the conditions that will continue to be necessary if we are to maintain our freedom and to grow in it: 'to act against their own sensuality, against their carnal and worldly love' (Exx 97). The term 'self-abnegation', without which the *Spiritual Exercises* and the Ignatian *Constitutions* remain meaningless, is destined to be meaningless, even harmful, if it is not experienced as an intrinsic requirement of love, as a determination to be free, as a precondition of growth in desire.

**What Is to Be Done?**

The questions that St Ignatius suggests in the colloquy before Christ on the cross—'What have I done for Christ? What am I doing for Christ? What ought I to do for Christ?' (Exx 53)—are a powerful element in the dynamic of growth in faith and desire. Exercitants find their source of growth in gratitude. The active and generous elements in St Ignatius' temperament, the practical sense of being engaged in an enterprise of moment, were taken up and taken into, purified and reinforced by, his mystical experiences at Manresa. The Exercises are for those who have those dispositions even in some small degree. 'Yes,

but what is to be done?' is never far from the forefront of St Ignatius'
mind. These questions are the practical articulations of desire. They
are as dynamic as the level of love and desire that prompts them, as
powerful as the degree of openness to, of surrender to, the power of the
Spirit who is at work.

It can be seen how all this is, step by step, one thing at a time, all
the time, pointing towards decision, or to what St Ignatius will call
the Election. It points towards the personal discovery of all that is
implicit in the highest degree of spiritual freedom. As the exercitant is
moved forward into the Second Week, the indifference of the
Principle and Foundation begins to disclose itself as a freedom to
desire to respond to the call of Christ, and to be contemplatively
identified with him and with his work, 'should your most holy
Majesty be so gracious as to choose and receive me to such a life' (Exx
98). 'Might it be ...? If only I could ...?' It is part of the experience of
this dynamic that such a gift is given, not contrived, that it can be
desired and received but not grasped. It is not at our command. It is a
contemplative gift. In every hour of prayer in the Exercises, desire
experiences petition as a need.

## The Dynamic within Each Hour

Within that overall dynamic there are other subordinate dynamics at
work. As the exercitant begins the Second Week, there is a dynamic
within each hour and a similar dynamic within each day. Within each
hour there is a movement from asking at the beginning for 'what I
want and desire' to colloquy. Every hour of prayer in the Exercises
begins with a time of quietness in which the body is engaged and where
the exercitant allows himself to 'become aware of how God my Lord is
beholding me' (Exx 75). Nothing could more clearly remind us of the
necessary perspective of all prayer, of the sovereign freedom and
initiative of God in the entire life of grace and faith, of God's desire on
our behalf. The exercitant begs at the beginning of every hour that his
whole being 'may be ordered purely to the service and praise of the
Divine Majesty' (Exx 46).

This general expression of his desire moves to a particular and
concrete petition. In the Second Week, this is:

… to ask for what I want and desire. Here it will be to ask for an interior knowledge of the Lord who is made man for me, that I may love him more and follow him (Exx 104).

This petition focuses and specifies the original and growing desire. Its force, its efficacy in disposing us to receive what God so desires freely to give, is as strong as the underlying desire. To the extent that it is real, it will be realistic. The exercitant is brought to ask himself before God: What do I really want? How much do I want it? How really do I want it?

It can be objected that this imposes on the exercitant a prayer for something that in his deepest self he may not want. Who is St Ignatius, who is a director, to suppose that this particular exercitant ought to want this? Will not this move him into alienation, confusion and conflict? The objection is a good one if it brings inexperienced directors to ask themselves what they are doing. But in fact it can be truly said that these focused petitions are all implicit in the gift of faith, that they are the 'natural' articulations of the original gift of the Spirit. A person who experiences within himself no desire at any level of the Spirit for these specific gifts should not be making the full Exercises. An experienced director will encourage an exercitant to come to his own expression of what he really wants. If the exercitant is as mature as the full Exercises require, he will know without being told that we may not lie to God.

### The Dynamic of *Lectio divina*

The movement from 'asking for what I want' to the colloquy can be seen more clearly by recognising the affinity of Ignatian contemplation with the movement of *lectio divina*. The four steps of the *lectio divina* are, so the tradition has long told us, like a ladder, and a ladder is a simple instrument to accomplish the dynamic of getting off the ground. *Lectio* corresponds to 'calling to mind the history' (Exx 102) of the particular mystery in Jesus' life in Ignatian contemplation. *Meditatio* corresponds to what St Ignatius, in this Second Week, calls 'contemplation'. *Oratio,* in which one asks or begs for or desires what has been seen as good or needed or desirable, is the same as the Ignatian colloquy. In the monastic tradition this was held to be as far as we can go, aided indeed by grace, in seeking God. *Contemplatio* is something that is simply given and cannot be acquired or induced; the corresponding term in St Ignatius is 'consolation'.

The terminology is of small importance. What is important is to recognise that reading is with a view to meditation; that meditation is with a view to prayer; and that prayer is with a view to that openness to God or readiness for His gift that disposes the spirit to receive what God freely desires to give. In the same way the preliminaries in Ignatian contemplation are with a view to prayer, to colloquy, to speaking 'as a friend speaks with a friend' (Exx 54). The Ignatian pedagogy of contemplation is designed to help the one who is praying to discern when and where to be still, to be able to receive:

> ... at the point where I find what I desire, there I will remain in repose, without being anxious to go forward until I have been satisfied.[4]

From the beginning the exercitant has been helped to trust his own desires, to come to recognise them in truth, to express them in an exchange that is direct, intimate and personal. The 'asking for what I desire' at the beginning, expressed by St Ignatius in the general and familiar language of the faith, becomes, through the movement experienced in the hour of prayer and in the light of what has happened—in the light, too, of the exercitant's personal history, experience and self-awareness—an exchange that becomes more and more concrete, particular and personal.

### The Dynamic within Each Day

There is, besides, a dynamic inherent in each day of the Exercises. There are five hours of prayer, beginning during the night. In the Second Week the first hour is a contemplation of, for example, the Three Persons beholding the earth and all humanity and the moment of the incarnation. On the same day, the second hour is a contemplation of the Lord's birth. The third and fourth hours are 'repetitions' of these contemplations, in which the exercitant returns, less diffusely and more simply, to 'dwell where I have sensed greater consolation or

---

[4] Exx 76; compare Exx 199.

desolation or greater spiritual savour' (Exx 62). This is a movement from what is wider and more detailed to what is simpler, more focused, less busy. The day follows what might be called the natural development of prayer. It is the Ignatian way or pedagogy by which the whole person is disposed to be led towards contemplation.

The Ignatian day ends with an exercise that St Ignatius calls 'applying the senses'—what in the tradition are known as the interior or spiritual senses. This prayer, when it is possible (it is hard to see how it can be made in desolation), is a further simplifying and focusing of the Spirit at a deep level. When the soul is quiet and recollected, it returns again to where it found itself invited to dwell (Exx 227), in a desire to be simply present to the mystery. During the course of the Exercises, the day can be seen as a movement towards the gospel event, towards Jesus in his relationship with the Father and with those who responded to him in love, or in hesitation, or in refusal. The whole person is engaged in looking and listening, not only to what the persons say but to 'what they might say' (Exx 123). All that is a preparing or disposing of oneself in desire to be drawn through the event into the mystery and, beyond the mystery, perhaps, into the silence and dynamism of the Divinity, the divine *dynamis*, the still and powerful interrelationship of Father, Word and Spirit.

## Reflection and Repetition

What seem to be original in St Ignatius are the repetitions and what has come to be called the review of prayer, in which after each hour of prayer the exercitant reflects upon what has happened during the hour. The review is made with a view to the repetitions. Both are essential factors in the dynamic of the Exercises. The review is, of course, or at least soon becomes, a prayerful exercise in discerning where the Creator and Lord in person is communicating Himself to the devout soul in quest of the divine will (Exx 15), and where, in Ignatian language, movements come from the good spirit or from the bad spirit or from one's own activity (Exx 2, 32, 331, 336). This attitude of discernment is itself dynamic. It is asking: Where is God's power at work? Where is God's love attracting and drawing me? It looks to decision, to resolution, to action. 'What ought I to do for Christ?' (Exx 53)

> Eternal Lord of all things ... it is my earnest desire and my deliberate choice ... to imitate you ... should your most holy Majesty be so gracious as to choose and receive me to such a state and way of life. (Exx 98)

The discerning movement of the review of prayer, in its attention and sensitivity to the movements of the spirits, presupposes the exercitant's desire to be entirely available in freedom to God in the dynamic of grace, in the interplay of desolation and consolation, of resistance and surrender, in which the exercitant is both exercising and being exercised.

## Relationships

This points to another element in the dynamic, to a series of relationships. There is first the paramount relationship of the exercitant with God, the free, initiating, sustaining and active relationship of God with the soul and the exercitant's intimate response. Secondly, there is the relationship of the director with God and of God with him; this seeking to find God in sensitivity to His will is the first duty of a director. Finally, there is the relationship of the director and the exercitant in the Spirit, in which, incomprehensibly, God works to accomplish His designs. The director in some sense represents the believing community, the whole Christ, the tradition, and is borne up by the faith of the Church, since,

> ... between Christ our Lord the bridegroom and the Church his bride there is the same Spirit that governs and guides ... because by the one Spirit who gave the ten commandments our Holy Mother Church is ruled and governed (Exx 365).

This relationship between the director and the exercitant is based on a trust that is freely given (and therefore can be withheld), in which the director reverences the sovereign freedom of God and the sacredness of the exercitant's freedom (Exx 22). It is in this trusting exchange that the movements of consolation or desolation and what seemed to occasion them, noticed by the exercitant in reflecting on his prayer and returned to in the repetitions, are articulated as best they can be, looked at and reflected on, and then cautiously interpreted— that is, discerned. The director discerns and tries to help the exercitant to learn to discern the significance of the movements. All the while the director is privileged to be present to and to be keeping in mind the whole process of growth, the movement of the dynamic as it unfolds in this particular exercitant, often in unpredictable ways: the hopes, the courage, the stumblings, the fears, the searchings, the resistances, the failings of heart, the waverings and recoveries that mark the painful strugglings of desire.

## Two Standards

Behind all this are always present the questions: Where is this pointing to? Where is it leading? Is there some action or decision or change that God is drawing the person to? What may be the next step of effective growth in desire? To what degree of closeness to Christ does 'your most holy Majesty wish to choose and receive me' (Exx 98)?

St Ignatius takes it for granted that, as God continues to elicit and strengthen the heart's desire, the exercitant will be drawn towards some decision that will affect the way they live. Such a decision, if it is 'from above, that is, from the love of God' (Exx 184), will be conformed to the pattern of Christ. 'Father, I want those you have given me to be with me where I am.'[5]

The way forward, however, is beset with possibilities of illusion. The aspirations of an exercitant may be beyond what God is desiring for him. Or his deeper and subtler attachments may induce him to cling to what is familiar and safe, and he will experience fear of the measure of closeness to Christ to which the Father is calling him. Or he may simply shirk decision at all. Either his fears or his unpurified desires may lead him to misinterpret what God is inviting him to. At this point the considerations of the Two Standards and the Three Classes have their place.

Why are they placed here and what is their place in the dynamic of the Exercises? 'We will begin, all the while contemplating his life, to explore and ask in what kind of life Christ desires us to serve his Divine Majesty' (Exx 135). The more there is at stake for the building of the Father's kingdom, the more the exercitant will experience the

---

[5] John 17:24; compare 12:26, 1 John 2:6.

turbulence of conflicting emotions, the onset of fear, the ambiguity of his desires, the alternations of light and darkness, of desolation and consolation. Soon he will be contemplating Jesus in his struggle in the desert temptations. When desire is drawn towards concrete decision, there are many ways in which we can be turned from the Way. So,

> ... as some introduction to this ... we will look at the intention of Christ our Lord and in contrast at the intention of the enemy of our human nature (Exx 135).

## The Enemy of Our Human Nature

There is no question here of a choice between the standard of Satan and the standard of Christ, between obvious good and obvious evil. What is in question is the way in which generous people, in seeking the good, can be led to choose the less good. What is more, they can be deflected from the values of Christ and misled into choosing what is opposed to the gospel. 'It is concerning good things', says St John of the Cross, 'that the soul must ever have the greatest misgivings, for evil things bear their own testimony with them'.[6]

The exercitant, recalling from the experience of the First Week the darkness in his heart, and asking here for 'what I want and desire', begs for light and asks that his spirit may be clarified and illumined by the Spirit of Jesus. The universal and total designs of the enemy are pondered: 'no province, no place, no state of life, no individual is overlooked' (Exx 141). Not even the holiest is immune. The enemy is envious of freedom; he casts nets and chains. He tempts people in seeking the good 'to desire riches ... that they may the more easily come to the empty honour of the world and then to great pride' (Exx 142). Everything that is not God can become the object of the heart's desire, 'riches'. What looks selfless, idealistic and noble needs scrutiny. We can cling out of fear to things that are small and trivial or exalted and spiritual. The more spiritual and patently good they are, the more easily we can make them a substitute for the living God. The holier, seemingly, the object, the more we are in

---

[6] *Ascent of Mount Carmel*, 3.37.1.

danger of idolizing it. There is no spontaneous desire of the human heart that does not need to be purified, especially the desire for God. The source cannot purify itself. It must turn its gaze continually to Christ until he becomes the source.

**The Way of Our Creator and Lord**

The way of Jesus in the gospel is to submit himself entirely to the loving will of the Father. By contrast with the enemy, Jesus is 'lovely and gracious' and 'chooses so many persons, apostles, disciples and sends them through the whole world to spread his holy teaching through all states and conditions of humanity'. He sends 'his servants and friends to help all by attracting them' to desire to be like him in his poverty and rejection, for from this desire comes humility (Exx 146). If we desire him, we desire his way. To desire him is to choose the way. Only a constant and loving contemplation of the light of the world can penetrate the darknesses that lurk in the thickets of our desires.

'All the while continuing to contemplate his life.' Godly decisions are not made by turning to ourselves but by keeping our contemplative focus on Christ. If God desires to make His will known, the discernment will probably take place in the day by day contemplation of Christ in the mysteries of his earthly life. It is in those hours of being with him that the movements of consolation and desolation will occur. The exercitant is moving, as it were, on two paths that run parallel; on one he begins to seek to know God's call or task; on the other he is immersed in Jesus in his ministry. What God may desire for him may at first be experienced as painful and fearful. At times this path may come close to what is given him to perceive of Jesus' way. At other times it may diverge and be experienced as desolation. These two paths, or perhaps these two themes, will, if it is what God desires, come into alignment or harmony with one another and perhaps into contemplative identity. The person's life comes to be united with Christ's life, Christ's way. There may remain at a surface level some sense of pain or fear. But at a deeper level of the spirit there will be a sense of rightness or wholeness. Should that sense of rightness and wholeness persist, it would indicate what St Ignatius means by 'confirmation', especially if it remains when sensible consolation is absent.

**Three Classes**

The prayer of the Two Standards is for illumination of the judgment. The prayer of the Three Classes looks to the will. What we ask for and desire is 'grace to choose what is more for the glory of the Divine Majesty' (Exx 152). The consideration tests the reality of our desires. If we truly desire the end, we choose the means. Our desires remain illusory so long as we refuse to embody them in concrete choice.

The first class of people confront us with the ways in which we postpone and evade decision. 'The hour of death comes and they have not taken the means' (Exx 153). The second class, too, desire to be free, but they also desire what is a burden upon their freedom. They want and do not want. They want to be free of the burden, 'but in such a way that they retain what they are attached to, so that God is to come to what they desire' (Exx 154).

> Such persons do not go directly to God, but want God to conform wholly to their ill-ordered attachments. Consequently, they make of the end a means and of the means an end. (Exx 169)

What we protest that we mean and what we actually mean are often out of phase. Our own designs masquerade as God's glory.

The third class, too, desire to be free. They do not presume that what they feel to be more difficult is what God desires for them.

> They desire neither to retain nor to relinquish ... they seek only to will and not will as God our Lord inspires them. ... Meanwhile, they will want to conduct themselves as though in their heart [*en affecto*] they had left what they are clinging to .... As a result, the desire to be better able to serve God our Lord will be the cause of their keeping or relinquishing. (Exx 155)

The fact that St Ignatius wants the exercitant to pray the triple colloquy and to continue to do so during the coming days is a sign that this degree of freedom, this deeper purification of our desires, is not something we can acquire of ourselves, but is rather a contemplative gift. We can only dispose ourselves to receive it by desiring to be placed with Jesus.

The indifference of the Principle and Foundation (Exx 23) begins to reveal itself as a freedom to desire to be identified with Christ who is poor and on the cross, a desire which is ready to enter into the consequences of doing his work and sharing his lot, 'since he is the way that leads men to life' (Examen, 4.44 [101]). Desire wants to be free. It wants to be unburdened of the wayward and illusory desires that impede and mislead it.

### Degrees of Freedom

To make a choice that is 'sound and good' (Exx 178) requires as a minimal disposition the grace of the second degree of humility, which is the gift of indifference.[7] Here St Ignatius introduces a deeper degree of freedom, the desire to be drawn into closer conformity with Jesus:

> To desire and choose poverty with Christ poor ... insults with Christ laden with them ... in order to be really more like Christ our Lord ... to desire to be looked on as worthless and a fool for Christ, who first was held to be that. (Exx 167)

And to desire this even when 'the praise and glory of the Divine Majesty would be equally served' by an easier way.

St Ignatius does not propose this for prayer, but as something to be pondered upon from time to time during the day. 'It will be very useful to consider and to give one's attention to the three degrees of humility before entering upon' the process of discernment and decision. One ponders this in order that 'the heart may be moved to love the true teaching of Christ our Lord' (Exx 164). St Ignatius says it will help very

---

[7] Dir 1.17: 'Care is to be taken during the elections (which ought to be made with entire resignation of the will, and, if it is possible, with a disposition that is close to the third degree of humility) that the exercitant prefer, should God be equally served, those things that are more conformed to the counsels and example of Christ. Someone who lacked that indifference of the second degree of humility should not make the election ....' For the Directories, see now *On Giving the Spiritual Exercises: The Early Jesuit Manuscript Directories and the Official Directory of 1599*, edited by Martin E. Palmer (St Louis: Institute of Jesuit Sources, 1996).

much to pray the triple colloquy if one desires to attain 'this third humility' (Exx 168).

St Ignatius could not have made it plainer that this is something we cannot grasp by willing it. We can only desire to be given it. 'If one desires.' There is no proposal here of a programme for behaviour. St Ignatius is speaking of a climate of the heart, an attitude that expresses itself in desire. He is inviting the exercitant to see if perhaps at some deep level of faith he finds it has been given him so to love Christ, to have the desire to be enabled so to desire.

To be given such a gift is to be free with the freedom of Christ to be entirely available to the Father. In the presence of such a disposition the Father can make His will known. It is the point towards which the dynamic of faith and grace tends. It is not something exotic or alien to the desire of the heart for God, but is intrinsic to the movement of all things towards their fulfilment in Christ. One cannot be more free than this to choose what is according to the mind of Christ. Beyond this one is now ready to be drawn by the Father into the experience of Christ in his passion and resurrection, to grieve with him in his grief (Exx 203) and 'to rejoice in our Creator and Redeemer' (Exx 229).

## From Exercise to Receptivity

In a person who in truth desires to be entirely open to God and to the designs of His love, the dynamic of grace and faith, especially during the Second Week of the Exercises, often tends to appear more and more as a movement from the exercitant's self-exercising, his own active responding to God's initial gift, towards a greater receptivity and passivity. It may be that this is experienced within a single hour of prayer or within the movement of the day. Something of it may be expected within the dynamic of the Exercises as a whole. This is so not because of anything special to the Exercises but because in a person who is striving to be wholly faithful to the intrinsic dynamism of his desire, that is how God works, 'labouring for me' and 'desiring to give Himself to me as far as He can' (Exx 236, 234).

It becomes clear that it is God who is the giver of growth, the energizer of the process, the one who first lovingly gives the spontaneous desire of the human heart for Himself. It is God who caringly invites and entices our hidden self into the open and watches over its unfolding, who Himself strengthens it through the pain and darkness, the hesitations and the taking heart, the struggles and surrenders, the angers and fears, the alternations of repugnance and joy. The dynamism of the Exercises is not the Exercises, though they have been a powerful instrument in preparing and disposing the heart, but God and His wise understanding of the heart He has created for Himself. That is the objective reality. Subjectively it is experienced as that pure consolation that can only be His gift, the gift of Himself (Exx 316, 330, 331, 336).

## The Dynamic beyond the Exercises

If we may be allowed to say that the fourth point of the Contemplation to Attain Love is an appropriate expression of the disposition of one who has completed the Exercises, it is interesting to note that its last word is *etcetera* (Exx 237).

This points towards the continuing dynamic that has been brought to light and has become familiar in the experience of making the Exercises. The Exercises are a point of departure. The seeds of the particular gifts of grace given in the course of the experience will burgeon in the living of daily life, in obedience to the pain and joy of living, in a refusal to be protected against the instructive experience of life, above all in the call to be spent in serving others. The discovered dynamic of desire is the disclosure of God present in all the details of His providence and in a person's inner fidelity to the movement and attraction of the Spirit, a fidelity expressed in a sensitive discernment of all reality.

The dynamic of the Exercises does not come from a cunning selection and ordering of a sequence of exercises and their inter-relationship. Those serve and are subordinate to the normal way of the human spirit and its desire in faith and grace. Their force for growth comes primarily from the dynamic interplay between God initiating and a person responding, an interplay between someone exercising themselves and striving and God responding, an interplay between our personal activity and God waiting and illuminating, inviting and freeing, allowing the pain of desolation for our maturing and consoling, an interplay between the human and the divine. It is a dynamic interplay of two freedoms: the sovereign freedom of God and the imperfect, crippled, blind, aspiring freedom of the human spirit: God wrestling with Jacob and Jacob with God.

# 4

# THE FIRST WEEK:
# PRACTICAL QUESTIONS

IN ANSWER TO THE BASIC QUESTION of what the director should do in the First Week, I imagine an experienced director would say 'I don't know', or 'I don't know what I am going to do until after the interview'. It is part of the incomprehensible dynamic of the Exercises that the Spirit works through the prayerful relationship of the director and the exercitant. What is said or not said is a function of the relationship and of what emerges in the conversation.

In practice there are three kinds of exercitant. There are those who have already met their director fairly frequently over a long period and who have been prepared by prayer and spiritual direction to begin the enclosed thirty-day retreat (this is closer to St Ignatius' practice). There are those who have been preparing themselves in the same way for the Exercises in Daily Life. Finally, there are those whom the director meets for the first time on the evening the thirty-day retreat begins.

This last kind would seem nowadays to be the most common. With such a person, the first few days of the retreat need to be given to getting to know him: to allaying feelings of apprehension and founding the possibility of trust; to establishing a prayerful atmosphere; and to discovering (as far as possible without asking questions) why he wants to make the Exercises, what he desires and is seeking, something of his situation in life, what the pressures of his work are, whether he has come to the retreat bone-wearied, whether he has been praying, how he prays, how important prayer is in his life, what he cares about, whether he has made this kind of retreat before, and who God is for him.

Fairly early in the first few days I suggest, firmly, that the retreatant begin each time of prayer as St Ignatius recommends (Exx 75), so that the time of prayer has a formal beginning; so that the body is brought into prayer; so that the perspective is right (*como Dios nuestro Señor me mira*, 'how God our Lord is beholding—contemplating—me'); so that the focus is on God rather than on self; so that he begins to feel reverence before the holiness and majesty of God. I will also try (often with limited success) to show him how to make the review of prayer, since it is essential to the dynamic of the Exercises, and without it he will not begin to learn what is helpful in order to reply to the standard question: 'Well, what has been happening … ?'

### Readiness for the First Week

During these days I will try to pick up the signs that will show me whether the retreatant will be able to make the exercises of the First Week. Negative indications will include: a defective image of God (demanding tyrant or wholly indulgent Daddy); a very defective self-image; a weak faith; a weak sense of God that makes a true sense of sin difficult; a weak hope that has small expectations of God's power and desire to give his gifts (Exx 5: 'to enter upon them with magnanimity'); an absence of mature relationships in his life; a Pelagian tendency to imagine the Exercises to be a technique.

I will want to encourage the retreatant to spend at least a day or two ruminating about (the term of the early Directories) or praying over the Principle and Foundation—in these times probably longer than that. Louis Beirnaert says somewhere that people today need to discover the very meaning of God's sovereignty; hence the Principle and Foundation cannot remain simply a set of ideas, but must become an exercise for acquiring an awareness of the absolute primacy of God. By this time I will be hoping that he has begun to pray, to experience something of God's goodness and love in prayer. Until that has begun to happen, I should be unwilling to go into the First Week.

The retreatant's response to the Foundation is something of a touchstone for his readiness to make the Exercises and especially for his readiness to begin the First Week. The closer he comes to the dispositions of the fifth and twentieth Annotations, the more I will have hoped that he has discovered some growth in desire to give himself wholly to God. Moreover, in the light that comes from God and in the light of some previous glimpse of what interior freedom is, there should also be a growing desire to be 'indifferent', the desire to experience the freedom of the Spirit (2 Corinthians 3: 17), the desire to participate in the freedom of Jesus before the Father and before all other things.

However, the person needs to be tempering this with some realistic sense of their own capacities. As they hear St Ignatius' casual statement 'therefore it is necessary to make ourselves indifferent', they should be aware of a power within themselves to expand somewhat the area of their own human freedom. At the same time, they should realise that we cannot 'make ourselves indifferent'. Only the power of the Spirit can do that. They should be realising, 'I do not know how to find God's particular and concrete will for me', and indeed, 'were I to know it, I do not have the moral strength to do it'.

The early Directories seem to be clear on this, that the exercitant should experience the difficulty (*para que sintais la difficultad*) of becoming that free. Both Ignatius' own directory dictated to Vitoria and that of Eduardo Pereira speak of the fruit of the Foundation as 'resignation':

> Indifference is a 'resignation'; a man places himself in the hands of his God and Lord .... When the whole heart does this really and in truth, it greatly disposes him for God's communication of Himself, because it opens the door of the heart, so that the Lord can work great things in him.[1]

All this has something to do with readiness to begin the First Week. I believe that in the coming years the director of the enclosed thirty-day Exercises will have much to learn from the guide of the Exercises in daily life; indeed the latter may (in practice if not in principle) become the paradigm of our direction of the Exercises. For Fr Maurice Giuliani, the transition into the First Week is one of the moments in the Exercises which comes into sharper relief when the process is being undertaken in daily life:

> ... after several weeks of the Exercises, a real attitude of 'indifference' shows that the retreatant is ready to enter into the mystery of mercy and salvation .... A distance develops between being and action, between the fundamental desire of his heart and the manifold desires which swarm around, to the point of paralyzing him; between the vital attachment he feels for people and the invitation to break with all love that is

[1] Dir 4: 21; 10: 30-31.

possessive. Some sort of order begins to emerge among his feelings; superficial movements of sensitivity die down and give way to movements that the person sees to have another origin … at the very heart of everyday living, a power is leading the person's consciousness, making him pass from selfishness to the gift of self … in the sense, so to speak, that his daily life is 'ruled' by Another …. Is this what we call 'indifference'? I think so. In the Exercises in daily life, this is a threshold, the very threshold which marks the beginning of the experience of the Exercises.[2]

## Entering the First Week

A director knows that he cannot contrive or bring about these insights or dispositions. And since he cannot do this, he should not try. All the director can do is to propose or to urge or to suggest those dispositions that open us to receiving the gifts of the Spirit, to be alert to signs of such dispositions that may as yet be obscure to the exercitant himself, to clarify them, perhaps to suggest that he return to them in prayer, and to point the way forward. The director prays for the exercitant. He tries to discern and to help the exercitant to discern what is happening. He may certainly encourage the exercitant to be grateful for what he has been given and encourage him to be confident that it is a favourable disposition for the rest of the Exercises.

The more the exercitant desires to have the dispositions of Annotation 5 and the more he has entered into interior silence and has really begun to pray, the more I should expect him to begin to be moved towards a sense of his sinfulness. The other side of the Principle and Foundation is a sense that I am not free, that I cling to many things whether they are God's will for me or not, that my capacity to love is imprisoned in a thousand ways. Before moving into the meditations of the First Week, I should be waiting for some sign that the exercitant was being moved in that direction. If the Exercises seem to be less effective than we might hope, it may be that people are being moved prematurely into the First Week, and that the Spirit has not been given time to prepare them or to dispose them. Of course, if in praying the

---

[2] Maurice Giuliani, 'The Exercises in Daily Life', *Progressio*, Supplements 18-19 (November 1981), 36, 14.

Foundation an exercitant were clearly and markedly moved in an unexpectedly different direction, or moved to remain in consolation in an attitude of adoration or worship or surrender to the goodness of God, then a good director would not interfere (Exx 15).

Fr William A. Barry in a well-known article says:

> ... we have taken a stance of not leading retreatants through the Exercises .... We try ... to help the retreatant to pray spontaneously, to enjoy this kind of prayer, and to find his own way and content .... The stance we take means that we do not introduce the 'First Week' ideas after a certain period of time. Rather we let the dynamic of prayer and of God's dealing with the person do the 'introducing'. What does this mean? We have found that many of our retreatants are led into what might be called a 'First Week experience' ... the retreatant begins to experience a sense of alienation, of impotence, of desolation .... He feels himself unworthy of God.[3]

Ideally it is the exercitant who discerns and decides when he should move into the First Week exercises, as into any further stage of the Exercises. It is for this reason, among many, that the Exercises in daily life are beginning to look like a privileged way, since there is plenty of time in which to allow an insight or a grace to go deeper before moving ahead. Fr Giuliani is insistent that it is the exercitant who must decide when it is time to go forward.[4]

**The Director's Own Understanding**

Among the things I keep in mind in presenting the First Week are:

- The grace of the First Week is a grace of profound consolation.
- St Ignatius' way of putting it is given in the fourth Annotation: 'contrition, sorrow and tears for sin'.

---

[3] See 'The Experience of the First and Second Weeks of the Spiritual Exercises', in *Notes on the Spiritual Exercises of St Ignatius of Loyola*, edited by David L. Fleming (St Louis: Review for Religious, 1981), 95-102, here 96, 97.

[4] Guiliani, 'The Exercises in Daily Life', especially chapters II and VIII.

- What is customarily called the *id quod volo*, asking for what I desire, focusing on a particular grace to be begged for and desired in prayer and throughout the day, is essential to the dynamic of the Exercises.

- The terms 'shame and confusion' can easily be misunderstood by a contemporary exercitant. I see no such problem with 'a growing and intense sorrow'.

- It is better that the exercitant come to his own expression of the grace to be desired. Time is not wasted if he can come truthfully to answer the question 'What do I really want?'

- The terms in which St Ignatius proposes the Colloquy indicate the kind of grace he hopes will be given: the grace of being deeply moved *de arriba*, from above, to wonder and gratitude before the mercy and goodness of God.

- The director will expect the path to the consolation of the First Week to be an experience of desolation.

- The director will not want, through mistaken kindness or because of his own discomfort, to try to move the exercitant prematurely away from that desolation.

- Desolation is a turning in on oneself, a being imprisoned in isolation from others, from the world, from oneself, from God. The director will be alert to sense if such a state is in danger of taking hold, of becoming a settled and barren self-preoccupation. Then he will try gently to shift the exercitant's focus from self to Christ.

- 'Only God speaks well of God.' Only God speaks well of sin. Only God can reveal my sin to me. Apart from the light and presence of God my unworthy behaviour may remain only a sense of pervading guilt at breaking laws, of acting unethically, of betraying my self-respect and undermining my self-esteem. (We need a new word to help us distinguish between healthy and unhealthy guilt.) For many retreatants nowadays, much prayer in the presence of God's goodness may be needed to liberate them from such substitutes for a realisation of what their sinfulness really is. The grace of the First Week is a liberation from *ersatz* guilt.

- The grace of the First Week is a new knowledge of God. I do not see how we can come to know God without a deep sense of our sinfulness and our absolute need for salvation. The more closely a soul is drawn to God the more it will experience layer upon layer of self, of the false self. In the continuing experience of finding God in all things, the further discovery of unexpected sinfulness can become, in the light of the First Week grace, a joyful means of entering into a deeper knowledge of God.

- The grace of the First Week leads to a realistic facing up to the reality of oneself. It undermines our sinful need of self-justification. It places us naked and unprotected before the goodness and the love of God.

The director will want to have a clear grasp of his own understanding of the dynamic of the Exercises. The more he has this, the more he will be free to sit easily to the letter of the *Spiritual Exercises*; equally, the more he will be free to use the text unaccommodated, if that is what will help the exercitant more. The dynamic of the First Week is understood by grasping the movement from the *id quod volo* to the colloquy. The points in between in the text are of secondary importance. The parts of the First Week that I should tend to look on as essential are:

- the second preludes in the first two exercises;
- the colloquy before Christ on the Cross;
- the triple colloquy;
- the additions that recommend a sober environment and interior climate, a calm urgency of desire;
- the repetitions;
- Exx 46: the petition before every hour of prayer for the grace of the Principle and Foundation.

## The First Exercise

Should one use the three points as given by Ignatius or not? I do not know. A director has to ask himself whether these points will help or hinder the exercitant, whether they will help the exercitant find the fruit of 'shame and confusion' and open him to an intimate and personal speaking with Christ on the cross. Scripture passages will be more helpful to some. The Ignatian principle should always prevail: have a contemplative grasp of the end and be flexible in your use of the means. The points are means.

There are some parts of the text that it may be helpful to keep in mind. St Ignatius does not at first ask the exercitant to look at his own sin or sins. He first presents him with the pervading contagion of sin in the world. The exercitant meditates first on sin 'out there' as it were. It would not be un-Ignatian to have the exercitant recall to his memory and imagination the effects of sin in the world as he has experienced and observed them. This would, besides, be in keeping with the dynamic of the First Week, which looks towards the contemplation of the Incarnation. In these days one would want the exercitant to be livingly aware of evil in his contemporary world, lest his sense of sin be individualistic, or lest the angels and Adam and Eve be too detached from the reality of his experience. There is a sufficient hint of this in 'and the great corruption which came upon the human race' (Exx 51). We are more and more likely to meet with two types of exercitant: those who, for whatever reason, are anaesthetized to the sin in human structures; and those who are deeply moved by injustice but imperfectly aware of it as sin. Of course those exercitants who are deeply moved by injustice and feel their powerlessness are already disposed for the prayer of the First Week.

However, for all that, St Ignatius does move towards consideration of one's own sins. This he does by a series of comparisons: 'When I compare the one sin … with the many sins I have committed … for one sin, and the number of times I have deserved … because of my numerous sins'. His stress here is on frequency, as much as to say that the multitude and frequency of my sins, whether venial or mortal, ought to be a painful reminder of my heedlessness and ingratitude. We cannot grasp our solidarity in grace if we do not see our solidarity in sin. It is our antidote to the professional hazard of Pharisaism.

Ignatius wants to help the exercitant to begin to realise the intrinsic 'gravity and malice of sin against our Creator and Lord'. Many exercitants may need much time to seek to be given a sense of this, given that our contemporary climate gives us many reasons for justifying ourselves in our own eyes (and, we hope, in God's eyes), and for diluting our responsibility. It is a mode of thinking that can coexist with a need to cling to a sense of one's worthlessness. And, note, the colloquy with Christ on the cross is indispensable.

Should one use the first prelude, 'a composition, seeing the place', in which I 'consider that my soul is imprisoned in this corruptible body' (Exx 47)? Or how might one use it? How might one suggest that it be used? For all our fastidiousness about possible dualism or about a disordered sense of evil in the world, it seems to me that the images St Ignatius uses are scriptural. It may help some exercitants greatly to stay with, to steep themselves in, some of the scriptural images of imprisonment, of unfreedom, of constriction, of exile, of alienation, of the absence of light, of blindness, of falsity and untruth, of the felt absence of God, of hopelessness, of the weight of sin and its oppression. 'And a great famine arose … and he began to be in want …. And he would gladly have fed on the pods that the swine ate; and no one gave him anything.' (Luke 15: 14-16)

**The Second Exercise**

For the *first prelude* here, where St Ignatius simply sends us back to the first exercise, it may be helpful to gloss St Thomas to the effect that God is offended by our sins only in so far as they hurt ourselves and each other.[5]

In the *second prelude* the grace asked for is foundational to the gospel ('Repent and believe …'). There is therefore no need to apologize for or to transpose the words here—'great and intense sorrow, and tears for my sins'—into another idiom. However, it is good not to present the second prelude too rigidly or absolutely. It may help some exercitants more to suggest that they beg for a sense of God's eagerness

---

[5] *Summa contra Gentiles*, 3. 122: *Non enim Deus a nobis offenditur, nisi ex eo quod contra nostrum bonum agimus.*

to forgive, or for a sense of their need of the compassion of Christ. There are some who may need to spend much time in praying the parable of the prodigal son and his elder brother before making the second exercise.

The *first point* is about *el processo de los pecados*. Many retreatants, though this is becoming rapidly less common, will be used to frequent confession, and will need to be told that this exercise is not an examination of conscience in preparation for a general confession. One of the earliest Directories stresses this: 'To arouse sorrow, it does not help so much to go into details, but rather to picture the overall view of their gravity' (Dir 3: 10). At the same time, St Ignatius would not be content with vagueness but would want us to be concrete and specific.

The *second and third points*, weighing the sins with their foulness and malice, and seeing myself as a sore and an ulcer, are not intended to encourage people to depress themselves into a state of disordered self-abasement. The director needs to be alert, and to shift the focus away, if necessary, from a barren self-preoccupation. Should we allow our contemporary nervousness at phrases like 'the corruption and loathsomeness of my body' to force us to be silent about these points? Clearly if such imagery will be an obstacle rather than a help to being open to the grace of 'growing and intense sorrow', or will prevent the exercitant from entering into a colloquy 'extolling the mercy of God our Lord ... giving thanks to him that up to this very moment he has granted me life', then it should not be suggested. But perhaps many exercitants are tougher than we think. It seems to me that a sense of sin is likely to remain superficial and, in these times, too privatised, if we are too squeamish to accept that as a sinner I am a 'source of corruption and contagion'.

The *fourth point* is an invitation to contemplate God, to turn the focus firmly to Him, His wisdom, His power, His justice and His goodness. Together with the *fifth point* it is a repetition of the Principle and Foundation. The affective insight that St Ignatius seems to hope for here is something like:

> It could have been otherwise. It ought in all justice to have been otherwise. If the roots of the capital sins in me have not taken

control, that is not due to me but to Christ. I am loved. I am alive. And I am free.

The director knows that he is impotent to teach that lesson. It is not his work.

### The Third and Fourth Exercises

This is not the place to expand upon the crucial importance of 'repetition' in the Exercises. Whether one presents for meditation the Ignatian points as they stand or equivalent passages from Scripture is of secondary importance. The petitions of the triple colloquy are indispensable. The words may need some exegesis. There should be a sense of calm urgency about the asking.

In the dynamic of the Exercises St Ignatius is looking ahead towards the degree of freedom of the Spirit that is a prerequisite for finding God's will. Any act of discernment requires that I be aware of my particular disorder, my ill-ordered affectivity, my bias (Exx 21: 'without being determined though any affection that might be disordered'), so that I may constantly take it into account in practical judgment and decision.

What is being sought here is an interior knowledge (*para que sienta interno conocimiento*). Where Ignatius introduces 'the mediators', it is an indication that what we are desiring is not something acquired by willing and thinking, or rather by simply willing and thinking, but a knowledge which is given and is the work of the Spirit. What is being asked for is a sense at a deep level of the particular sinfulness that is at the root of my sins. St Ignatius would not be content with a vague and generalised sense of sinfulness, but would want us to be particular and concrete. But the grace is sought and desired in the confidence expressed by Julian of Norwich:

> He, in his courtesy, limits the amount we see, for it is so vile and horrible that we could not bear to see it as it is. In his mercy our Lord shows us our sin and our weakness by the kindly light of Himself. (*Revelations*, Long Text, c. 78)

Without this repeated prayer it is hard to see how we can give any genuine or effective meaning to St Ignatius' doctrine of self-abnegation.

The conjunction of 'the disorder of my actions' and 'a knowledge of the world' may find some affinity with a contemporary theology of sin that sees man as structuring his world by his choices and being made by the world he structures.

## The Fifth Exercise

If an exercitant has been experiencing great dryness or desolation I should not feel compelled to suggest this meditation on Hell. If he has experienced something of the consolation of compunction, I should certainly ask him to pray the colloquy of thanksgiving 'that up to this very moment he has always shown himself so loving and merciful to me'. A director might legitimately add 'and that he will continue always to save me by his mercy'. If he has had experience of desolation and is willing to recall the taste of it, he will know what the possibility of separating himself from God is like. That, together with the authority of the Lord's words, 'Lord, Lord, did we not prophesy in your name? ... I have never known you' (Matthew 7:21-23) and 'I do not know where you come from' (Luke 13:25-27), and the parable of the judgment in Matthew 25, may be sufficient as a preparation for the colloquy. If we are too nervous about presenting this fifth exercise, it is no harm to look at St Ignatius' robust theology of fear and love in the final statement of the Exercises (Exx 370) as a complement to the second prelude:

> ... to ask for interior sense of the pain which the damned suffer, in order that, if through my faults I should forget the love of the Eternal Lord, at least the fear of the pains may help me not to come into sin. (Exx 65)

All the colloquies of the First Week open a person up to a realisation of mercy and love and goodness, to a sense of the gift of life, to the opportunity that remains to serve God, to release, relief and freedom, to gratitude and praise. There is a question, both here and earlier, as to whether St Ignatius' fiery imagery is compatible with this goal. I should refuse to be drawn into theological argument.

**All Five Exercises on One Day**

The text nowhere says that the massive First Week programme is to be repeated day after day. The second of the Directories going back to Ignatius himself is clear:

> Father does not think that the exercises of the First Week should be given him all together. He never did so, but gave them one at a time, until all five were given. (Dir 3:3)

If an exercitant is subjected to an introduction to all five exercises at one sitting, the result for most exercitants would be clutter. Clutter, a sense of being oppressed with too much matter, is to be avoided at all costs. Rather than that, it is better to simplify and to omit.

One assumes that the exercitant will spend some days at least on the First Week. Of course, if the grace is given without the apparatus of preludes and points, then there is no point in giving them; if the end is given, the means become unnecessary.

When the time has come to move forward from the Principle and Foundation, I should give the first exercise or its scriptural equivalent. If an exercitant has entered into prayer, that is quite enough material for one day's prayer. The second exercise can be given on the following day. I would want the exercitant to begin to make the repetitions and to pray the triple colloquy as soon as possible. Only then would I perhaps suggest spending a day going through the five, or four, exercises in succession. By that time they will tend, in any case, to be repetitions. But I see no especial virtue in doing all five exercises on one day in the order given. The contemplative shape of each day in the Second Week is quite another matter.

**The First Week—How Long?**

Another question to which there is no simple answer is, 'How long should the First Week last?' The director will be watching for a marked experience of the First Week consolation. As soon as that is present he will know that it is possible to move forward.

Why, then, should he delay at all? For two reasons. Firstly, so long as the exercitant is experiencing consolation, he is finding God and God is enlightening and strengthening him. 'Where I find what I desire, there I will rest, without anxiety to go forward until I am satisfied.' (Exx 76) Secondly, to remain a few days longer praying the prayer of the First Week will confirm and deepen the grace. I should expect, however, that with many exercitants the strong experience of consolation will begin to fade. The beginning of a certain distaste or dryness or weariness would be a good sign that it is time to move on.

Naturally the somewhat artificial arrangement in a retreat-house setting of an imminent repose day should not determine how long the exercitant remains in any of the weeks. But supposing that the exercitant, as far as one can judge, is not entering into the experience of the First Week and is not experiencing consolation, should one keep him there day after day for nine or ten or eleven days or more, until he is moved to sorrow and tears? I take it that most experienced directors would say 'no'. It may be that the exercitant has been entering sincerely into the prayer of the First Week and is, one may confidently hope, being given the grace he needs at the moment, and will perhaps be given a deep experience of conversion and contrition during the Third Week.

Alternatively, this may be the time to judge that the exercitant should not be making the full Exercises. Perhaps the exercitant would be more helped by spending the remainder of the month simply praying and being helped by daily spiritual direction. St Ignatius makes it clear that he would suspend the Exercises sometimes at the end of the First Week. The reason he gives is what he calls 'obstinacy':

> For all those who are not yet resigned into the hands of God our Lord so that He can act on them ... but who enter with certain plans and intentions, it is very fitting that all diligence be used in order that they be freed from such an attitude, because it is a moth that infests ... and prevents them knowing the truth. He who is known to be very obstinate in this way should not be encouraged to make the Exercises until he has become more mature. Nevertheless, after one who is thus obstinate has entered upon the exercises, it is necessary to try to help him .... If he has remained very obstinate for the First Week, it seems to me that I would not go forward with him. (Dir 4:20)

If someone has already made the full Exercises, then an eight-day retreat may often take the form of repetitions of some exercises, if that is what the exercitant wants or needs. If he is unfamiliar with the Exercises, then I see no value in trying to concertina the full Exercises into eight days. A director with a sense of the dynamic of the Exercises will be moved by that and will be able to sit more lightly to the letter of the text. There is a different dynamic in eight days, but I should find it hard to try to articulate that.

I believe that there is no one who cannot profit from prayer that seeks greater purification and conversion. We all continue to be sinners. Many priests and religious need the prayer of contrition and first conversion. The whole of an eight-day retreat may often be equivalent to the First Week of the Exercises. That does not mean that a director says so. Nor does it mean that he does not suggest matter from the gospel accounts of the infancy and ministry of Jesus, or of the passion and resurrection. It is obvious that what specifies the four weeks is not the points or the matter for meditation, but the grace needed and sought.

It is better in any retreat that the exercitant himself should discern and express the grace he needs. But a retreat would not be Ignatian in the absence of that clarifying and focusing of desire.

If a person asks to make the Exercises and knows what he is asking, then in a thirty-day retreat I feel an obligation to stay as close to the dynamism of the Exercises, and even to the text, as the leading of the Spirit allows. In the absence of any marked leading in a different direction I tend to trust St Ignatius' spiritual genius. But in a shorter form of 'some exercises' I tend to try to follow where the exercitant seems to be led rather than force him to jump through a series of Jesuit hoops.

# Part 2

## *The Ignatian Constitutions*

# Introduction

ADMIRERS OF JOE VEALE'S expertise in Ignatian spirituality have been left with one great regret: that he did not write a book on the Jesuit *Constitutions*. He had thought about it, and even sketched a provisional outline for such a work; but it never materialised. In spite of requests, encouragement and cajoling from his friends, he eventually decided to leave the project aside. The reasons behind this decision were complex, even opaque, and had more to do with his inner journey than with any lack of ability or competence. He had the raw material for such a book at his fingertips.

One reason that he occasionally offered was that he had said all that he had to say in his published articles. This is totally unconvincing when taken at face value, but it draws attention to a very important point: he was primarily interested in a methodology for reading the *Constitutions*. He wanted to open up the *Constitutions* in such a way that readers could find their own way through them. His aim was to offer a key to unlock what is a difficult text, and to show how it can brought to life. This is confirmed—though there are tapes of talks by Joe on the *Constitutions* that range more widely—by the titles of two of his three published articles: 'How the *Constitutions* Work' (1988) and 'From Exercises to Constitutions: A Spirit in Search of a Body' (1993). The third article, 'Ignatian Criteria for Choice of Ministries' (1986), deals with fundamental issues in Ignatius' understanding of discernment, and thus illuminates much more than the limited area indicated in the title.

Joe Veale's experience and research led him to two conclusions that then formed the presuppositions for everything he wrote. They might be expressed as follows. Firstly, one can fully understand Ignatius' experience, and hence Ignatian spirituality, only through a deep knowledge of *all* the Ignatian documents: not only the *Spiritual Exercises*, but also the *Constitutions*, the *Autobiography*, the *Spiritual Journal*, and the letters. These must be allowed to throw light on each other, and even to interpret each other. Secondly, the foundational Ignatian experience occurred at Manresa, and especially at the River Cardoner. Each of Ignatius' writings is an expression of that foundational experience, but in a different literary genre. These two presuppositions give a unity and even a particular form to Joe Veale's writing and teaching.

It is often said that while the *Spiritual Exercises* are for everybody, the *Constitutions* are specifically for Jesuits. Why then reproduce work on the *Constitutions* in a book aimed at a wider readership? They are, of course, of interest to those other religious who have taken them as their own, or at least used them as a resource. But beyond that? The two presuppositions mentioned above already give an adequate reason. It is a fallacy to think that one knows Ignatian spirituality if one only knows the Exercises. In fact, the *Constitutions* (the fruit of Ignatius' maturity) throw much light on the *Spiritual Exercises* (the fruit of his early post-conversion years).

But there is another saying: 'from the "I" of the *Spiritual Exercises* to the "We" of the *Constitutions*'. The *Spiritual Exercises* deal with personal spirituality; the *Constitutions* move towards a corporate spirituality. In our contemporary world, where many lament an exaggerated individualism, there is a desire to live a more corporate expression of Christianity. The *Constitutions* illustrate how one Christian group, the Society of Jesus, achieved and continues to achieve (however imperfectly) this aim. This in turn links with another contemporary issue, that of formation for ministry, whether it be lay or ordained. On this theme too, there is much to learn from the *Constitutions*. And the article on 'Ignatian Criteria for Choice of Ministries' will help many today, whether as individuals or as groups, as they wonder where best to focus in ministry, where to invest their energies, and how to incarnate their vision and generosity in a choice for the better (the Ignatian *magis*).

As there is overlapping between the 1988 and 1993 articles on methodology in reading the *Constitutions*, we reproduce here the first in full, but only an abridged version of the second. As they now stand, 'How the *Constitutions* Work' centres on the structure and genre of the *Constitutions*, while 'From Exercises to Constitutions' is chiefly concerned with how the *Constitutions* grow out of St Ignatius' generative experience at Manresa. The article on choice of ministries (1986) is published in full.

# 5

# HOW THE
# *CONSTITUTIONS* WORK

THE STORY OF THE EXPERIENCE of St Ignatius and his early companions, of the movement from Manresa to Rome, is the story of a process by which their experience is translated into the *Constitutions*. Their spirit is given a body. A charism is embodied in an institution.

But institutions can be a tomb of the spirit. In all human life, and especially in the life of the Church and of religious orders, there is a tension between the charism and the institution. How can you harness an earthquake or regulate a tiger? If you try to domesticate a tiger, do you risk turning it into a kitten? St Ignatius was well aware of the fact that religious enterprises which begin with spiritual energy can, with the passing of years, become humdrum and depleted of life. Routine and legalism can choke the original vitality. Efficient administration can try to impose by regulation what in the beginning had its source in a shared spirit. Impersonal authority can supplant spiritual government. Obedience, in response, can grow dispirited. Or, indeed, the body can continue with some juridical semblance of life while from within it can simply disintegrate and decompose.

## The Decision to Be a Body

The document that we call the Deliberation of the First Fathers describes what happened when the early companions came together in Rome in 1539 'to seek the gracious and perfect will of God according to the scope of our vocation'. They could not go to Jerusalem as they had planned. They had offered themselves to the Pope to go wherever he might send them. He was about to send them to different places:

> Would it be better for us to be so joined and bound together in one body that no physical dispersal however great could separate us? ... Finally we decided affirmatively, namely that since the most kind and loving Lord had deigned to unite us to

one another and to bring us together—weak men from such different places and cultures—we should not sever God's union and bringing together, but rather every day we should strengthen and more solidly ground it, forming ourselves into one body.[1]

That was quickly decided. It took longer to decide whether 'to pronounce a third vow, namely to obey one of us'. Their eventual decision to obey one of themselves was the equivalent of deciding to become a religious body. It was a decision to be permanent. They expressly wished to pass on to later generations the particular experience they had shared with one another.[2]

The only way to do that is to institutionalise. How, otherwise, do you communicate and conserve the original spirit? Spirit needs to be incarnated, to be given a local habitation and a name. But how do you wed the charism and the institution without killing the charism?

## The Divine and Supreme Goodness

'We think it necessary that Constitutions should be written' is a clear statement at the opening of the document (Preamble, 1 [134]). The Formula says:

> They had become companions ... [and] exerted themselves in the Lord's vineyard for many years ... performing with much praise in whatsoever countries they journeyed, and each one according to the grace granted him by the Holy Spirit Himself, all the services of charity which pertain to the edification of souls. *Therefore* our predecessor approved, confirmed and blessed their Institute ... *that thus* the bond of charity and the unity might be preserved both among the companions themselves and among others who would desire to follow that same Institute.[3]

'Therefore ... that thus ...': the object of the institution is to aid the bond of charity to be preserved. You institutionalise in order to sustain

---

[1] Deliberation of the First Fathers, translated in John Carroll Futrell, *Making an Apostolic Community of Love* (St Louis: Institute of Jesuit Sources, 1970), 189-190.

[2] See Formula of the Institute, 2; Examen, 4. 1 [53]; 4. 27 [82].

[3] Formula of the Institute, 2; emphases JV.

love. The *Constitutions* are, in a sense, a Contemplation for Obtaining Love addressed to the body of the Society of Jesus. The bond of love is *de arriba*. This quintessentially Ignatian phrase points to what St Ignatius experienced as entirely given from above, as something that could never be the object of human achievement or striving.

> The chief bond to cement the union of the members among themselves and with their head is the love of God our Lord. For when they are closely united to His Divine and Supreme Goodness, they will very easily be united among themselves, through that same love which will descend from the Divine Goodness and spread to all other men and particularly into the body of the Society. Thus from both sides charity will come and in general will come all goodness and virtues through which one proceeds in conformity with the spirit. (VIII 1.8 [671])

The companionship and the mission are a participation in the love of the Three Persons, 'as rays descend from the sun and waters from a fountain' (Exx 237):

> The Society was not instituted by human means; and neither is it through them that it can be preserved and developed, but through the omnipotent hand of Christ .... (X. 1 [812])

At all important junctures of the *Constitutions* the same theme recurs: the primacy of the divine initiative and activity. The vocation is experienced as being totally contemplative.

The response to the love of the Supreme Goodness is, therefore, *Deum primo semper ante oculos habere*:

> ... first of all to keep before his eyes God and then the nature of this Institute which he has embraced and which is, so to speak, a pathway to God; and then let him strive with all his effort to achieve this end set before him by God—each one, however, according to the grace which the Holy Spirit has given to him ... (Formula of the Institute, 3)

The first movement is from God, and the constant response to that is to keep God always before one's eyes. *Deinde*, in the second place, is the Institute; the particular way of living, and the law that endeavours to put words on it, are secondary and subordinate. 'And then let him strive': the ascetical comes third; it is consequent upon and dependent on the previous contemplation of God. 'To achieve this end set before him by God': it is God who gives the vocation and specifies the end.

The whole movement of the *Constitutions* is here. It can be seen in particular parts and chapters and within single paragraphs as well as within the document as a whole. The movement is from God to the human means, then to the person's appropriation of the means, and finally back again to God.

There too is the characteristic Ignatian emphasis on being clear about the distinction between the means and the end. It is helpful to notice how frequently St Ignatius reiterates the end:

> This is the order which will be followed in the *Constitutions* … while keeping our attention fixed on the end which all of us are seeking, the glory and praise of God our Creator and Lord. (Declaration on the Preamble [137])

The end is absolute and invariable. Then, so long as one purely desires the end, one can be flexible with regard to the means. Besides, not all the means have the same importance; they have a hierarchy of value.

### The *Constitutions* and the *Spiritual Exercises*

The *Constitutions* do not stand alone. They are an elaboration of the Formula of the Institute, which expresses the outcome of the Deliberation of 1539. They are linked with the preceding General Examen. They presuppose, above all else, the experience of making the Spiritual Exercises, which was the experience the early companions had shared, the experience by which 'the most kind and loving Lord had united us to one another and brought us together'. It is not surprising, then, that the *Spiritual Exercises* are printed as part of the Institute:

> To maintain faithfully the grace of our vocation as described in the Institute, the *Spiritual Exercises* of our holy founder stand in first place, both as a perennial source of those interior gifts upon which depends our effectiveness in reaching the goal set before us, and as the living expression of the Ignatian spirit which must temper and interpret all our laws. (GC 31, d.4, n.1)

The *Constitutions* are unintelligible apart from the experience of making the Exercises. Indeed, without that experience the *Constitutions* are dead. There is an organic relationship between the two. It is helpful, as one reads the *Constitutions* and tries to live them, to see the Exercises coming through and to see the differences—to see how the *Constitutions* cast light on the Exercises and how the Exercises cast light on them.

'To seek God and to find Him in all things.' St Ignatius' own words are the best summary of his relationship with God. From the beginning, in Manresa, his mystical experience was of the Three Persons. In the contemplation on the Incarnation at the opening of the Second Week of the Exercises, the Three Persons behold, contemplate the world, the whole of creation and of human history, the reality of all our human experience. St Ignatius never sees the Three Persons apart from creation, *todas las cosas*. He never sees creation apart from the Three Persons.

It is integral to St Ignatius' experience of God that the smallest event in our human lives is governed by the providence of God. God manifests His concrete and particular will, His providence for our lives, in many ways: through the gospel; through the believing community, the Church; through the circumstances of our lives; through the demands of service, the needs of God's people; through obedience; and also through the interior leading of the Spirit.

**The Freedom of the Spirit**

What did St Ignatius hope would be the outcome of making the Exercises? Of the many ways in which an answer might be given, the one closest to his expectation would be: someone who had been given the freedom of the Spirit, the inner freedom that enables one to be led by the Spirit in all situations and circumstances: '… through that same love which will descend from the Divine Goodness … in general will come all goodness and virtues *through which one proceeds in conformity with the Spirit*'.[4] To one who is familiar with the *Spiritual Exercises* and the *Constitutions* it is evident that behind them is always present a distinctive or particular experience of God. For St Ignatius, this experience of God, rooted in his time in Manresa, found a focus in the meditations

---

[4] VIII. 1.8 [671]—emphasis JV.

on the King and the Two Standards. One cannot read the *Constitutions* without being aware of them.

### Exercises and Experiences

There are three stages, inseparable and interdependent, of entering into a spiritual appropriation of the Jesuit vocation. Firstly, making the Exercises. Secondly, doing what St Ignatius called the experiences or experiments. Thirdly, returning from these two experiences to the text of the the the Constitutions.[5]

The Exercises without the experiments could be detached, olympian, antiseptic, self-centred, self-preoccupied, individualist. If that is what they become, then this is not in harmony with St Ignatius' hope and intention. The whole thrust of the Exercises is towards mission, towards the apostolic contemplative life: 'that filled with gratitude for all, I may in all things love and serve the Divine Majesty' (Exx 233). For St Ignatius, 'to love and serve His Divine Majesty' is inseparable from 'to love and serve people', and from 'helping souls'— *ayudar a las ánimas*. What ensures that the fruit of the Exercises does not lapse into spiritual egoism or a disembodied spiritualism is the experience of finding God in the limited, messy, disordered, unsatisfactory, illogical and passionate reality of people's lives.

It is the interplay of the Exercises and the experiments that, in the intention of St Ignatius, reconstitutes the contemplative experience of the early companions. What comes first is the experience, what they

---

[5] *Editor:* Technically the Exercises themselves are the first of the six experiences or experiments named in the *Constitutions* but (as here) the word is more commonly associated with the other five: ministry in hospitals, pilgrimage, humble service in the novitiate house, teaching catechism to boys and the illiterate, and (where appropriate) priestly ministries of preaching and hearing confessions. See Examen, 4.10-15 [65-70]. St Ignatius was aware that by introducing experiments as an integral part of Jesuit formation he was breaking new ground. So it is helpful to see the rationale that he offers in a preliminary document written in 1541: 'The reason which impels us to give greater importance to experiments and to devote more time to them than is customarily employed in other congregations is the following: if someone enters a well-ordered and well-organized monastery, he will be more separated from occasions of sin because of the cloister, tranquillity and good order there than he will be in our Society. For this Society does not have that cloister, quiet and repose, but travels from one place to another. Moreover, if one has bad habits and lacks some perfection, it suffices for him to perfect himself in a monastery so ordered and organized. But in our Society, it is necessary that one be well experienced and extensively tested before being admitted. For as he travels about later on, he must associate with men and women both good and bad. Such associations require greater strength and greater experience, as well as greater graces and gifts from our Creator and Lord.' (MHSJ Const. 1, 60)

were accustomed to call *nuestro modo de proceder*, our way of proceeding. It was this that they articulated in the process of election (discernment) that is recorded as the Deliberation of the First Fathers, and then put into words in the Formula of the Institute. The Formula is the substance of the papal document that founded the Institute. The *Constitutions* are, in turn, an elaboration of the Formula.

The *Spiritual Exercises* and the *Constitutions* are typically Ignatian in that they are not concerned to expound a doctrine; they avoid the abstract and look to concrete living and choice. They embody a dynamic. The *Constitutions*, like the *Spiritual Exercises*, lead into a set of experiences or, more properly, suggest the conditions under which such experiences may be given. For St Ignatius, this began with mystical experiences in Manresa, which then led to his pilgrim searching alone for the particular way of service those graces entailed. This involved his constant prayerful reflection on experience, leading to decision and action; his discovery that the Exercises could dispose others to be given the same kind of grace; the experience of companionship in grace in Paris, issuing in the months of menial service and poverty and street preaching in Venice and Vicenza and the northern towns; the decision to go to Rome, to the Pope, and then, as Paul III was about to scatter them, the Deliberation, the election to form a body and to pass on the founding experience to later generations.

There are evident differences between the *Spiritual Exercises* and the *Constitutions*. The *Exercises* are addressed to all Christians; they engage individuals; they may, as happened from the beginning, issue in a Carthusian or a Dominican or a lay vocation. The *Constitutions* are addressed to a body in its members, each of whom has been given the same spirit, has experienced being called by God in the same way and towards the same end, to seek Him and to find Him in a life of service, to be an instrument of God's saving work in the world. The *Constitutions* have as their purpose the health, the well-being, the energy and growth in the spirit of the body.[6]

---

[6]  See the Preamble to the *Constitutions*, and all of Part X.

## Structure and Meaning

The *Constitutions* are like the *Spiritual Exercises* in that they cannot be described in terms of any literary genre. It is easier to say what they are not than what they are. Fr Pedro Arrupe wrote:

> The book of the *Constitutions*, though it contains juridical elements, is not a code. Though it possesses many ascetical-spiritual elements, it is not a book of devotion nor an ascetical manual. Though it offers many directives that are apostolic on the human level, it is not a simple textbook for the apostolate or for pastoral ministry.[7]

Jean Beyer, formerly Dean of the Faculty of Canon Law in the Gregorian University, said of the *Constitutions*, 'We have a law that is not a law, a code that is not a code'.[8] If they are not any of the above, then what are they? The key to understanding them and to interpreting any part of them is their structure.

The *Constitutions* are so structured that if we want to understand them we need to see each part in the whole and each part in organic relationship with all the other parts. The Summary of the *Constitutions* served us well, but it was defective. It was as though someone had taken *King Lear* and extracted the great speeches and lyrical passages, arranged them in some rough logical order, dismembered the text, dislocated the dramatic structure and destroyed the story, and had then said: 'there you have the essence of *King Lear*'. Moreover it is as though the dismemberer of *King Lear* had omitted: 'And take upon's the mystery of things as if we were God's spies'. Unaccountably, the Summary left out three of the most characteristically Ignatian passages in the *Constitutions*: the reference in the context of apostolic training to the need for the unction of the Holy Spirit, with the suggestions offered in the text presented merely as opening a way (IV.8.8 [414]); the flexibility of the directives regarding the prayer and austerities of the formed members (VI.3.1 [582]); and the passage

---

[7] Pedro Arrupe, in an address at Loyola, Spain, September 1974.

[8] Jean B. Beyer, 'Originalità e dipendenza delle Costituzioni', in *Introduzione allo studio delle Costituzioni SI* (Rome: CIS, 1973).

already quoted about the love of God our Lord serving as a bond
between the members and their head (VIII. 1.8 [671]).

### The Road, a Path, the Way

The General Examen explores the level of desire of one who wants to
enter the Society (Examen, 4.44 [101]). To desire the end is to have a
desire to set out. It is the beginning of a journey. The image of the road,
a path, the way, recurs throughout the text. It recalls the *Autobiography*,
where St Ignatius speaks of himself always as 'the pilgrim'. That
metaphor came naturally to men who knew that it was to be their
vocation to be constantly on the road, moving from place to place,
never settling or putting down roots, always to experience the
insecurity of having no permanent roof, to live 'in journeyings'.

The Institute, *via quaedam ad Deum*, is, as it were, one road to God.
'We think it necessary that *Constitutions* should be written to aid us to
proceed better ... along the path of divine service on which we have
entered' (Preamble, 1 [134]). The novice or the young scholastic will
'endeavour always to go forward in the path of the divine service'
(III. 1.10 [260]). But he may 'run too rapidly' and may need to be
restrained; or he may need to be 'stimulated, urged on and
encouraged' when he flags (IV. 6.15 [386]). The formed members will
be 'men who are spiritual and sufficiently advanced to run in the path of
Christ our Lord to the extent that their bodily strength and exterior
occupations and obedience allow' (VI.3.1 [582]). In experiencing what is
characteristic of the poor,

> ... where the first members have passed through these
> necessities and greater bodily wants, the others who come after
> should endeavour, as far as they can, to reach the same point
> as the earlier ones, or to go farther in our Lord (Examen,
> 4.26 [81]).

The early companions,

> ... made that fourth vow ... in order that his Holiness might
> distribute them for greater glory to God. They did this in
> conformity with their intention to travel throughout the world
> and, when they could not find the desired spiritual fruit in one
> region, to pass on to another and another, ever intent on

> seeking the greater glory of God our Lord and the greater aid of souls. (VII. 1 . B [605])

> For he gave us an example that in all things possible to us we might seek to follow Him, since He is the way which leads men to life. (Examen, 4.44 [101])

The novice or scholastic begins with a desire to set out.[9] But it is as yet unclear what will be the conditions of the road, the climate, the encounters and adventures, the incidents, the hazards of the journey. He cannot know them until he meets them, and no one can tell him beforehand because no one knows. The constant interior climate of the pilgrim is to find his assurance and security only in the Supreme and Divine Goodness and in the certainty of being sent by obedience and guided by the Spirit. All the rest is uncertain; he lives with insecurity. He is freely undertaking to be led into, and accompanied in, an experience, to be incorporated step by step, integrated into the companionship of the body on mission.

It is this that underlies the ten-part structure of the *Constitutions* and the mode, without precedent, of its composition.

### How the Body Is Formed for Mission

In Part I the individual is admitted. It may be that he is dismissed (Part II). He is cared for that he may go forward in spirit and in virtue (Part III). He is given the equipment of learning that he will need and begins to be apprenticed to the mission of the body (Part IV). Part V treats of his final incorporation.

The first five parts deal, therefore, with the formation and growth of the one who will be sent on mission. In treating of the formation of the individual members, the *Constitutions* describe how the body is being formed in its members. They are approaching the point at which the body is dispersed in its members on mission. But first, Part VI treats of the fully incorporated members in their relationship with God and with the other members, with the body.

---

[9] See Ignacio Iparraguirre, 'Caminare in spirito per la via delle Costituzioni', in *Introduzione allo studio delle Costituzioni*.

Part VII deals with the ways in which the members are dispersed 'in Christ's vineyard and their relations with their neighbours'. This is the end towards which all the rest has been moving. It is the end for which the Society was brought into being. And so it is the heart of the *Constitutions*. It is also the most primitive part of the text and the most indisputably Ignatian. The body, now fully formed, is articulated in its mission.

The last three parts of the *Constitutions* deal with the whole body in its life and mission. First, how the members so dispersed are to be kept in union, in coherent and co-operative action (Part VIII). Then, in Part IX, how the body is to be governed and given a head who will send the members, keep them in union and care for their growth in the spirit of the body by being,

> ... closely united with God and intimate with Him in prayer and in all his actions, that from God, the fountain of all good, he may so much the better obtain for the whole body a large share of His gifts and graces and also great power and efficacy for all the means which will be used for the help of souls (IX. 2. 1 [723]).

The tenth and final part, 'how the body can be preserved and developed in its well-being', repeats those elements that are essential if the earthen vessel that holds the spirit is to be sustained in continual and constant growth.

**The Order of Execution**

This description of the process of formation of the body, of the dispersal and the union, of the good government and vigour of the body, follows what in the Declaration to the Preamble [137] St Ignatius calls 'the order of execution', not 'the order of intention or consideration'. The 'order of consideration first considers the end and then descends to the means to attain it'. Characteristically, St Ignatius rejects that way. He prefers to keep to the process of experience. He prefers the concrete to the abstract. He looks to the means in constant contemplation of the end: 'while we keep our attention fixed on the end which all of us are seeking'. He is therefore concerned with the less perfect on the road to the more perfect; he implies imperfection in the traveller at the start and makes allowance for it. Michael J. Buckley has pointed out how St Ignatius is not here presenting ideals; he insists rather on contemplating the end, something that is spiritually and psychologically different. This method has to be flexible to adapt itself to the person, to his capacity and pace, 'according to the measure of divine grace imparted to each'. God is found in the reality of our human condition, and one finds God and serves Him by obeying it. The more abstract 'order of consideration' tends to be rigid. The way favoured by St Ignatius demands flexibility, in that the prescriptions of the *Constitutions* are to be implemented 'according to the circumstances of persons, times and places'.[10]

The order of consideration would properly proceed by topics: a chapter on obedience, another on prayer, and so on. That St Ignatius does not express himself in that way has puzzled many a lawyer who comes to the *Constitutions* without the experience of trying to live them, and has led to misunderstanding and misinterpretation. St Ignatius' method entails repetition, requires him to take up the same topic in changing contexts and at different stages of a Jesuit's life. To the man who likes things clear and distinct or who is more at home in abstract thinking, or to the legalistic mind, this method is unsatisfactory. In 1551, when a first draft was submitted to the founding group in Rome, the peppery Nicolás Bobadilla said it was like 'a confused labyrinth'. Even Alfonso Salmerón, who was learned and wise, said it had too much repetition.

The same theme is treated more than once. A good example is obedience. Part X treats of obedience in its function in preserving the well-being of the whole body; Part IX of the correlative to obedience, good government; Part VIII in obedience's function of maintaining the union of the dispersed members; Part VII in its function for mission; Part VI of the obedience of the formed and incorporated Jesuit; Part IV in the context of studies; and Part III of the obedience of novices. It is made clear that the obedience of a novice is not the same as the obedience of one who has been 'long tested' and who has been given the responsibility of a mission. It does not follow, of course, that

[10] See  II. 1. C [208];  II. 2. A [211];  II. 4. C [238];  III. 2. C [297];  IV. 4. B [343];  IV. 5. 1 [351]; IV. 6. K [382]; IV. 7. 2 [395]; IV. 13. 5 [462]; VII. 2. H [626]; IX. 3. 8 [746]; IX. 3. 11 [754].

what is said of obedience for novices has no meaning for the older men. Indeed, the full Ignatian teaching on obedience of the judgment is given only in Part VI. The earlier teaching is to be taken up and transmuted by the maturer man at a different level of experience.

**The Preamble**

The Preamble is given to help us to understand the nature of the text and how to interpret it. It is to the *Constitutions* rather as the Principle and Foundation is in regard to the *Spiritual Exercises*. The reality that it expresses underpins all that follows and is to be kept in mind as a guiding norm of interpretation, as a compass to hold one on course.

It would seem, says St Ignatius at the beginning, that Constitutions are unnecessary. The Society was not founded by human means (X. 1 [812]); therefore it must be 'the Supreme Wisdom and Goodness of God our Creator and Lord which will preserve, govern and carry forward in His divine service this least Society of Jesus'. The principal means used by the divine Wisdom is 'the interior law of charity and love which the Holy Spirit writes and engraves upon hearts'. This interior law is effective 'more than any exterior Constitutions'. 'Although' all this is true, 'nevertheless ... we think it necessary that Constitutions should be written to aid us to proceed better ... along the path of divine service on which we have entered'. The interior law of the Spirit is primary. The exterior law is useful and necessary.

There is the same relationship here between the human means and the divine initiative and activity as we find in all the central statements of the *Constitutions*. 'Nevertheless, since the gentle arrangement of Divine Providence requires cooperation from His creatures ....' Our created and redeemed reality must be true to itself; we do what we can do; the human must be reverenced and its goodness honoured.

A passage concerning the apostolic formation of young Jesuits, omitted from the Summary, is one of those that shows St Ignatius' sense of the relationship between the human and the divine. In the eighth chapter of Part IV, which deals with 'the learning and other means of helping their fellowmen', it is said that towards the end of their studies the scholastics should begin to accustom themselves to the spiritual arms they will employ. Since they will have to associate with so great a diversity of persons throughout such varied regions, they need to learn about the Society's way of proceeding. They should be able to foresee the opportunities which can be grasped for the greater service of God by using some means at one time and others at another. They are to be flexible and adroit in using a variety of human means. St Ignatius comments on the purpose of the text:

> Although all this can be taught only by the unction of the Holy Spirit and by the prudence which God our Lord communicates to those who trust in His Divine Majesty, nevertheless the way can at least be opened by some suggestions which aid and dispose one for the effect which must be produced by divine grace (IV.8.8[414]).

Such an approach is especially familiar to anyone who has given the Exercises. He knows that he can 'open the way by some suggestions'. What is humanly done is itself the fruit of the action of the Spirit and what is accomplished is wholly God's. As in the opening of Part X (X.1-3[812-814]), and in the Preamble, and in VIII.1.8[671], the spirituality calls to mind the eighteenth-century aphorism which attempted to capture the uncapturable:

> Trust in God as though nothing depended on Him but all on you. But so give everything you have to the work as though God alone were doing it and you not at all.

## Incarnation

At the heart of all Ignatian spirituality is a vision of the goodness of created reality and of the earthly and earthy reality of the Incarnation. It is, as one might say, a concrete and contemplative experience of the continuing Incarnation, of the Church. St Ignatius takes creation seriously; he never disdains the human, the real, the concrete, the historical, but sees them as sacramental, the channel of God's presence and power. All human reality, all human experience, is sacramental. The spirit seeks a body.[11] '…[N]either a disincarnate spiritualism nor a

---

[11] See Dominique Bertrand, *Un corps pour l'Esprit: Essai sur les Constitutions de la Compagnie de Jésus* (Paris: Desclée, 1974).

merely secular activism truly serves the integral gospel message.' (GC 33, d. 1 , n. 36)

Here we come back to St Ignatius' contemplative grasp of God's action in the world, of the creating and redeeming action of the Three Persons *ad extra*, of the supreme Wisdom and Goodness as our Providence. On 11 February 1544 he wrote in his Spiritual Diary:

> There came to me further understandings, namely how the Son first sent the apostles to preach in poverty, and then the Holy Spirit, giving His spirit and tongues, confirmed them, and so the Father and the Son sending the Holy Spirit, all three persons confirmed that mission.

God is the one who enters into, and is present to, and cares for our lives in every detail, who has a will in regard to our lives and mission, if only we can learn to seek and find it by 'proceeding in conformity with the spirit' (VIII. 1. 8 [671]).

### Experience Discerned

So, to return to where we were at the beginning. The writing of the Formula, the General Examen and the *Constitutions* is a human means designed to pass on to future generations the contemplative experience of the first companions. But it is not raw experience. It is prayed experience, reflected upon together and discerned in the Deliberation, before it is written down. Between the experience and the text comes the election, *discretio*, a process of discernment.[12]

An analogous process, in reverse, is required if the text is to be understood, interpreted and lived. It is the same with the *Spiritual Exercises*, and indeed with the other Ignatian documents. To interpret the text, to bring it to life again, to continue to found the order, to animate and to deploy the body demands, in a post-Enlightenment, post-Darwin, post-Freud, post-Marx world, a sensitivity to 'the interior law of charity and love' which is the Holy Spirit. Between the text and the living of it comes the election, a process of spiritual

---

[12] See Maurizio M. Costa, 'Costituzioni: esperienza ed ermeneutica' in *Introduzione allo studio delle Costituzioni*. To anyone who has read that article it will be clear how greatly my reflections throughout are indebted to it.

discernment repeatedly named in the text itself, *discreta caritas*. The written law is a useful means, an instrument. But the primary instrument is the body in its members, to the extent that they are *instrumenta coniuncta cum Deo* (X.2[813]). The *Constitutions* are not for speculative contemplation but for contemplative decision and action. It is this that embodies them, gives flesh again to the word, always 'according to the circumstances of persons, places and times'.

To bring this about one needs to be in tune with the text, with the *Autobiography* and the letters, above all with the *Spiritual Exercises*. A little erudition can help us to be somewhat more exact in understanding the sixteenth-century language, its culture and its theological assumptions. That knowledge will be imperfect at best. We need, too, naturally, to be as clear as we can about our contemporary world and the direction in which it is moving, its different cultures and theologies, the sense of the believing community and the needs of God's people now. Those are the human means. At least as important is the need to be affectively involved in the *Constitutions* and their satellite documents. We learn their meaning by living them.

It is in deeds more than in words that the *Constitutions* come to be understood. Their meaning comes alive in an experience together of 'proceeding in conformity with the spirit', of our way of proceeding. It is *discreta caritas* in action that opens the *Constitutions* to us. It is in that contemplative procedure that we are to seek and find God in what we are brought to decide and to do as we seek to meet new needs in a different world, in missonary action that embodies the same spirit in another time.

### Not a Rule

In that sense the Ignatian *Constitutions* are not a rule, a law that would prescribe in detail what must, as a rule, be done. For example, in Part VI, where you would expect to find some description of what it would be like for a formed Jesuit to live in a Jesuit house, all you find is the following:

> In regard to the particular rules which are employed in the houses where they happen to be, it is proper that they should endeavour to observe the part which is expedient either for their own progress and edification or for that of the rest among whom

they find themselves, and which is proposed to them according to the judgment of the superior (VI. 3. 3 [585]).

And in Part VII: 'What pertains to the offices of a house and other things more particular will be seen in the rules of the house' (VII. 4. 12 [654]).

The fact that the *Constitutions* do not prescribe details of common life does not mean that there is no common life. St Ignatius held common life to be important. He would expect common life to be arranged by the local superior in communication with the Provincial, in the light of circumstances, and in view of the particular apostolic function of the members who happen to be residing in the house. Nowadays, too, the arrangements would certainly be made in consultation with them. That Ignatian obedience is with a view to mission does not mean that one's day-to-day living does not come under obedience. There are some structures that have to be in place in order to ensure the human and spiritual well-being of people who live together and so as to ensure the vitality of the mission.

The *Constitutions* are to be observed and implemented. 'Hence all of us should exert ourselves not to miss any point of perfection which we can with God's grace attain in the observance of all the *Constitutions*.' (VI. 1. 1 [547]) But that implementation is not a mechanical or literal conformity. The *Constitutions* do not say what must invariably be done; they are not in that sense a juridical code. They are aimed at dealing with concrete realities. They are to be pondered rather than to be executed unthinkingly. They cannot substitute for *discreta caritas*; they require it, demand it, ground its necessity. They provide criteria for that discernment. They describe and prescribe those interior attitudes and dispositions before God that are needed if one is to use *discreta caritas* according to the circumstances of persons, places and times. They are not just useful spiritual counsels lacking all authoritative and juridical value. They are meant to be prayerfully used.

### The Body Discerning

The *Constitutions*, then, are a kind of law. But they are a law that provides explicitly for the transcendence of the law by giving first importance to the interior law of charity and love, to the Holy Spirit.

They are an instrument for missionary discernment, decision and action.

This discernment is never carried out, of course, independently of the body to which one has been joined as a member. Certainly a man must take responsibility for himself; that ultimate responsibility to God may not be supplanted by law or by obedience. He must stand over all his choices and be open to being led by God—yet always as a member of the body. Discernment is always done in the body. One's mission needs to be in harmony with the mission of the body. To be made a member of the body is to surrender one's unredeemed preferences and desires. The link between personal responsibility and the mission of the body is the communication and relationship between the member and his superior.

We come back once again to the relationship between the *Spiritual Exercises* and the *Constitutions*. The *Constitutions* presuppose the apprenticeship to discernment experienced in making the Exercises. It can be said that the primary note of Ignatian spirituality and of the charism of the Institute is *discretio habitualis* (GC 33, d. 1, n. 13). Just as the *Spiritual Exercises* are not a treatise on spirituality or prayer, but rather a programme initiating a person into an experience of seeking God in seeking His will, and just as the various prescriptions in the *Spiritual Exercises* are various ways of disposing the person to receive gifts from God, so the various prescriptions in the *Constitutions* are designed to facilitate an experience of the body, to dispose the body of the Society to receive gifts from God 'through that same love which will descend from the Divine Goodness and spread to all other men and particularly into the body of the Society'. It is a contemplative experience of the whole Society in apostolic action. The prescriptions, the themes, the topics are functional; they are means to something different, namely to the growth in the spirit of the body of the Society in doing what it was called together and sent to do, to respond in love to God as an *instrumentum conjunctum* in serving His people.

**A Tension of Opposites**

It has been shown by a French commentator that the *Constitutions* and their Parts, the chapters within the Parts and even single paragraphs within the chapters, have a structure that is *genetic, relational and dialectic.*[13] *Genetic,* in that the *Constitutions* are so structured as to show a process of growth. *Relational,* and therefore personal, since the individual member grows through a series of relationships. You could say that the whole *Constitutions,* certainly Parts I to V, are a document on formation, a set of guidelines aimed at forming a certain kind of man who will be an instrument united with God. The process of formation and integration into the body is, like St Ignatius' own formation, a process of reflecting on experience and praying it. But that is not done alone. It is done in relationship with a guide who, as in the Exercises, has been travelling the same road, and it is done within a wider network of relationships with the other members of the body. The formation is individual and personal, not an assembly line. Without that, the essentially contemplative nature of the life is almost certain to atrophy or disappear.

Then, finally, the structure of the *Constitutions* and the reality it reflects are *dialectic.* They operate through seeming contradictions that are in fact opposites in interplay. It is easily seen how, for example, Part VI, which treats of the personal life of the incorporated member, moves into Part VII, in which the members are dispersed. And that in turn gives place to Part VIII, in which the scattered members are sustained in union, a juridical union of the body and a spiritual union of hearts. The dialectic can be shown in operation in the language itself. We have seen how frequently St Ignatius expresses his sense of that in the characteristic verbal construction 'although ... nevertheless ...' whenever he confronts the mystery of the relationship between the freedom of God and human freedom.

We began with one of those pairs of apparent incompatibles, the charism and the institution, and wondered how they might be wed. The divine and the human we have also seen. There are many others: the individual member and the body; the discerning body and the Church; the spirit and the body; the mystical and the ascetical; passivity and activity; the freedom of the gospel and the law; the union and the scattering; a personal life and mission that require the

---

[13] François Roustang, 'Introduction à une lecture', *Constitutions de la Compagnie de Jesus*, volume 2 (Paris: Desclée, 1967), 122.

deepest level of freedom, responsibility and initiative in seeming contradiction with total obedience; inner enlightenment and rationality; the norms of intelligent reflection and discernment that are at one and the same time subjective and objective; contemplation and action; the most efficient and professional employment of the human means, whether of learning or of skill, and at the same time the realisation that it is only God who can make the fruit grow.

St Ignatius was too realistic, he had too keen a vision of the concrete, to be unaware of the tensions between these polarities. The human tendency is to grasp one pole strongly and to relax one's grasp of the other. What St Ignatius wanted was that both be held both gently and strongly. Our minds tend to think in terms of either-or. It is never easy to sustain our grasp of both-and. However, it is not a question of balance or compromise between two opposing poles; balance and compromise can lead to dilution and apostolic debility and then you have neither one nor the other. It is rather a question of holding firmly to both and waiting upon God to work in us a transcendence of the polarities, a resolution of the tensions, a compenetration of one with the other.

This points inescapably to the difficulty, the pain and the challenge of the life we are called to. We live in the insecurity that lies at the heart of the tensions, the most familiar of which is between action and contemplation. It is somewhere at the intersection of those apparent opposites that we are crucified to the world and the world is crucified to us. But it is also somewhere in that tension that imagination is set free and enlarged, and that prophetic creativity takes place.

# 6

# FROM EXERCISES TO CONSTITUTIONS

## The Spirit in Search of a Body

THE *CONSTITUTIONS* AND THE *SPIRITUAL EXERCISES* form a unity. Both have their origin in the same experience. The original experience is narrated in the document we generally call the *Autobiography*. There (nn. 28-30) Ignatius the pilgrim simply names the series of graces that culminate in the illumination by the banks of the Cardoner.

First, 'his understanding began to be elevated so that he saw the Most Holy Trinity'. Second 'the manner in which God created the world was revealed to his understanding with great spiritual joy'. Third, 'he saw clearly with his understanding … how Jesus Christ our Lord was there in the most holy sacrament'. Fourth, he tells us that 'often and for a long time, while at prayer, he saw with interior eyes the humanity of Christ'. Finally:

> … as he was going out of his devotion to a church … called St Paul's … the road ran next to the river … he sat down for a little while with his face toward the river, which was running deep. While he was seated there, the eyes of his understanding began to be opened … he understood and knew many things, both spiritual things and matters of faith and of learning, and this with so great an enlightenment that everything seemed new to him.

This account is not meant to be taken as chronological. What it tells us is that St Ignatius' mysticism is an experience of the Three Persons seen in relation to the world. And it is within that context that Ignatius experiences the sacramental reality of Christ in the Eucharist and the humanity of Christ. The sequence is significant: the Three Persons: the created world; sacrament; the humanity of Jesus. The trinitarian mysticism of St Ignatius is centred in incarnation. The Word is made flesh. Human and material realities are now seen to be sacramental. Spirit, from the beginning, it would seem, seeks to be given a body.

## All Things Seen New

St Ignatius tells us rather little about the fifth experience. He 'did not see any vision' but the eyes of his understanding began to be opened and he understood many things, both spiritual things and matters of faith and of learning. And everything, *todas las cosas*, the whole of reality, 'seemed new to him'.

We learn a little more through what Ignatius confided to Laínez, Polanco and Nadal.[1] Jerónimo Nadal tells us:

> The eyes of his understanding were opened by such a fullness and wealth of interior light that in that light he understood and contemplated the mysteries of faith and spiritual things and things pertaining to natural enquiry [*quaeque ad scientias pertinent*]. The reality of all things seemed to be manifested to him and a wholly enlightened understanding.
>
> Ignatius always set a high store by this gift and as a result of it conceived a profound modesty and humility; from it there began to shine in his countenance a certain spiritual joy and light.
>
> Whenever questions were put to him on matters of import-ance or when something was to be determined regarding the character of the Society's Institute, he would refer to that grace and light, as though he had there seen the guiding principles and causes of all things [*quasi rerum omnium ibi sive rationes sive causas vidisset*].
>
> He was raised above himself, in such a way that all the principles of things were opened to him.

St Ignatius gave Nadal to know that the understanding in which the whole of reality looked new was for him an insight into *rationes et causas*, the connections and relations of things. All things, human and divine, take on a shape, a pattern, and are moving toward an end. The text of the *Autobiography* is so familiar that it can escape us how

[1] MHSJ FN 1, 83 (Laínez); 2, 152, 239-240, 406 (Nadal); 2, 528-529 (Polanco).

strange it is that this mystical experience should have given him to understand 'both spiritual things and matters of ... learning'. In the one illumination he grasps together something of the things of earth as well as the things of heaven, a conjoining of the human and the divine.

### A Foundational Experience

This one experience is then communicated through three documents, which are otherwise very different: the *Autobiography*, the *Spiritual Exercises* and the *Constitutions*. In all three, St Ignatius attempts to embody in words an experience that is beyond words. And the putting into words is a kind of rudimentary incarnation of the communication of the Spirit.

The *Autobiography* does not pretend to give us a complete account of St Ignatius' life. What St Ignatius agreed to do was to recount the way God had dealt with his soul. It is not a simple chronicle of a sequence of happenings. It is experience reflected on, sifted and discerned; it is purposefully selected and shaped.[2] Nadal saw the telling and recording of the story as foundational: 'the Society develops in the same way as the life of the Father unfolded'.[3] The nature of the narrative and the circumstances of its telling allow us to say that St Ignatius saw it in that way too.[4] When the telling of the story was under way, Gonçalves da Câmara tells us in his preface that,

> Fr Nadal ... [was] very pleased that it was begun and bade me urge the Father, telling me many times that the Father could do nothing of greater benefit to the Society than this and that this was truly to found the Society. He himself spoke to the Father many times in this way.

It almost seems as though Nadal, the trusted expounder of the *Constitutions* throughout the Society in Europe, is saying that the

---

[2] See Leonardo R. Silos, 'Cardoner in the Life of St Ignatius of Loyola', *Archivum historicum Societatis Iesu*, 33 (1964), 3-43.

[3] MHSJ FN 2, 9.

[4] Laínez reports Ignatius as saying 'that when God chooses a person for the foundation of a religious order, He guides him in the way that He wants him to guide others' (MHSJ FN 2, 137).

*Autobiography* is of greater value than the *Constitutions* for the founding and the future well-being of the Society.

What is clear is that St Ignatius himself always understood the experiences at Manresa to be foundational. It is Nadal who tells us that when in later years St Ignatius was asked why this or that was in the *Constitutions*, he would reply: 'The explanation will be found in something that happened to me at Manresa'.[5]

## The Exercises and the Cardoner

Laínez, Polanco and Nadal are agreed that the Exercises were the fruit of those graces and especially of the Cardoner illumination. They say this expressly of the factors that are peculiar to the Exercises: the meditations on the King and of Two Standards; the process of election, of discernment, of the meaning of the movements of the spirits and of the guidelines for discriminating between the spirits. It is Nadal who suggests the origin in Manresa of what we would tend to see as especially original in the *Spiritual Exercises*: the shape, the sequence, the structure that in some measure accounts for their power. Nadal expressed the point in a striking phrase. He said that St Ignatius was moved by God *quasi in spiritu quodam sapientiae architectonico*.[6] A version of that in English might go something like: 'He was given a kind of spirit of wisdom that was architectonic'.

Architectonic? The primary sense comes from building, from architecture. It says something, not about exterior ornament or outward shape, but about an inner structure, an inner cohesion or coherence that gives proportion and unity to the parts. It is like the inner rhetoric that controls the order, sequence and coherence of an argument and that gives it its force.

We have to speak in metaphors. To capture something of that inner unity of the Exercises we tend nowadays to speak of their dynamic. That adds to the idea of an inner principle of unity the idea of movement. It suggests the image of a living organism whose life is

---

[5] MHSJ FN II, 240, 406.
[6] Nadal, *Scholia in Constitutiones S.I.*, edited by Manuel Ruiz Jurado (Granada: Facultad de Teología, 1976), 163.

not derived from itself, but whose factors and parts in their relationship and interaction make for movement and growth.

The *Constitutions* presuppose that we are familiar with the dynamic of the Exercises. The *Constitutions* continue and prolong that dynamic through the members who make up the body that is the Society of Jesus.

## Companions in Grace

The *Constitutions* express how the grace of the *Spiritual Exercises* and the *Autobiography* can be lived corporately. The spirit is given a body. What makes both the *Spiritual Exercises* and the *Constitutions* typically Ignatian is that they are not concerned to expound a doctrine; they avoid the abstract and look to concrete living and choice. Just as both documents come from an experience, they both lead into an experience. To speak more properly, they both state the conditions in which a particular experience may be given by God.

The first companions' decided to form a body with a view to sharing their way of living with others who might be given the same grace. They expressly wished to pass on to later generations the particular experience they had shared with one another.[7] The purpose of their new Company was mission.

Thus the divine freedom which they sought to live out was above all a freedom to do. God was understood as one whose providence has a task to be accomplished in the world. The *Spiritual Exercises* culminate with a contemplation of God at work in His world: '... how God works and labours for me in all things created on the face of the earth' (Exx 236). To be shown the detail of the task is to be united in the doing of it with the master of the 'work'.[8]

## The Kingdom and Two Standards

All this presupposes that the formed Jesuit companion has experienced the process of election in making the Exercises, and

---

[7] Formula of the Institute, 2; Examen, 4. 1, 27 [53, 82].

[8] These reflections are indebted to many articles of Michael J. Buckley, especially to '"*Sempre crescendo in devotione* ... ": Jesuit Spirituality as Stimulus to Ecumenism', *CIS*, 66 (1989), 63-101.

appropriated its dynamic deeply. And this process of election is inseparable from the two meditations that Nadal saw as specific to the Exercises and as deriving from the graces of Manresa. They are the meditations on the King and on Two Standards.

The meditation on the King looks back to the Principle and Foundation. The concluding words of the Principle and Foundation were, 'we should desire and choose only what helps us *more* towards the end for which we are created' (Exx 23). This is now transposed and becomes:

> Those who want to respond in a spirit of love, and to distinguish themselves by the thoroughness of their commitment to their eternal King and universal Lord, will not only offer themselves bodily for the task, but rather by going against their sensuality and their carnal and worldly love will offer *greater and more important* sacrifices .... (Exx 97)

There is always more. That is the nature of desire.

The Principle and Foundation is, as we know, christological. But the text is pared and bare, and the words are laconic and abstract. In the meditation on the King the words are given flesh. The desire to be drawn to 'desire and choose only what helps us more' is disclosed in Christ the eternal King as having flesh and blood. What seemed abstract in the Foundation is made concrete and personal. What seemed so rational is discovered to be an attraction, a personal invitation and call, a person.

At this point in the Exercises the exercitant may perhaps be moved to generous self-offering, but he does not know as yet to what degree of closeness to Jesus the Father may wish to draw him. The offering is made 'should your most holy Majesty wish to choose and admit me to such a state and way of life' (Exx 98).

Here St Ignatius touches on an important reality which is constant in the tradition and is crucial to Ignatian spiritual formation and government. It was said of St Ignatius that he followed the Spirit who was leading him and did not run on ahead. In the *Constitutions* there is a frequent refrain that everything is to be done 'according to the measure of God's grace imparted to each'. And in the Deliberation of the First Fathers, out of which the

Society was born, the companions recalled how they had worked 'each one according to the grace granted him by the Holy Spirit'.

From the meditation on the King onwards, exercitants are not only doing or making exercises; they are also beginning to be exercised. They are learning to attend to the movements of consolation and desolation and to what seems to occasion them. They are being helped to begin to judge something of the meaning of the movements. The dynamic of the growth of faith unfolds in a particular exercitant in unpredictable ways; in an alternation of hope and failings of heart, of courage and stumbling, of mistaken paths, of wavering and recovery, of fears and resistance: all the changes that mark the painful struggling of desire.

The attempt to live the *Constitutions* requires the prayer of Two Standards as a permanent attitude of the spirit, as a familiar way of beholding one's life in the world as it is. A person's experience will have shown him how his desire may run beyond his capacity or beyond what God is desiring for him. He sees how his deeper and subtler attachments induce him to cling to what is familiar and safe. He will have learnt something of the ways in which he simply shirks decision-making completely. He will have known fear at the measure of closeness to Christ to which he is being called. He will have begun to discover in his own history the particular and recurring patterns of the ways in which his fears and his unapproved desires can lead him to misinterpret what God is calling him to.

All this is a personal learning of the stratagems of the Enemy. For those who are encouraged in Part X to use all the human means with as much efficiency and effectiveness as they can, this prayer is crucial. It is in making the Exercises that a person learns the particular ways in which he, in using the human means, can insensibly be led to make a means of the end, to make the means a substitute for God. The experience of the Exercises teaches us the infinitely subtle variations, in each individual, of the terms 'riches' and 'honours'; how everything that is not God can become riches; how, the more an enterprise is selfless, idealistic and noble, the more it needs scrutiny; how the more spiritual and patently good are the objectives of our desire, the more easily, in clinging to them, we can be betrayed. We learn the devices by which good and prayerful people are led to courses of action that subvert the gospel.

These two dynamic meditations, on the King and the Two Standards, lead into the process of the election, the apprenticeship, as it were, to lifelong *discretio*, the art of discernment. Entailed in that process is an experience of the freedom of the Spirit (indifference) that the election requires. Without such an apprenticeship, a statement in the *Constitutions* such as 'to hold fast to this thoroughly right and pure intention in the presence of God our Lord' (VII.2.1 [618]) is likely to remain a harmless piece of piety.

## The Third Mode of Humility

Desire wants to be free. It wants to be unburdened of the wayward and illusory desires that impede and mislead it. It is in the course of making the Exercises that it begins to be clear that the freedom (indifference) of the Principle and Foundation is a freedom to desire to be identified with Christ who is poor and on the cross, a desire which is ready to enter into the consequences of doing his work in his way and to share his experience 'since he is the way that leads men to life' (Examen, 4.44 [101]).

It is toward this point that the dynamic of the Exercises has been moving. St Ignatius makes it plain that this is something we cannot grasp by willing it. We can only desire to be given it. To be given it is to be free with the freedom of Jesus to be entirely available to the Father. In the presence of such a disposition God can make His will known. One cannot be freer than this to choose what is more according to the mind of Christ.

What is a culminating point in the *Spiritual Exercises* is found, in the *Constitutions*, at the gateway into the Society. The applicant is asked, before he is admitted to be a novice, how he responds to the account of this grace of the third mode of humility given at the end of the fourth chapter of the Examen: '... the candidate should be asked whether he finds himself in a state of desires like these ....' The passage describes a climate of the heart, a state of desire:

> ... they desire to clothe themselves with the same clothing and uniform of their Lord because of the love and reverence which He deserves, to such an extent that where there would

> be no offence to His Divine Majesty ... they would wish to
> suffer injuries, false accusations, and affronts, and to be held
> and esteemed as fools ... because of their desire to resemble
> and imitate in some manner our Creator and Lord Jesus
> Christ .... For he gave us an example that in all things possible
> to us we might seek ... to imitate him, since he is the way
> which leads men to life. (Examen, 4.44[101])

For many this is a dragon in the gate. St Ignatius would not want a
man to go forward unless he could glimpse some sign of his having
been moved towards that level of faith, or at least to the grace of
desiring to be moved to desire it. It has been said that this grace is an
indispensable key to the *Constitutions*. In the absence of some affinity
with that grace, the *Constitutions* remain a closed book, a dead letter. It
is this reality of Christ poor and humble, the Christ of the cross, who
is present on every page of the *Constitutions*.

**The Single End**

It is significant that St Ignatius was content to express the essence of
his way as 'to seek and find God in all things'. It was left to Nadal to
coin the phrase 'contemplative in action'. The terminology was
certainly available to St Ignatius and Polanco. The words would
seem to have been appropriate for use in the *Constitutions*. We might
ask, then, why St Ignatius did not use them.[9]

To say 'contemplative in action' at once places a distinction
between the two. It suggests a separation. In the Jesuit way of proceeding the two are not separate. Neither is there a division between the
saving and perfecting of one's own soul and the 'giving aid toward the
saving and perfecting of the souls of their fellowmen'. Both are the fruit
of the 'same grace' (Examen, 1.2[3]). The way of the *Constitutions* has
one end: *ayudar a las almas*, to help souls.

The *Constitutions* presuppose that the formed members 'run in the
path of Christ our Lord' (VI.3.1[582]). Time and the self-abnegation
demanded by the labours of the apostolate and by daily living have
allowed the graces of the Exercises to bear fruit. Given the graced
dispositions that are the fruit of the Exercises, then to labour for the

---

[9]  See Rodrigo Mejía Saldarriaga, *La dinámica de la integración espiritual* (Rome: CIS, 1980), 339.

sanctification of others is at one and the same time to be united with God. The action and the union are one. They coincide. One includes the other. As Michael J. Buckley wrote:

> … Joseph de Guibert's division between union and service ultimately breaks down in Ignatian spirituality. It is not that 'the orientation of this mystic [is] toward service rather than union'. It is rather that God is at work; and that to be united with Him the way that He is, is to be with Him in this labour. In this understanding of the providential God, the dichotomy between union and service is collapsed into a single *conmigo*. One is with God in His work.[10]

Works or activity are not what St Ignatius means by mission if they are not the actions of an instrument united with God (X. 2 [813]). The sanctification of the instrument and the operation of the instrument are indivisible. Apostolic action is intrinsically contemplative. What is done with what St Ignatius means by 'a thoroughly right and pure intention' becomes purgative, illuminative *and unitive*. The end of the Society is so to be united with God that He can use the body in its members as a flexible instrument to do whatever the Spirit leads them to discern to be needed to complete His work on earth.

It seems that St Ignatius' mystical experience of the whole of creation in its relation to God as new led him to refuse to settle for separation, opposition, disjunction. His contemplative spirituality expresses a spirit of reconciliation of opposites, principally because, despite the immensity that separates human being from Divine Majesty, 'the same Lord desires to give Himself to me' (Exx 234). St Ignatius' foundational experience would seem to have been one of conjunction, of connection, of relating, of movement towards synthesis and union. Towards union with God. Union hereafter, certainly, but also union now, with the God who is at work to create and to redeem. It is for that purpose that the divine Spirit in His providence for us seeks incarnation.

---

[10] Buckley, '*Semper Crescendo in Devotione*', 72.

# 7

# IGNATIAN CRITERIA
# FOR CHOICE OF
# MINISTRIES

THE IGNATIAN CRITERIA for choice of ministries are found in Part VII of the *Constitutions*, entitled 'The Distribution of the Incorporated Members in Christ's Vineyard, and their Relations with their Fellowmen'. The text which we know as the 'Deliberation of the First Fathers' gives us an account of how the companions came together to pray and to find God's will for them:

> Near the end of Lent the time was drawing near when we would have to be dispersed and separated from one another. We were very eager for this, recognising it as necessary in order to reach the goal we had already fixed upon and thought about with intense desire .... We decided to come together for some days before separating to discuss with one another our vocation and manner of life.[1]

It was from those weeks of busy apostolic work together, with 'prayers and sacrifices and meditations with greater than usual fervour', and 'casting all our concerns upon the Lord', that the universal scope of their vocation became clearer. They had been called together, and united in a single desire 'to help souls', in order to be separated again. The Deliberation culminated in the companions' decision to remain together as one body, and to promise obedience to one of their own number. In the *Constitutions* which were eventually written for the body, Part VII treats of the different ways in which they, and the others who soon joined them, were to be distributed throughout the world.

---

[1] See 'The Deliberation of the First Fathers', translated in Appendix I of John Carroll Futrell, *Making an Apostolic Community of Love* (St Louis: Institute of Jesuit Sources, 1970), 188.

## The Four Ways of Mission

The four chapters of Part VII name the four ways of being sent:

- they may be sent to some places or others by the supreme vicar of Christ our Lord (chapter 1);

- they may be sent by the superiors of the Society, who for them are in the place of His Divine Majesty (chapter 2);

- they may themselves choose where and in what work they will labour, when they have been commissioned to travel to any place where they judge that greater service of God and the good of souls will follow (chapter 3);

- they may carry on their labour not by travelling but by residing steadily and continually in certain places where much fruit of glory and service to God is expected (chapter 4).

## The Means of Helping Souls

The first companions were in no doubt as to the kind of things they were to do. These are named in the 'Formula of the Institute':

> ... public preaching, lectures, and any other ministry whatsoever of the word of God, and further by means of the Spiritual Exercises, the education of children and unlettered persons in Christianity, and the spiritual consolation of Christ's faithful through hearing confessions and administering other sacraments. Moreover, this Society should show itself no less useful in reconciling the estranged, in holily assisting and serving those who are found in prisons or hospitals, and indeed in performing any other works of charity, according to what will seem expedient for the glory of God and the common good. (Formula of the Institute, 3)

The means which the Society uses are named again in chapter 4, where residences and even houses of Jesuit studies are seen as centres from which Jesuits would go out and be constantly on the move in exercising a vigorous and varied apostolate. In summary form these means are:

- the good example of a thoroughly upright life and of Christian virtue;

- desires in the presence of God our Lord and prayers for all the Church;

- Masses offered, especially in gratitude for benefactors;

- the other sacraments;

- the ministry of the word, proposed to the people unremittingly both in the Society's church and in other churches, squares or places of religion;

- spiritual conversations and the Spiritual Exercises;

- corporal works of mercy (to the extent permitted by the more important spiritual activities and the members' own energies);

- writing books.

The selection of these means is to be made 'according to the opportunity which exists and the decision of the superior'.

## Criteria

We may find it surprising that no mention is made in Part VII of the founding of schools. Already, while St Ignatius was sifting his criteria for sending men, the bishops and authorities of towns in which Jesuit missioners had been converting the people were pleading with him to start boys' schools. With fewer than a thousand men to send, he saw the apostolic value of schools and accepted the need and the demand as a sign of God's will.

The second chapter does not look to the question of founding professed houses, or colleges, or places where Jesuits would reside 'steadily and continually', but to missions that would ordinarily take two or three months (VII.1.6[615]). Characteristically, St Ignatius requires flexibility in determining the length of such missions:

> One should attend to the first characteristic of our Institute.
> Since this is to travel to some regions and to others, remaining
> for a shorter or longer time in proportion to the fruit which is
> seen .... (VII. 2. H [626])

Travel as the first characteristic of Jesuit life is at the heart of the
Ignatian project. The early companions envisaged a body of men, in
dispersal and in motion but united in mind and heart, in imitation of
Jesus on the road with his apostles. Nadal, in particular, frequently
focuses on this theme.

> They consider that they are in their most peaceful and
> pleasant house when they are constantly on the move, when
> they travel throughout the earth, when they have no place to
> call their own, when they are always in need, always in
> want—only let them strive in some small way to imitate Christ
> Jesus, who had nowhere to lay his head and who spent all his
> years of preaching in journeying.
>
> The principal and most characteristic dwelling for Jesuits is
> not in the professed houses, but in journeyings ... by which
> they diligently seek to gain for Christ the sheep that are
> perishing.[2]

Within this context of a radical availability to be sent, thought
should be given to the nature of the spiritual affairs to be dealt with;
to the need and the fruit which is reaped or expected; to the
opportunities available in other places; to the obligation that there is
to take up these works; to the resources which the Society possesses to
provide for these undertakings. These suggest certain Ignatian
criteria that are permanently valid for choosing ministries: the actual
resources of personnel and their particular talents; the greater
opportunity elsewhere that we may be neglecting; the need and fruit

---

[2] MHSJ MN 5, 773, 195. The central importance of Jerónimo Nadal in the early Society of
Jesus lies in the fact that he is the one whom Ignatius chose to promulgate and explain the new
*Constitutions* throughout Europe. In sending him Ignatius said: 'He altogether knows my mind
and enjoys the same authority as myself' (MHSJ MN 1, 144). Polanco wrote of Nadal: 'He
knows our father, Master Ignatius, well because he had many dealings with him, and he seems
to have understood his spirit and comprehended our Institute as well as anyone I know in the
Society' (MHSJ EI 5, 109). See John W. O'Malley, 'To Travel to Any Part of the World:
Jerónimo Nadal and the Jesuit Vocation', *Studies in the Spirituality of Jesuits*, 16/2 (1984), 1-20.

which is being reaped or expected, as against a greater need elsewhere or a greater fruit that these particular people might meet or
gain elsewhere.

### For One Purpose Rather than the Other

When the demands for men were many and the men few, the criteria
for sending one or two or three Jesuits for a time to a place for a
particular work are given in VII.2.E[623]. A series of alternative
kinds of work is given, and in each case the first is to be preferred to
the second.

Firstly, superiors are to prefer work of more importance,
urgency and need:

> When there are some things which are especially incumbent
> upon the Society, or it seems that there are no others to attend
> to them: and there are other things in regard to which others
> do have a care and a method of providing for them; in
> choosing missions there is reason to prefer the first to the
> second.

Nadal sees the meeting of those needs 'where there are no others to
attend to them' as the *raison d'être* of the Society.[3] It is a view that is
central to his teaching and which recurs insistently:

> And this is indeed the distinctive mark of our vocation: that
> we accept from God and the orthodox Church the care of
> those for whom nobody is caring .... This is a work that is at
> the same time of the greatest difficulty, labour and danger, as
> well as the greatest utility and necessity. It is hence that the
> Society seems somehow to imitate the condition of the
> Church of the Apostles ....

Elsewhere Nadal writes:

> ... these [ministries] are more to be preferred, in that they are
> what the Lord has specifically called the Society to. For our

---

[3] Antonio de Aldama, a leading modern expert on the *Constitutions*, writes more cautiously: 'It
must be noted, however, that this is only one of several criteria. It is neither the only one nor the
main one, if we keep in mind Ignatius' other writings.' See Antonio M. de Aldama, *The
Constitutions of the Society of Jesus: Missioning*, translated by Ignacio Echaniz (Rome: CIS, 1990), 76.

vocation has as its aim that those souls be helped for whom
support from other ministers is not expected.[4]

Ignatius' second criterion is about safety:

> Among the pious works of equal importance, urgency and
> need, when some are safer for the one who cares for them and
> others are more dangerous; and when some are easier and
> more quickly dispatched ....

This curious criterion of 'safety', and how Ignatius could in some
circumstances overrule it, is well illustrated in the following incident.
When Fr Diego Mirão and later Fr Luis Gonçalves da Câmara were
asked to be confessors to King John III of Portugal, they refused
firmly, partly on grounds of safety. Ignatius was equally trenchant in
insisting that they accept the ministry:

> I can see, of course, your reasons, based on humility and the
> security which is more easily found in lowly than in prominent
> occupations, and I cannot but approve and be edified by your
> motives. But, all things considered, I am convinced that you
> are ill-advised in this determination, if you consider the
> greater service and glory of God our Lord.[5]

The third criterion is that what aids more of our fellow human
beings, such as preaching or lecturing, is to be preferred to other
work concerned more with individuals, such as hearing confessions
or giving Exercises, 'unless there should be some circumstances
through which it would be judged that to take up the second would
be more expedient'.

The final criterion is about the durability of the good that can
be hoped for:

> When there are some spiritual works which continue longer
> and are of more lasting value, such as certain pious
> foundations for the aid of our fellow men; and other works less
> durable which give help on only a few occasions and for a
> short while ...

---

[4] MHSJ MN 5, 195; *Scholia in Constitutione*, 442.
[5] Ignatius to Diego Mirão, 1 February 1553, in *Letters of St Ignatius Loyola*, translated by William
J. Young (Chicago: Loyola UP, 1959), 282.

The 'spiritual works' in question are organizations which a Jesuit, during a short stay, could begin and then leave to the care of their members.

These are the criteria, centred on what is done, that are most familiar to us. What may not be so familiar is that Ignatius prefaces them with a rubric about need; and the fact that this comes first suggests that it takes priority over the criteria just named. That part of the vineyard ought to be chosen in which there is greater *need*, 'because of the lack of other workers or because of the misery and weakness of one's fellowmen in it and the danger of their eternal condemnation'; or hope of greater *fruit* 'through the means which the Society uses'; or a greater debt of *gratitude*; or hope of a greater *multiplying effect*; or where there is need to counteract *opposition* to the Society (VII.2.D[622]). All these are prefaced by a clause relativising them: 'when other considerations are equal (and this should be understood in everything that follows)'.

## The Governing Principle

These criteria are simply articulations of the governing principle that St Ignatius repeats over and over again. The Society does not exist to serve this or that local or particular need. The Society's mission is to look to the more universal good, and it is for this reason that the Society 'has placed its own judgment and desire under that of Christ our Lord and his vicar'. 'The more universal the good is, the more it is divine.' (VII.2.2[606]) 'One should keep the greater service of God and the more universal good before his eyes as the norm to hold oneself on the right course.' (VII.2.D[622])

What is most important is the general norm. The articulations of it are an attempt to show how the norm might be applied in concrete situations. They are not to be taken absolutely or rigidly, since it was always in St Ignatius' mind that the more particular a prescription is, the more flexibly it should be implemented in view of the end and in the light of circumstances. But neither are these more specific norms to be easily dismissed, since St Ignatius and Polanco laboured long in refining them.

Explicitly, and in their narrowest interpretation, they deal with the question of temporary missions. However, the Society has always and rightly taken them in a more general sense as a valuable indication of St Ignatius' mind regarding better choice of ministries—especially when they are confirmed by what we know of his mode of decision-making in his own practice and from his letters. The recent Jesuit General Congregations have also given them authoritative confirmation and interpretation:

> The Spiritual Exercises can pour into us a spirit of magnanimity and indifference, of firm decisions and reformation, a renewal of our activity or of the means for reaching our goal more successfully through the light of those well-known principles: the greater service of God; the more universal good; the more pressing need; the great importance of a future good; and special care of those significant ministries for which we have a special talent. (GC 31, d.21, n.4)

### What the Criteria Presuppose

But the criteria are simply aids to 'hold oneself on the right course' in a process of prayer that we learnt in the election in the Exercises, a prayer that looks to decision and is governed and directed by 'the unction of the Holy Spirit'.[6] Just as the criteria are subordinate to the general norm (the more universal good), so even that criterion is subordinate to a process or procedure that St Ignatius has at heart here in Part VII and throughout the *Constitutions*:

> Although it is the supreme providence and direction of the Holy Spirit that must efficaciously guide us to bring deliberations to a right conclusion in everything … still this can be said in general …. (VII. 2. F [624])

> Therefore the superior general … ought to bestow much careful thought on missions of this kind in order that … that procedure may always be used which is conducive to the greater service of God and the universal good … while holding fast to this thoroughly right and pure intention in the presence of God our Lord …. (VII. 2. 1 [618])

---

6  See VII. 2. F [624]; IV. 8. 8 [414]; I. 2. 13 [161].

This is the language of the *Spiritual Exercises*. Here, as throughout, the *Constitutions* presuppose that the Jesuit who reads them and is trying to live them has made the Exercises, is familiar in practice with all that is said there about making right and good decisions, and is living by the *discretio* that they dispose him to receive.[7]

That these dispositions are not seen by St Ignatius to be required only by superiors who send on missions, but by all Jesuits as well, is shown in his luminous statement on the formation of scholastics:

> In general they ought to be instructed about our manner of acting .... Hence they should foresee ... the opportunities which can be grasped ... by using some means at one time and others at another. Although all this can be grasped only by the unction of the Holy Spirit (1 John 2: 20, 27) and by the prudence which God our Lord communicates to those who trust in his Divine Majesty, nevertheless the way can at least be opened by some suggestions which aid and dispose one for the effect which must be produced by divine grace. (IV. 8. 8 [414])[8]

The 33rd General Congregation confirms this where it says, 'In order that we are able to hear God calling us in this world and respond to Him, we need the habit of discernment [*habituali discretione*]' (d. 1, n. 12). We know from the Exercises that the precondition for such *discretio habitualis* is the gift of indifference, and that the disposition for receiving that degree of freedom is self-abnegation:

> We cannot attain this discerning attitude [*hunc discretionis habitum*] without self-abnegation, which is the fruit of our joy in the

---

[7] In the document entitled 'Our Mission Today', the 32nd General Congregation, calling the Exercises 'the wellspring of our apostolate', wrote: 'We are also led back again to our experience of the Spiritual Exercises .... Thereby we gradually make our own that apostolic pedagogy of St Ignatius which should characterize our every action.' (GC 32, d. 4, n. 38) And again, 'The pedagogy of the Exercises is a pedagogy of discernment. It teaches a man to discover for himself where God is calling him, what God wants him to do, as he is, where he is, among his own people.' (GC 32, d. 4, n. 57)

[8] The construction 'although ... nevertheless ...' is found wherever St Ignatius wishes to indicate his reverence for the usefulness of the human means and their entire subordination to the unction of the Holy Spirit. The Preamble to the *Constitutions*, which is their 'Principle and Foundation', and determines their interpretation in practice, is constructed in that way. Though the words are not used, the key passages that are found in paragraphs 813 and 814 of Part X express the same relationship between the human and the divine.

presence of the coming kingdom …. Today our interior freedom will show itself in a greater availability on the part of the
whole body of the Society as well as of each one of us, an availability by which we will respond in obedience to the changes
and diverse cultures of the world (GC 33, d. 1, nn. 14, 15).

## Mobility

Even a cursory reading of Part VII brings home St Ignatius' concern
for mobility. Jesuits were to be set free so that they could leave a work
when a greater need could be met or a greater good be obtained:

> They did this in conformity with their desire to travel
> throughout the world and, when they could not find the desired
> spiritual fruit in one region, to pass on to another and another,
> ever intent on seeking the greater glory of God our Lord and
> the greater aid of souls. (VII. 1. B [605])

Since Fr Janssens said in 1947 that a better choice of apostolates
was 'the most important task of all', the Society has been painfully
trying to regain its mobility. Now, it is not geographical mobility that is
called for so much as mobility of imagination and enterprise. Now, it is
not only individuals who are called to mobility, but also institutions.

The *Constitutions* are, in large part, a set of guidelines for forming
members of the body with those attitudes and dispositions which
would ensure that the body should have a high degree of *freedom,
obedience, responsibility* and *initiative*. The recent General Congregations
call communities and institutions to take the means necessary for
acquiring the same dispositions. They provide for each community or
team an inbuilt principle of change, in that they ask men to come
together prayerfully in order to assess whether their work is meeting
the criteria of greater need and greater fruit. A province of apostolic
teams like that would be free, adaptable, available and mobile. When
the *Constitutions* were written, the problem of long-established
institutions had not arisen. They do not deal with the question.
Jesuit houses were places where Jesuits lived, not settled
communities in which they worked. Even houses of studies were
places from which men went out to meet local apostolic needs.

Nadal again reminds us of the ideal of mobility in the early Society:

> Houses of the Society must be like quarters for squadrons, from which soldiers leave to skirmish and to make various sallies against the enemy, and then regather there. Thus it will be that from the Society's houses those of the Society will go out to one or other region in order to fight against vices and against demons; while others will remain and will make up the main corps for battle. There our people will gather *et requiescent pusillum,* to quote our Lord's words to his disciples: they will regather in order to refresh themselves, and others will go in their place.[9]

### Obstacles to Mobility

However, quite early in the Society apostolic institutions (such as colleges) were found to be a way to respond to needs. And institutions will continue to be suitable means serving a purpose of mission. It is necessary to take account of the deeper and more lasting good they can do. Nevertheless, it is also necessary to look from time to time at the ways in which they can in practice reduce Jesuit mobility, Jesuit freedom to move to meet a more pressing need or to gain a more universal good. We are all familiar with the multiple and subtle ways in which what we begin to use as a means insensibly becomes the end:

> They make a means of the end, and an end of the means, and so they put last what they ought to put first ... nothing ought to induce me to take up or reject such means except the service and praise of God Our Lord and the eternal salvation of my soul (Exx 169).

More easily than other means, the institutions to which we happen to be assigned can become the end for which we live and work. Since the 1940s the Society has been asking us to look beyond the horizon of our particular work and to cultivate responsibility for the mission of the whole body. There can be unspoken pressures in any settled apostolate to give all one's energies and ingenuity to defending the

---

[9] MHSJ MN 5, 470, quoting Mark 6: 31 in the Vulgate.

work against other Jesuit institutions hungry for men, or against General Congregations or Generals who are pointing out that the world has changed, and that other demands may be more urgent.

The freedom that the Spirit gives includes a freedom from prejudice, whether in favour of relinquishing a work or of keeping it. It gives the freedom to retain what is discovered to be reaping more spiritual fruit:

> In the meantime … they draw upon all their powers to want neither this particular thing nor anything else, unless it be solely the service of God Our Lord that moves them. Thus it is the desire to be better able to serve God Our Lord that will move them to accept the thing or leave it. (Exx 155)

The freedom to keep something is found only when there is freedom to let it go.

### Indifference

The secret of the Society's mobility is indifference. Indifference is everywhere presupposed in the *Constitutions*, and it is expressly referred to in Part VII where St Ignatius says that a 'thoroughly right and pure intention' will keep us on the right course. Indifference is the constant and purifying search for 'the interior law of charity and love which the Holy Spirit writes and engraves upon hearts' and which is more important than 'any exterior constitution' or any part of one.

The 33rd General Congregation also speaks about indifference: 'today our interior freedom will show itself in rising above individualism'. The Congregation refers to the individualism that is an obstacle to integration into the mission of the community. But retreat houses, schools, institutes of spirituality or of justice, parishes, any kind of work embodied in any kind of institution, can suffer from an analogous individualism that is an obstacle to integration into the mission of the whole body. It is a way in which the Society itself experiences the oppression of structures. It is all the greater an obstacle because it is less recognisable and less tractable than our individual clinging to comfort, convenience, prestige and influence and all the other clamouring egoisms that face us daily.

That is why the recent Congregations prescribed that responsibility for apostolic initiatives be shared by all. When an apostolic community becomes aware, together, of the urgency of an apostolic need, and labours to come, together, to an apostolic choice and shared purpose, then it has to discover its need to work and pray for a continued deepening of spiritual freedom. The pain of that and the fears it arouses are something that each of us experiences.

## A Spirituality of Risk

The spiritual freedom that is at the heart of the *Spiritual Exercises* and the *Constitutions* seems to have been the secret of the early Jesuits' ability to undertake new and daring enterprises. It liberated their imagination to seize opportunities 'now using one means, now another', to create new ventures, to realise possibilities previously unimagined. It may also be the secret of the disproportion between their small numbers and small talent on the one hand, and the great spiritual fruit God worked through them on the other. It freed them to be supple instruments through which the Spirit could blow where He willed (X. 2 [813]).

Both the *Constitutions* and the *Spiritual Exercises* embody the conviction that God can make His concrete and particular will known when we take the means to be made free. The *Spiritual Exercises* are a school of discernment for the individual. The *Constitutions* are a school of discernment for the whole body of the Society. Part VII gives the norms for discerning missions and, in our times, for adapting apostolates. The *Constitutions* give guidelines for the exercise of *discreta caritas*. That is not an invitation to imprudence. But in practice discretion can be so emphasized that the *caritas* evaporates. We have to go to St Ignatius' practice to understand it properly. In Luis Gonçalves da Câmara's *Memoriale* it is said of him:

> Our father often gives the impression that in his undertakings he is not at all concerned with human prudence, as in the case of the college that he started without having any definite income at his disposal .... As, at the beginning of such undertakings, he seems to go beyond human prudence, so he uses

divine and human prudence to look for the necessary means to maintain them.[10]

In Part X we are told that 'the human or acquired means ought to be sought with diligence' (X. 3 [814]). But the measured judgment and sanity of the *Constitutions* are also a clear indication that good decisions are not made by confining ourselves to the level of reason. St Ignatius wrote in a letter to the Duke of Alba:

> For it may often be that those things which do not seem to fit in at all with human prudence are perfectly compatible with the divine prudence. For this cannot be bounded by the laws of our reasonings.[11]

Hugo Rahner's judgment on this text is that 'these words are the best commentary on the Three Times of the Election. They sum up the whole of Ignatius.'[12] In the same place he quotes as an accurate reflection of the mind of St Ignatius some words attributed to him by Ribadeneira:

> In the things of God, those who are over-prudent will hardly ever achieve anything really great. For those who are always thinking about difficulties and who are constantly brooding and vacillating because they fear the possible outcomes which they foresee, will never turn their hearts towards things of real beauty. (MI FN 4, 898, 899)

---

[10] Gonçalves da Câmara, *Memoriale*, n. 234.

[11] Ignatius to Fernando Alvarez, Duke of Alba, 16 February 1556, MHSJ EI 11, 7-8, here 8.

[12] Hugo Rahner, *Ignatius the Theologian*, translated by Michael Barry (London: Geoffrey Chapman, 1968), 225.

# Part 3

## *Retrieving Ignatian Wisdom*

# Introduction

JOSEPH VEALE LIVED AND WORKED during a period which straddled two rather different traditions of Ignatian spirituality. These two traditions were propounded by what are described as the 'ascetics' on one hand and the 'mystics' on the other. We can understand how the author speaks about a 'radical revision of spirituality' when he states that 'the official spirituality of the Order and the institutional structures that shaped the regime of living and formed the internal experience of Jesuits were in place from, roughly, 1600 to 1965'. This period was dominated by the 'ascetical' approach to Ignatian spirituality.

The two essays in this section were written during the years when the Society of Jesus was revising its understanding. 'Ignatian Prayer or Jesuit Spirituality' dates from 1976, when Joe Veale was just beginning to develop his major insights, and is still quite recognisably the work of a distinguished teacher of English literature. 'Dominant Orthodoxies', based on a seminar paper given for the Ignatian jubilees in 1990-1991, is in its substance more developed but in its style more direct, more raw; and there is more than a hint of sheer anger in the writing.

One senses both anguish and joy in these pieces. Joe Veale evokes the 'pain and bewilderment' felt by many Jesuits as the spiritual culture in which they had come to maturity was dismantled, and as they were called to make changes in their spirituality. There is the unmistakable ring of personal experience when the author describes the Pelagian asceticism in which he himself had been formed, with its,

> ... depressing climate, its mean hopes and small expectations, its inhumanity and pessimism about what is in humanity ... its opening to desolation, its anxieties and stresses.

For someone to describe his years of theological study as a time of 'dreadful theological aridities' when the very word 'experience' was frowned upon indicates something of the pain that was felt by him then, and maybe never completely eradicated.

Some of what the reader comes across here may seem to have 'the stale taste of battles long ago', but someone alert, with an open mind, will uncover nuggets of wisdom born out of the experience of a sensitive and intelligent man who lived through the transition, reflected deeply on his experience, and learned important lessons from it both for his own living and for the spirituality and ministry of the Society of Jesus to which he belonged.

At one level, Joe was seeking to dissolve false traditions by getting at the real ones, and to promote confidence in the authenticity of the renewal that was taking place as he wrote. That said, he was acute enough to be aware of the charge that modern Jesuits were simply refashioning Ignatius in their own image, perhaps a decadent one. He could, indeed, be as critical of contemporary Jesuit trendiness as he was of past Jesuit traditionalism. The postconciliar Society of Jesus was perhaps too fond of committees, and lacked apostolic incisiveness. Joe's point was not so much that we in our time had a privileged access to the authentic Ignatius, but rather that such authenticity as is possible for us comes not from texts alone. It is in our ongoing efforts to live out of the experiences and questionings generating the texts that we will come to appropriate their message. And the process will involve costs which, perhaps, contemporary Jesuits have been unwilling to pay.

These papers also reveal something of the author's relief and indeed exhilaration as he came in middle life to know God in a new way:

> It is remarkable what one learns about the ways of God when one spends time each day with one exercitant listening to their experience in prayer and trying to discern together where it may seem the Spirit is leading.

The mystery of God, who cannot be neatly summarised in our limited human concepts, can lead us to a life-giving freedom of spirit.

Again and again, we are called back to meet Ignatius himself, even as we are encouraged not to be afraid at seeing how quickly his immediate successors led the Society he founded in another direction. Joe Veale rejoices in how the present generation can return to the sources, thanks to the pioneering work of those scholars who have made these texts available in our time.

# 8

# DOMINANT
# ORTHODOXIES

WHEN THE 1991 MILLTOWN INSTITUTE SEMINAR to celebrate the fifth centenary of St Ignatius was over, a friendly observer mused along the following lines. The Jesuit contributors at the seminar all seemed to take it as read that in recent years there has been a new understanding of Ignatian spirituality and that the man we know now is quite unlike the St Ignatius of Loyola of half a century ago. But not everyone is so familiar with this change, or so clear on how it may be accounted for.

It may, then, be useful to take the occasion to reflect on this new understanding, and to look at questions that it raises about history, spirituality and renewal. How do we really know we have an authentic picture of a founder? Will the real St Ignatius please stand up?

## The Change since 1940

What must strike observers as strange is that the Church's request to us to go back to our sources has not issued in a somewhat modified or slightly adjusted picture, but in a revolutionary one: a totally different picture. This may have puzzled friendly observers looking on from outside; it has caused pain and bewilderment to many Jesuits. Ignatian spirituality now is in many of its features the reverse of what has been associated with St Ignatius in the folklore of Catholic culture.

The change cannot be captured in a sentence. But it might, without too crude a simplification, be described as a shift from the anti-mystical to the mystical, from a stern ascetical regime to something more contemplative. Crudely, a question is raised: is this change a response to fad or fashion, an accommodation to contemporary needs, a forcing of the evidence to make St Ignatius say what suits our present flabbier mood, to make him say what he did not mean to say and would not wish to have said? Is it no more than the replacing of a healthy asceticism with an uncostly mysticism?

*The Heroic Image*

Every generation recreates its heroes in its own image. Religious orders are no exception. The simple qualification that needs to be made to that is that the stern and strong-willed Ignatius had a long run for his money. That was the picture by and large that has been dominant since the Order was suppressed and restored at the beginning of the nineteenth century. It goes even further back, at least to the early years of the seventeenth century. A more human Ignatius was depicted in the first published biography, the one written with enthusiasm and admiration soon after his death by Pedro Ribadeneira, who had lived and worked closely with him since 1540. But Ribadeneira's portrait did not please, and a new biography was commissioned. It was around this time that Fr General Francis Borja required all the manuscript copies of Ignatius' dictated life story, the Autobiography, to be returned to Rome. The Society was already painting an official portrait, composed through the lens of how it saw itself and how it was desiring to be.

In Ignatian spirituality more generally, there has been recently a similar shift in understanding, one that needs to be accounted for as far as possible. Again it is not a question of a small adjustment here or a fairly large correction there. Both the official spirituality of the Order and the institutional structures that shaped the regime of living and formed the internal experience of Jesuits were in place from, roughly, 1600 to 1965. That was largely the work of Fr General Claudio Acquaviva (1581-1615). The Acquavivan settlement crumbled in the 1960s. 'Overnight' is only a shade too strong to describe the swiftness of the dismantling.

*Healthy Traditions*

In *Perfectae caritatis*, Vatican II's decree on religious life, the Church required us to return to the sources, to identify and to preserve the spirit of the founder and the *sanae traditiones* (healthy traditions) which are the patrimony of each Order. An earlier draft had said *venerabiles traditiones* (venerable traditions). The change of terminology opened the door to a recognition that not all traditions are *sanae*. It was an acknowledgement, new in the history of the Church, that Orders within the Church, and the Church itself, can become encrusted with layers of misinterpretation, can come to carry a heavy baggage of custom, custom that may once have been healthy, necessary and life-giving, but that is now found to be a dead hand, a chill on the spirit, a constriction upon God's work.

## How Are We to Judge?

But how are we to judge what is healthy tradition and what has become unhealthy? By what criterion? Is it not arrogant of the present generation simply to dismiss a regime and an understanding that stood firm for three and a half centuries? On what grounds was our generation justified in deciding that many things in the venerable Acquavivan traditions wereno longer *sanae*?

To decide which traditions are a natural development of the original charism and which are foreign to it would seem to suppose that we are in possession of a clear and authentic grasp of the original charism. To take the particular case of St Ignatius. On what grounds can we claim to know him better now than we did sixty years ago? The best historical evidence from the origins is at its best partial, fragmented and patchy and, besides, composed by men with different axes to grind. Do we find in the evidence merely what we want to see? Do we discover only what we expect to find? Are we inevitably blind to facts that escape our attention because what we attend to is circumscribed by what we are interested in? Do we look only for what serves our immediate purpose, for what meets our needs, for what happens to enliven us?

Perhaps St Ignatius, if we may be allowed to imagine him looking down at us, quizzically or bemusedly, is amused to observe that contemporary Jesuits paint him as a congenial and warm-hearted member of a group of companions who were friends in the Lord. So he was. But it is striking that this should be how he is seen in a democratic time when we are unenamoured of autocracy and of institutions.

## The Nineteenth-Century Ignatius

The St Ignatius we inherited from the nineteenth century was stern, more than a little inhuman, a soldier, militant, militaristic, an organiser of genius on soldierly lines, a martinet expecting prompt and unquestioning execution, the proposer of blind obedience, not greatly given to feeling or affection, rational, a man of ruthless will-power, hard in endurance, of a sensibility (if it were there at all) under stern control, heroic. That was when he was not a superhuman, Olympian figure just this side of apotheosis, remote among baroque clouds and shafts of light and gambolling cherubs. If this is a caricature of the personality for a long time commonly propounded by Jesuits, it is not too grossly exaggerated. It could not have had currency at all if there were no warrant for it in the sources.

### The Late Twentieth-Century Ignatius

But there is warrant in the sources, too, for the picture that is now more popular. It has come about in part through attending to the person who shows himself to us in the document misleadingly called the *Autobiography*. There we see a man of feeling, often given to tears; a spirit of soaring imagination; a dreamer with sensitive self-awareness, attentive to the subtle movements of his sensibility; a man of strong affectivity with a gift for friendship and affection; a companionable person.

The narrative of the *Autobiography* breaks off in 1540, soon before Ignatius is chosen by his companions to govern the new Order. The older man of the last sixteen years of his life is not essentially different from the younger man of the *Autobiography*. His friend Diego Laínez describes him:

> The busy general was observed at prayer … he used to go up to the terrace where he could see the open sky. He would stand there and take off his hat. Without stirring he would fix his eyes on the heavens for a short while. Then, sinking to his knees, he would make a lowly gesture of reverence. After that he would sit on a bench, for his body's weakness did not permit him to do otherwise. There he was, head uncovered, tears running drop by drop, in such sweetness and silence, that not a sob, no sigh, no noise, no movement of body was noticed.[1]

---

[1] MHSJ FN 4, 747, cited by Charles E. O'Neill, in '*Acatamiento*: Ignatian Reverence in History and in Contemporary Culture', *Studies in the Spirituality of Jesuits*, 8/1 (January 1976), 7.

Towards the end of his life he said, in conversation with some of the companions, that he did not know how he could go on living without consolation.[2]

The two pictures are incomplete. It is not possible here to indicate the qualifications that should rightly be made to the first or the shadings that could be suggested to the second. What interests us is not to justify one picture as against the other, but to ask why one should have been current for so long and the other so accepted now. Is the second one, which our times prefer, simply the fruit of our subjectivity?

*The Charges against Jesuit Spirituality*

There is a similarly strong contrast between the Jesuit spirituality of fifty years ago and the style of spirituality now more commonly termed Ignatian.

Fifty or more years ago it would commonly have been charged against the spirituality purveyed by Jesuits that it was rationalist, voluntarist, Pelagian, moralistic, individualistic and desiccating. It was a bully; it would force the free play of the spirit into a strait-jacket of method. Besides, it was accused of forming many religious who were anxious, scrupulous, intense, introspective, self-preoccupied. (Interestingly, it would probably also have been granted that the pastoral work of Jesuits with lay people, in the confessional or the pulpit, was hopeful, optimistic, an allayer of scrupulosity, a dissolver of fears.)

Of course a case can be made to defend Jesuit spirituality against these charges. In an Order so widespread and so varied in its pastoral experience over four centuries, there were many writers whose doctrine rebuts the charges. From within twenty years of St Ignatius' death there were two contending tendencies which, to oversimplify, may be called the 'ascetics' and the 'mystics'. The point of interest for our purposes here is that the dominant orthodoxy in the generation before the Second Vatican Council was the 'ascetic' one.

---

[2] Ribadeneira, in MHSJ FN 2, 338, recounts Ignatius explaining what he meant by consolation: 'On a certain topic when I was present, he said that he thought he could not live if he did not feel in his soul something which was not his, nor could be his, nor was it a human thing, but a thing purely from God'.

## Jesuit Spirituality before the Council

A confirmation of this is found in the history of Jesuit spirituality by Joseph de Guibert. Fr General Wlodimir Ledóchowski (1914-1942) commissioned the work for the fourth centenary of the Order's founding in 1940.[3] A short fifty years later, with the celebration of the 450th anniversary of the same event, papers read in celebration present a picture of Jesuit spirituality that is quite unlike the one de Guibert presents.

De Guibert's book reads like a work composed by two different men. The same contention that existed in the Society from the 1570s, between the 'ascetics' and the 'mystics', is at work in the author. The two tendencies are not composed or integrated; they exist side by side, often in the same paragraph.

The portrait de Guibert draws of St Ignatius and of his spirit was bold enough for its time. After all, de Guibert had been the first, in 1938, to publish a serious reflection on the fragment of St Ignatius' diary of 1544-1545.[4] There he had not only shown St Ignatius to be a mystic 'led by God in ways of infused contemplation to the same degree, though not in the same manner, as a St Francis of Assisi or a St John of the Cross', but he had given us a language in which to begin to understand the significant difference between the nature of Ignatius' mystical graces and those of St John of the Cross or of St Francis. It was no longer possible to assume that the mystical journey was all of one kind.

It has been pointed out that de Guibert also gives us a domesticated saint, finicky about 'observance', meticulous about rules and common life. There is no sense of the magnanimity of vision, of the daring of enterprise, of the urgency of mission. There is a curious hiatus between

---

[3] Joseph de Guibert, *La spiritualité de la Compagnie de Jésus: esquisse historique* (Rome: Jesuit Historical Institute, 1953). The author died unexpectedly in 1942. Fr General Ledóchowski was disappointed with the manuscript and the work was only published under his successor, Fr Jean-Baptiste Janssens, eleven years later. There is an English translation by William J. Young, *The Jesuits: Their Spiritual Doctrine and Practice* (Chicago: Loyola UP, 1964), which is clumsy and misses the nuances of the original, consistently reinforcing its Pelagian-ascetical tone. But for convenience, the page references that follow are to this English version.

[4] Joseph de Guibert, 'Mystique ignatienne: À propos du "Journal Spirituel" de Saint Ignace de Loyola', *Revue d'ascétique et de mystique*, 19 (1938), 3-22, 113-140, largely reproduced in *The Jesuits*, 44-66.

the saint's interior life and the work he did, the first naturally looming larger. Questions that de Guibert could well have raised about the intrinsic interrelationship of the saint's mysticism and mission remain simply unasked.

### Double Authorship

The third part of *La spiritualité de la Compagnie de Jésus*, written when de Guibert was presumably a sick man, and left unrevised upon his death in 1942, is an extended essay on the specific characteristics of Jesuit spirituality. It is here that the double authorship stands out and distorts the reality. There is, for example, a good section on the ways in which Jesuit authors have treated of questions of contemplative prayer and infused graces. De Guibert knew well the strong current of personal mystical experience and teaching on contemplation among the Spanish Jesuits from the 1570s onwards: Antonio Cordeses (1518-1601), Balthasar Alvarez (1533-1580), Diego Alvarez de Paz (1560-1620) and Luis de la Puente (1554-1624). De Guibert had been of that generation in France that had been quietly producing scholarly articles on these matters since 1920 in the *Revue d'ascétique et de mystique*. Nevertheless, on this terrain the writer strikes a marked note of caution in *La spiritualité de la Compagnie de Jésus*. He seems not to want to speak too loudly.

The second author, the 'ascetic' de Guibert, speaks with a different voice. He sets out to defend Jesuit spirituality against the charges of being a mere moralism, excessively rationalist, voluntarist, Pelagian. The terms in which he conducts the defence confirm the case made by the prosecution.

### The Language of Rationality

Since de Guibert's work was published in 1953 we have learnt a different language with which to explore our experience and to understand the Spiritual Exercises. We speak a different idiom. Here it is possible only to give a sketchy idea of the ways in which we should now find de Guibert's vocabulary dismaying.

De Guibert sees a chief characteristic note of Jesuit spirituality in the combination of enthusiasm with reason.[5] From meditation on the Principle and Foundation, 'Jesuits would henceforth ceaselessly recall that strong-willed indifference in the face of everything which is not the end'.[6] In his exposition here of what Jesuit spirituality owes to the Exercises he gives one sentence to the Election:

> To the *principles* and *counsels* regarding the Election is related the very clear relish for *well-considered* action which is the fruit of mature *thought*.[7]

Today we should see the whole process of election, the apprenticeship to discernment in making the Exercises (Exx 135-189) as not only what gives the Exercises their peculiar nature, but also what gives a Jesuit's spirituality its contemplative missionary character. It is linked intrinsically with the Contemplation to Obtain Love (Exx 230), an exercise which, in its bald language, expresses something of the culminating mystical grace by the Cardoner in 1523. But in de Guibert's account, the finding of God in all things, familiarity with God in the daily experience of living, is presented merely as being '*among* the … *traits* of Jesuit spirituality …':

> Among the most constant traits in Jesuit spirituality—traits which also were numbered among those which St Ignatius most earnestly desired to find in his sons—are several which have *sprung from the suggestions* in the Contemplation for obtaining Love; the finding of God in everything, familiarity with the Master ….[8]

And then the finding of God in all things is dropped. The rhetoric sees as marginal and accidental what we now see to be central and constitutive. Instead, it is rationality that dominates.

In the chapter 'Reformation of Life and Ascetical Effort', the two authors are at work side by side. The 'mystic' de Guibert, the man who had drawn out the deep things of St Ignatius' diary, writes:

---

[5] de Guibert, *The Jesuits*, 595.
[6] de Guibert, *The Jesuits*, 534.
[7] de Guibert, *The Jesuits*, 536. Emphasis JV.
[8] de Guibert, *The Jesuits*, 536. Emphasis JV.

> Prayer is a means by which the soul can be penetrated with the supernatural spirit, united with its Creator and Lord, and placed completely under the influence of his grace.[9]

The other de Guibert, the 'ascetic', who labours to make a case and at much greater length, writes:

> What appears first ... is the pitiless struggle against love of self, attachment to comfort and one's own judgment and will. Ignatius carried on this struggle without truce, by giving trials and reprimands not only to beginners but also to his most faithful companions ....[10]

> The Society has in truth never deviated from the line thus drawn. The acquisition of solid virtues and the struggles against self have been the themes which the generals have ceaselessly reverted to in their letters .... This courageous and incessant struggle against themselves .... Another characteristic to be noticed in these programmes to overcome defects and acquire virtues is that there is question above all of *direct* struggle and a *direct* effort.[11]

De Guibert argues at length that it is an essential Jesuit characteristic, stemming from the Exercises, to refuse to rest content with the maxim *Ama et fac quod vis*—'love and do what you want'. The Jesuits have preferred to insist on the necessary practice of particular virtues and have urged others to a direct effort to acquire them. The other de Guibert (the real one?) writes in the terms that we would tend to use now:

> If we are dominated by the love of Christ, we shall spontaneously take on his thoughts and tastes, we shall judge and act according to the example he has given. St Francis de Sales' affectionate comparison is well known. On entering into the soul, charity, like the 'king of the bees' brings her whole people with her, that is, the whole troop of other virtues whose queen she is.

---

[9] de Guibert, *The Jesuits*, 571.
[10] de Guibert, *The Jesuits*, 565.
[11] de Guibert, *The Jesuits*, 569. Emphasis JV.

But then in the next paragraph the author wrestles with himself and returns to the claim that 'nowhere in his spiritual directions and counsels' is St Ignatius satisfied 'with the indirect struggle against faults'.[12] It is a prescription for self-absorption. That alone is enough to explain why many religious may have taken refuge in what seems a healthier way of living in activism.

Two rhetorics are at work. There are two languages, each issuing from a different kind of experience and from different presuppositions. It is as though the 'ascetic' is afraid to concede that God might have his own gentler ways of drawing people into union with Himself. De Guibert concedes that there have indeed been Jesuits who have advocated a less grim way of Christian living,

> No doubt, just like so many spiritual writers of other schools, more than one Jesuit also has written about facile paths to union and the shortened roads to the love of God.[13]

But it would be dreadful to leave the reader with the impression that the way to God might be enjoyable.

At one point the 'ascetic', who is concerned at all costs to defend the grim version of Jesuit spirituality, sets out to refute the imputation of Pelagianism by the astounding argument that the spirituality could not have been Semipelagian because Jesuit theologians taught a sound theology of grace, as though the one necessarily had anything to do with the other.[14] Fr Paul Dudon, in commenting on the instructive affair of Fr Balthasar Alvarez, whose practice of direction was delated to the General in Rome by the watchdogs of authenticity and who was forbidden by superiors to pray contemplatively or to recommend affective prayer to others, observes that in these matters it is easy to be wrong when the only ground for one's judgment is *une science livresque* – 'knowledge from books'.[15]

---

[12] de Guibert, *The Jesuits*, 569-570.
[13] de Guibert, *The Jesuits*, 572.
[14] de Guibert, *The Jesuits*, 570.
[15] Paul Dudon, 'Les leçons d'oraison du Balthasar Alvarez (1573-1578)', *Revue d'ascétique et de mystique*, 2 (1921), 37-57, here 56.

## Which, Then, Is Authentic?

What interests us here is not the arguments for or against the positions that de Guibert found he had to defend at the time he was writing. Those have been dealt with in many places. And indeed, they may have the stale taste of battles long ago, long since fought and won. What concerns us here is the questions raised about authenticity and the confidence we may have in the current orthodoxy.

Throughout de Guibert's account, there is an operative assumption about the course of Jesuit spirituality over its 400-year history. It is that certain directions that were taken, especially those determined by generals like Acquaviva and Roothaan, were the work of providence, and that therefore they must be the faithful evolution of the spirituality and spirit of St Ignatius. Those were prayerful and holy men, and besides had the authority of office. It is not to be imagined that the directions they chose not to take might have been more authentic. The historian's imagination does not encompass a conjecture of discontinuity. We should all be agreed (at least while we wait for a better study of the time) that what Acquaviva did was probably necessary. It was an achievement to hold the Society of Jesus together when it could easily have fragmented, and a tighter regime of living was probably required to deal with a surge in numbers. De Guibert simply takes it, as we all did in those days, that what was done was inevitable and irreversible.[16]

It has become a commonplace to observe that, when we question history, the historical evidence answers us within the limitations of the words we use and the assumptions latent in our terminology. When de Guibert was writing it was not easy, indeed it was virtually impossible, to put certain questions to the evidence or to the tradition. The culture did not favour a freedom to imagine things becoming otherwise. Consequently it did not encourage us to explore the paths of development that were *not* followed, to imagine how things might have been otherwise. It is not that questions were disallowed or officially

---

[16] John W. O'Malley, 'De Guibert and Jesuit Authenticity', *Woodstock Letters* (1966), 103-110. 'It is rather disconcerting to find him simply assuming that because our superiors were sincere and prayerful men, trained in the Society, that they were *eo ipso* successful in capturing St Ignatius' meaning and in translating it into forms which presumably explored all its possibilities.' (108)

forbidden. That was not necessary. The dominant orthodoxy tends not to hear awkward questions and they die by silence. It is not surprising that the stern version of Jesuit spirituality defended by de Guibert happened to coincide with the preferred doctrine of the General, Fr Ledóchowski.

## The Factors that Undermined the Old Orthodoxy

The most subversive statement of the Second Vatican Council may well have been, 'since the ultimate norm of religious life is the following of Christ as given us in the gospel, this is to be held by all institutes as their supreme rule'.[17] There were always some religious who cheerfully acted on that principle anyway. What is hard to imagine now is the way in which we saw the gospel through the lens of the categories of the books and not the other way round.

The Pelagian asceticism defended by de Guibert at such length, and somehow without the ring of conviction, as being authentically of St Ignatius, cannot stand long in the presence of the gospel. It is seen for what it is, and crumbles in the light. Besides, its depressing climate, its mean hopes and small expectations, its inhumanity and pessimism about what is in humanity, its capacity to induce a permanent aridity of the spirit, its opening to desolation, its anxieties and stresses, could not long survive the largeness of mind and generosity of heart that we find in chapter five of *Lumen gentium* on holiness.

*Experience*

In my lifetime, the change with the most revolutionary consequences was the discovery that it was respectable to use the word 'experience'. I do not know if this can be attributed to the Council, or simply happened around the same time. In my four years of studying theology between 1949 and 1953 I never heard the word. It was not imagined that it might have anything to say to the dreadful theological aridities of those days. The dominant orthodoxy at the time frowned on it.

But the making of the Spiritual Exercises depends on being able to articulate what God is working in one. It seems incredible now that

---

[17] *Perfectae caritatis*, 2.

experience should have been a bad word in a Jesuit theologate. The dynamic of the Exercises is connected with being able to be aware of what is happening in the spirit and to reflect on those subjective realities with the help of the one giving the Exercises. It has been pointed out how both Karl Rahner and Bernard Lonergan found the root of their theology in the experience of the Exercises.[18]

*The Exercises as St Ignatius Gave Them*

By the time of the Council, Jesuits had begun to take seriously St Ignatius' directives about giving the Exercises. There had always been an awareness that it was an adaptation of the Exercises to give them to groups with a number of lectures each day. There was a kind of floating assumption that to give them to one person at a time was not practicable.

It is remarkable what one learns about the ways of God when one spends time each day with one exercitant listening to their experience in prayer and trying to discern together where it may seem the Spirit is leading. The trim garden paths of the spiritual treatises begin to look unreliable. One is brought to wonder at the largeness and generosity of the infinite variety of ways in which God sanctifies souls. God discloses God's self as sovereign in all that God does. God is not confined by our categories. God is no respecter of our refined distinctions or labels. God makes our cautions look shabby. For each person God determines the proper pace. God ignores our maps and schedules. Methods of prayer are seen simply for what they are: useful devices that may or may not be a means to open this or that person to God's action. Some of the venerable generalisations of the tradition are seen to be useful, some false, some pointless.

*Beyond Rationality*

All that began to spell the end of rationalism in spirituality, the poor relation of a rationalistic theology. We began to stop distrusting subjectivity and instead to become suspicious of mere rationality. But in those days before Vatican II, it was as though objectivity and reason

---

[18] For example in Avery Dulles, 'Jesuits and Theology, Yesterday and Today', *Theological Studies*, 52 (1991), 524-538, at 535.

could save us from the illusions that attend upon feelings, from the *ignis fatuus* of the imagination, from the subterfuges of self-deception. I do not recall that it was ever observed that rationality is the stoutest ally in evading painful decision, and a chief tool of the self-serving spirit. The truth is that rationality stands in as much need of purification as the heart or the imagination do.

Experience has shown that if abstractions are to be our servants and not our masters, we need constantly to be bringing them into a friendly encounter with experience, and continually to be checking them out and adjusting them in the light of the real. Otherwise they too easily take on a life of their own and determine too much how we see reality.

### A Questioning of Fear

Attention to experience, too, and reflection on it began to dissolve the inherited burden of Pelagianism. Even a small presence to the power and generosity of God's action in a person begins to dissipate the clouds of pessimism about human nature that had been looming too long over Counter-Reformation spirituality. The kind of fear and mistrust masquerading as a wise prudence implicit in the official version of Jesuit spirituality defended by the 'ascetic' de Guibert is seen to be a begetter of pusillanimity—a small-minded placing of human limitations on the power of God, a timid hedging around of a person's expectations of how God desires to act and how generous His bounty is.

### Contemplation

Before the mid-1960s, the dominant orthodoxy did not encourage us to use the word 'contemplation'. I recall Fr James Walsh, co-founder and for so many years editor of *The Way*, telling me how in Rome, in the 1950s, at the end of a seminar on late medieval writers, he said to the presiding professor, 'Isn't it clear that their use of the term contemplation is what St Ignatius meant?' The professor replied, not quite looking over his shoulder, 'Yes, of course. But you can't say so.'

Now at any rate we can speak more freely of contemplation. Some may say too freely, given the rapid deterioration of the currency of good words in the field of spirituality in these days. We may feel, indeed, that words such as 'mystical' are too cheaply used. Be that as it may, it is clear from the experience of being present to a person's prayer in the Spiritual Exercises that very often one quite soon becomes aware that something has intervened, and that the exercitant is aware of being the receiver of something given. In St Ignatius' language that would coincide with the experience of consolation (Exx 316).[19]

All that is no more than to say that when we begin to attend to what actually happens in persons under the working of grace we discover the importance of those places where St Ignatius expands on his warning to directors to avoid getting in God's way (Exx 15).

> Our father wanted us in all our activities as far as possible to be free, at ease in ourselves and obedient to the light given particularly to each one.[20]

> When they judge in the Lord that someone is growing in prayer and is led by the good spirit, they are to avoid interfering. They should rather give him heart and confidence, so that he may grow with ease and strength in the Lord. (MHSJ MN 4, 652)

## Beyond Categories

Ignatius confessed to being irritated by *decretistae*, conversation partners who laid down the law.[21] The authorities in the Order who early on wished to lay down prescriptions as to how Jesuits should pray, insisting on a narrow understanding of meditation, had lost the Ignatian empirical sense of dealing with persons 'according to the measure of God's grace imparted to each', the sense of a wariness about categories and absolutes that Ignatius never articulated but that he manifested in his way of acting, a distancing from distinctions and analysis, a preference for synthesis. If he had had the word 'mystical' to use, I am fairly sure he would have refused to use it. Even

---

[19] The term 'mystical' is used throughout in its larger sense to designate 'the aspect of passivity that is found again and again in every interior life'. See Joseph de Guibert, 'Mystique', *Revue d' ascétique et de mystique*, 7 (1926), 14. Quoted by Ignace de la Potterie in *The Christian Lives by the Spirit* (Staten Island: Alba House, 1971), 191.

[20] Gonçalves da Câmara, *Memoriale*, n. 357.

[21] Gonçalves da Câmara, *Memoriale*, n. 204.

more, if he had been challenged to say, 'Come now, do you mean mystical in the strict sense or in the broad sense? Are you talking here about acquired or infused, ordinary or extraordinary?', he would have kept his counsel. He would say that it is enough to know how to respond and, for the rest, to rejoice in 'more spiritual visitations or fewer' (III. 1. 10 [260]). He would have been at one with Balthasar Alvarez in his patient efforts to persuade Fr General Mercurian that there is a great spectrum of degrees of unitive grace.[22]

*Scholarship, Experience and Challenge*

The renewed grasp of the *Spiritual Exercises*, and of the other Ignatian sources, would have been impossible without the scholarship of the men who have been editing and publishing the more than 100 volumes of the *Monumenta Historica* since 1894. This means that we have access to the early documents and to the witness of those who were close to St Ignatius and knew his mind. It is a resource that the second and third generations of Jesuits did not have, apart from a dwindling oral tradition and a handful of manuscripts. For the first half of the twentieth century the *Monumenta* were quietly mined, scholars secretly burrowing away, undermining the dominant orthodoxy of the generations. Since the 1960s, this mining of the sources has grown to a great volume. Besides, the scholars have made a beginning in the labour of alerting us to the presuppositions inherent in sixteenth-century language and culture. As John W. O'Malley says,

> Documents do not speak to any of us, most certainly not when they are from an age other than our own. With a professional finesse reminiscent of the worst legends of the Spanish Inquisition we must *torture* their meaning out of them.[23]

But the renewed understanding of Ignatian spirituality owes most to a wrestling with the text of the *Spiritual Exercises* in the light of the experience of making and giving them. Experience puts questions to

---

[22] In a report to the General's visitor to Spain (Dudon, 'Les leçons', 50 n. 6). The text has now been published in English, as Balthasar Alvarez, 'Beyond the Train of Ideas', *The Way Supplement*, 103 (May 2002), 43-54.
[23] O'Malley, 'De Guibert and Jesuit Authenticity', 108 n. 7.

the text and invites the text to check and to challenge the experience. It is in that active dialogue that the Exercises yield their secret. The text on its own is dead.

## The Same Contention Soon after 1556

The dominantly ascetical reading of the tradition already had its advocates within twenty years of St Ignatius' death. From quite early the 'ascetics' and the 'mystics' were in contention. The 'ascetics' were fearful that the 'mystics', especially in Spain, might compromise the apostolic character of the new Order and turn it into a community of cloistered contemplatives or hermits. They were zealous to protect the tradition. The 'mystics', like Balthasar Alvarez, at 26 the director of St Teresa, understood St Ignatius better.[24] They insisted that prayer must not supplant the apostolate. They held that God gives contemplative gifts especially to those called to apostolic work.[25]

Both sides were aware that the charism of the Order was new and that it needed to be defended against being assimilated to older forms of consecrated life. But neither is at all clear in what the newness consists. Neither has a language in which to articulate the difference. Neither side quotes Nadal's 'contemplative even in activity', nor uses the Ignatian idiom of seeking and finding God in everything. Neither argues a case from the text of the *Spiritual Exercises* or from their experience of making them. Neither refers to a process of discernment or to *discreta caritas*.[26]

---

[24] Balthasar Alvarez was St Teresa's confessor from 1559 to 1564. He entered the novitiate aged 22 in 1555 and four years later, newly ordained, he became one of St Teresa's directors. Fr Brian O'Leary has reminded me that Alvarez was 'thrown in at the deep end'. St Teresa wrote of him, 'I believe he is the confessor who has done me the most good'. The references are given in E. Allison Peers, *Handbook to the Life and Times of St Teresa and St John of the Cross* (London: Burns and Oates, 1954), 111.

[25] Balthasar Alvarez, in an account of his teaching on prayer written for the General, refers to Exx 76 'where I find what I desire, there I will be quiet, without being anxious to go on until I have been satisfied'. That is a main point of St Ignatius' delicate pedagogy of contemplation. Alvarez in the same place says, 'To the ideas of my opponents I will oppose [St Ignatius'] example'.

[26] 'God usually grants this gift of contemplation to those who have long laboured at the purification of their hearts, at overcoming their passions and meditating on the truths of the gospel, *especially* when they labour zealously to sanctify and save others' (emphasis JV): Luis de la Puente, *The Life of Father Balthasar Alvarez* (London: Richardson, 1868), chapter 14.

Already before St Ignatius died in 1556, the Exercises were under attack. Their fiercest opponents were two of the foremost Spanish Dominican theologians of the time, Melchor Cano and Tomás Pedroche. In a study of sixteenth-century Spain, a fellow Dominican, Emilio Colunga, calls them the 'intellectualists' and distinguishes them from the 'mystics'.[27] As 'intellectualists' they were fearful of anything that savoured of subjectivism. Orthodoxy would be saved by rationality.

For men like these, strong fighters for the purity of the faith, anything that looked mystical was too close to the *alumbrados* for safety. Above all they were wary of whatever gave importance to the interior illumination of the Spirit. Pedroche's censure of the Exercises accurately pin-pointed those places in the text that are mystical. He wrote perceptively,

> These words manifest and clearly contain and affirm and teach a proposition that is temerarious and scandalous and heretical …. Preaching has no place, nor a preacher, to persuade [the exercitant] which particular choice among many goods he ought to make …. It is clear to me that this doctrine belongs to the *dejados* and *alumbrados*; the written word is left aside, with all the teaching and doctrine which good and wise men have given. These men give themselves over to what the spirit and God tells them there in the recesses of the soul.[28]

It is the natural fear of the inquisitor that when people attend to the leading of the Spirit they escape control.

The fascinating historical fact is that the Jesuit spirituality defended by the 'ascetic' de Guibert, an accurate account of the official spirituality of the order fifty years ago, is in almost all respects the same as that of the 'intellectualist' Cano and Pedroche. What is even more interesting is that within twenty years of St Ignatius' death

---

[27] Emilio Colunga, 'Intelectualistas y místicos en la teología española en el siglo XVI', *Ciencia tomista*, 9 and 10 (1914), cited in Iparraguirre, *Práctica de los Ejercicios*, 92.
[28] See Iparraguirre, *Práctica de los Ejercicios*, 99 n.20.

the Pedrochean tendency was becoming the dominant orthodoxy within the Society of Jesus.[29]

In those early times, under the Generals Francis Borja (the third General, 1565-1572) and Everard Mercurian (1573-1580) and for many a decade to come, what was exercising the contenders was the question of authenticity. The 'ascetics' were zealous to protect the stripling Society from what was alien to the true tradition and spirit.[30] There was a fear on the part of some that they might not be taken seriously as real 'religious'. Clearly the generals feared that the spiritualising tendencies among some Spanish Jesuits might dilute or radically change the apostolic character of the charism. They may have been right, though at this distance they seem to have over-reacted; the overworked Jesuits in northern Europe were unlikely to be excessive in the time they gave to prayer. The generals argued that contemplative forms of prayer were alien to the authentic charism. And, having a right sense that the charism is intrinsic with the Exercises, they insisted that it was improper for Jesuits to pray in any way that was not recommended in the Exercises. What they seem to have meant by that was the method of prayer as suggested in the First Week of the Exercises.

*External Pressures*

When eventually it becomes possible to write the history of Jesuit spirituality that de Guibert did not write (because the groundwork had not been done), it will have to show how the fortunes of a spiritual teaching like St Ignatius' are determined by the different cultures it lives through, by the currents of secular mood and thinking as well as by the religious culture of different times, by the Church's self-understanding, by dominant theological styles, by the aspirations and needs of the faithful, by passing religious fashion, by the fears that move authorities, as well as by the deeper movements of the Spirit of God. A decisive influence that changed the course of Jesuit

---

[29] Juan de Polanco had given a mystical interpretation to the Ignatian application of the senses. When the official Directory was published in 1599, Polanco's interpretation was not included although it had been taken account of by the compilers. See Dir 20. 66; 43. 154-158.

[30] See Michel de Certeau, 'La réforme de l'intérieur au temps d'Acquaviva, 1581-1615', in *Les jésuites. Spiritualité et activités. Jalons d'une histoire* (Paris: Beauchesne, 1974), 55.

spirituality was the Church's fear of illuminism and its uneasiness with mysticism.

It becomes clear that the second and third generations of Jesuits, who were passionately concerned with protecting the authentic spirit of the order, had no adequate grasp of it. This is more than simply to say what is obvious, that the disciples of a spiritual genius are pygmies compared with him. They did not have a theology, a theological culture, a vocabulary or a language which would have enabled them to grasp the new nature of what they were faithfully living. They clung, rightly, to the conviction that in some way the *Spiritual Exercises* were a key; they never referred to the *Constitutions*.

In fact the Exercises, had they known them better, would have provided a language in which to understand the questions at issue: the vocabulary of consolation and desolation, of the movements of the spirits, of activity and passivity, of the interior senses, of consolation without preceding cause, of the process of *discretio* in the making of a choice under the guidance of the Spirit and, from the *Constitutions*, the implications of *discreta caritas*. But neither side used this language. The charism was known in the living of it and known to be new. But there had not been time to reflect in depth on the experience or to grasp clearly what constituted its newness.[31]

The conceptual tools were not to hand to express the newness of a charism of consecrated life in which the single end is 'to aid souls'. Trent, in so far as it had considered the nature of priesthood, had been unable to encompass the long experience of priests whose consecrated life was entirely given to ministry.[32] In so far as there was any reflection on religious life, it was seen in monastic terms as the pursuit of personal perfection. The dominant theology in no way engaged with the reality of religious priests whose whole life was dedicated to the apostolate. Nor, indeed, in *Perfectae caritatis* has the

---

[31] 'The official documents of religious orders, including the documents of the founders themselves, express even the ideal only imperfectly. In particular those documents find it easier to articulate how they are in continuity with the tradition than how they are innovating within it, for by the nature of the case the latter reality lacks as yet a precise vocabulary': John W. O'Malley, *Tradition and Transition* (Wilmington: Michael Glazier, 1989), 134.

[32] O'Malley, *Tradition and Transition*, 154.

Church yet articulated that part of the Church's experience.[33] Nor have the official statements of the Church been able even yet to find words for that reality of Christian life in which action and contemplation compenetrate, and in which the apostolic task is unitive.[34]

### Where Do We Find the Tradition?

When we look at the anxiety of the early generations of Jesuits to ensure the purity of the authentic tradition, it forces us a stage further back, to the writings of the founder himself. Every deep human experience is traduced in the process of translating it into words. We know that that is trebly true in the case of mystical graces. There was something of the poet in Ignatius, but nothing of the poet's art with words. He was not one to forge a new language. He had to make do with the language to hand. As with any mystic, he can only communicate the ineffable within the limits and categories of his time. The same limits constrained him when he came to express the new charism in his *Constitutions*.[35]

It follows that in our search for the original spirit we have to live contentedly with some realities that attend the limitations of our creaturehood. The first reality is that authenticity cannot depend on the historical evidence. Such evidence as we have is fragmentary and our view of it coloured by our time. It is a fundamentalist fallacy to suppose that more knowledge of the sources or the discovery of new documents would ensure a more authentic grasp of the original spirit. The other truth is that, as John O'Malley points out, those early documents 'are incapable of rising above the historical realities in which they are immersed. Only with the hindsight of generations or centuries does the *sensus plenior*, the full implication, emerge.'[36] But

---

[33] O'Malley, *Tradition and Transition*, 161: 'Of the 25 sections of *Perfectae Caritatis* only two (8 and 20) are devoted to ministry'. It will be evident how much all of this part is indebted to the thinking of O'Malley.

[34] Yet in *Lumen gentium* 41, bishops 'will make their ministry the principal means of their own sanctification' and a priest should 'not be undone by his apostolic cares, dangers and toils, but rather led *by them* to higher sanctity' (emphasis JV).

[35] 'We must, in any case, reckon that even religious geniuses like Dominic, Francis and Ignatius may not have been fully capable of expressing what they were doing or hoped to do': O'Malley, *Tradition and Transition*, 168 n. 25.

[36] O'Malley, *Tradition and Transition*, 134.

how, by what means, may the *sensus plenior* emerge? This casts a new light on Part X of the Ignatian *Constitutions*, 'How the whole body can be preserved and developed in its well-being'.

St Ignatius was no historiographer of the kind that has become familiar at the end of the twentieth century. But he had a sense of history. The mobility and flexibility he knew the mission of the Kingdom would require he built into the *Constitutions*. Vastly different cultures in his own time, and changing cultures in the times ahead, would demand an inbuilt principle of adaptation. The mission was to be accomplished always 'according to the circumstances of persons, places and times'. The determining principle that was to govern the ongoing mission and the spiritual vitality of the body was to be no written document, but—as the Preamble to the *Constitutions* puts it—the interior law of love that the Holy Spirit writes in the heart. St Ignatius enshrined the way to authenticity in *discreta caritas*.

The written word, especially the word of the *Constitutions* and its satellite documents, is helpful and indispensable. The same is true of the historical evidence. Erudition can help us to be somewhat more exact in understanding the sixteenth-century language, its culture, its theological assumptions, and the limitations of its categories, as well as the literary aims of the contemporary witnesses who recorded their memories, the ecclesial climate, the fears and desires of the people. That knowledge is invaluable. But even at best, it is imperfect. Those are the human means and St Ignatius taught us to reverence them. The human means are to be used with diligence and always in the clear awareness that they are secondary.

The primary instrument of authentic interpretation is the living body in its members. Interpretation is authentic to the extent that they are *instrumenta conjuncta cum Deo*—'instruments united with God' (X.2 [813]). To the extent that the members are not united with the source, the spirit that is incarnated is inauthentic. The sources are not for speculative contemplation or for academic discourse but for contemplative decision and action. It is discerning love made concrete in apostolic action that embodies the original spirit, gives flesh to the word.

I take it to be a commonplace that authentic interpretation is a function of the authenticity of the interpreter. Moral integrity is needed. *Discreta caritas* goes further. The spirit, too, needs to be purified. The authentic understanding of the original charism needs certain dispositions in the interpreter. These are: 'a thoroughly right and pure intention', which in turn presupposes in the searcher 'his greater abnegation and continual mortification in all things possible'.[37] Freedom from self-serving motivation is given only in the context of a continuing affective and contemplative relationship with the one who is 'the way that leads men to life'. What constitutes the Ignatian charism is the habitual exercise of discerning love in the work of the Kingdom now. In that ongoing process the only guarantee of authenticity, of not being misled or deluded by the stratagems of the Enemy, is a continuing contemplative adherence to the Jesus of the gospel in his poverty and rejection. The grace of the meditation on Two Standards (Exx 136) and the desire of the Third Degree of Humility (Exx 165) are the preconditions of being made free to be led by the Spirit (VII. 1. 8 [671]). The final hermeneutic is the cross.

Far from being abashed or dismayed by the lessons that history teaches us about the fragility of evidence and the human capacity to get things wrong, we should live contentedly with the fact that our interpretations, too, are partial and myopic, and with the fact that God would have it so. 'There are no static answers to questions of historical authenticity.'[38] There was a deeper wisdom in the request of the Council that our approach to the sources should be a *reditus continuus* (a continual return). The authentic source is a daily rediscovery and an unending search.

---

[37] VII. 2. 1 [618 ]; III. 1. 26 [288 ]; Examen, 4. 46 [103 ]; Examen, 4. 44 [101].
[38] O'Malley, *Tradition and Transition*, 106 n. 7.

# 9

# IGNATIAN PRAYER OR JESUIT SPIRITUALITY

S PIRITUALITIES ARE AFFECTED BY THE CULTURES they live through. To see Ignatian prayer as it was in the beginning, it is necessary to understand something of the shifts of culture and consciousness that have occurred since the sixteenth century. William Blake saw the cause of all the ills of his day in the 'two-horned heresy', the heresiarchs being Bacon, Locke and Newton. Somehow man had become more at odds with his world and at odds with himself, his head in disharmony with his heart, the cerebral with the affective. 'Imagination' would put him together again and reunite him with the world. T. S. Eliot coined the phrase 'dissociation of sensibility' to describe something similar.[1] Changes in the language of poets pointed to a shift in consciousness that occurred at some time in the seventeenth century.

For Eliot, the sixteenth-century poets were able to incorporate 'their erudition into their sensibility':

> … their mode of feeling was directly and freshly altered by their reading and thought. … There is a direct sensuous apprehension of thought, or a recreation of thought into feeling …. A thought to Donne was an experience; it modified his sensibility.

By the end of the seventeenth century, 'wit' and 'feeling' had been divorced; the poets 'thought and felt by fits, unbalanced':

> Tennyson and Browning are poets, and they think; but they do not feel their thought as immediately as the odour of a rose.

In many ways Ignatian prayer is like an old painting covered with layers of varnish and touched up by inferior hands. The art of removing varnish in order to disclose the living colours of the original

---

[1]  T. S. Eliot, 'The Metaphysical Poets', in *Selected Prose* (London: Faber, 1953), 111-112.

is a relatively recent one. Similarly, it is only recently that the writings of Ignatius, apart from his *Spiritual Exercises* and the *Constitutions*, have been edited and to some extent studied. Future generations will see us to have had our proper biases and distortions. But we are in a better position to see what Ignatius was saying about apostolic contemplation than any generation since the death of the first companions. We have documents that they could not have had and we can see him more clearly in the current of the tradition that he reverenced, selected from and changed.

In his teaching on prayer, as in his conception of a group of consecrated men wholly given to apostolic work, he was both more innovative and more traditional than has usually been realised. His immediate successors did not quite see how revolutionary he had been.

Ignatius and the men who knew his mind best, like Jerónimo Nadal, were well aware how open the Exercises were to the charge of illuminism. In the text of the *Spiritual Exercises*, reference to the Holy Spirit is notably absent where you would expect it. In the Spain of the sixteenth century, it was not comfortable to be found guilty of illuminism. Melchor Cano had his fellow-Dominican Cardinal Carranza imprisoned for sixteen years on the charge.

The fear of being charged with illuminism, and later the fear of illuminism itself, especially in the period between the Church's condemnation of quietism and the condemnation of modernism, helped to distort Jesuit understanding of Ignatius' teaching. Tomás Pedroche, the Spanish inquisitor, was accurate in pin-pointing those places in the *Spiritual Exercises* that seemed to smack of illuminism: the fifteenth Annotation; the parts on indifference; everything to do with election; the description of spiritual consolation. Those parts, if you add the remaining guidelines on discernment, are the heart of the Exercises and of Ignatian teaching on apostolic life. When they are given small importance, Ignatian spirituality easily becomes an asceticism only.

The dangers of illuminism, the well-founded fear of the early Jesuit Generals that some Spanish Jesuits would turn the new Order from its apostolic calling and make it purely contemplative, the silliness occasioned in Spain and France by the fashionable fervour for mysticism: these reasons largely explain the reserve of Borja, Mercurian and Vitelleschi as Generals of the Society of Jesus towards certain Jesuit contemplatives. Largely, but not entirely: something else was at work that does not emerge explicitly in the documents of the time.

St Francis Borja, himself a mystic, ordered Fr Antonio Cordeses, one of the Spanish Provincials, to stop teaching his subjects a simple affective prayer. The terms of Borja's letter to Cordeses are surprising:

> I understand that your reverence requires your subjects to make acts of love in their daily prayer, and that you desire to lead them all by this way. I praise your zeal and your good desires, for it is quite true that that is the best and loftiest spiritual exercise. But I warn you, my Father, that not all are developed enough for this exercise, and that not all understand it or are capable of it. To teach them how to pray, the Lord has given us a good guide in the Spiritual Exercises of the Society. Later, some will continue in this manner of praying, others in another .... For the movements of the Holy Spirit are different, and different the characters and minds of men.[2]

Borja's successor, Everard Mercurian, the fourth Jesuit General, went further. He was a Fleming, formed in a climate of anti-protestant polemic and fear of illuminism, with a liking for what was logically coherent and systematic in spirituality. His character and government are well conveyed by his statement that the Society needed 'not so much to be reformed as to be formed'. He forbade Jesuits to read Tauler, Ruysbroeck, Mombaer, Herp, Raymond Lull, Gertrude, Mechtilde of Magdeburg and 'others like them'. It was by his authority that the saintly director of St Teresa, Fr Balthasar Alvarez, was ordered to stop praying contemplatively and to bring back those he was directing to safer ways.[3]

The incident helps us to understand the climate in which the definitive 1599 Directory could say:

---

[2] Paul Dudon, 'Les idées du Antonio Cordeses sur l'oraison', in *Revue d' ascétique et de mystique*, 12 (1931), 97-115, here 97-99 ; de Guibert, *The Jesuits:* 198.

[3] Dudon, 'Les leçons d'oraison du Balthasar Alvarez', 36-38.

> Applying the senses is different from meditation, since meditation is more intellectual and consists more in reasoning. Meditation is altogether higher, since it reasons concerning the causes and effects of those mysteries .... (Dir 43.156)

The president of the commission which completed the text of the Directory was Fr Gil González Dávila, one of the first to be alarmed by Balthasar Alvarez' way of prayer. The observation on meditation did not go unchallenged, and was ignored in practice by men like Gagliardi, La Palma, La Puente, Alvarez de Paz and Suárez. For the moment, however, the men wary of contemplation had prevailed. In the nineteenth century, in a Church even less favourable to contemlation, the authority of the Directory was to carry more weight than that of the Spanish writers.

Jesuit folklore tends to cast Fr Jan Roothaan, the General who re-established the Society after its restoration in 1814, in the role of the man who influenced Jesuit spirituality along an excessively rationalist path. The truth is not so simple. A man who wanted, in the midst of the labours of government, to edit and publish Gagliardi's commentaries on the Exercises, was certainly familiar with the contemplative Jesuit tradition.[4] It is true that Jesuits in the nineteenth century interpreted the Exercises in a rigid and literalist way. But it is more accurate to say that their lack of flexibility,

> ... is due less to a single man or a single doctrine than to institutional forces: the formation of scholastics (with numerous borrowings from Sulpician seminary practice), the long years when young men, just emerging from adolescence, were daily exposed to the care of men whose specialism was formation and isolated from the normal life of the Society.[5]

It is through such fortunes as these that the Jesuits came to be accused, some rightly and some wrongly, of an intellectualism or rationalism in spirituality and theology that is at the opposite pole from all that Ignatius taught about apostolic prayer.

---

[4] Henri Bernard-Maître, 'Le Père Jean-Philippe Roothaan et la Vulgata latine des Exercices de saint Ignace', in *Revue d'ascétique et de mystique*, 37 (1961), 199.
[5] Pierre Vallin, 'La compagnie rétablie en France 1814-1950', in *Dictionnaire de spiritualité*, 8. 1047.

It is possible to read the text of the *Spiritual Exercises* in an excessively quietist or in an excessively Pelagian way. Ignatius gave those he trained to give the Exercises no theory of prayer or spirituality. He apprenticed them to the art, and they acquired it in a living tradition. He would have wanted them to be neither doctrinaire Pelagians nor doctrinaire quietists, neither anti-mystical nor anti-ascetical, but capable flexibly of guiding a particular man 'according to the measure of God's grace' given at any particular time, away from inert passivity or anxious activity.

The somewhat useful theoretical distinctions we are familiar with—'ordinary', 'extraordinary', 'acquired contemplation', 'infused contemplation'—are all tools of the seventeenth century. Had he known them, Ignatius might still have refused to use them. They can be of some use to directors. It is another question whether they have been of more help or hindrance to learners. It is clear that Ignatius was well aware of the invitation to illusion and self-deception entailed in a certain kind of chat about 'mysticism'.[6] Yet, had he lived in the aftermath of the quietist rumpus or in the bleak aftertaste of the Age of Reason, he might well have been trenchant in his comments on those who, like Bossuet, insisted on the great rarity of 'more visitations' and the dogged expectation of 'fewer'.[7]

It is not a question of conjecturing how many there are whose prayer remains fallow, how many succeed in emerging from spiritual or emotional self-centredness, how many reach a high degree of charity without exceptional gifts of prayer. These are speculative questions. It is rather a question of the effects a particular style of pedagogy may have on limiting or expanding the expectations and preconceptions of those who embark on a life of prayer. Ignatius would keep his counsel. He would place the responsibility for encouragement or deflation where it belongs, on the director.

The evils that Jesuit spirituality has sometimes committed would have been avoidable if succeeding generations had taken Ignatius' directives seriously. When the Exercises are given a Pelagian inter-

---

[6] Gonçalves da Câmara, *Memoriale*, nn. 195, 196.
[7] See III. 1. 10 [260], where it is said that the novices should 'apply themselves to the pursuit of the true and solid virtues, whether this be with many spiritual visitations or with fewer'.

pretation, and when the role of individual direction is diminished or precluded, whether in the making of the Exercises or in the living of the *Constitutions*, manipulation is at once a danger and the invasion of the Spirit's freedom is to some extent inevitable.

It is possible to find a purely ascetical meaning in the Exercises. It is easy, since it has often been done. It would be possible, though not so easy, to give an excessive mystical reading to the text. A logician coming innocent to the text might possibly be puzzled by the incompatibility of the active and passive verbs: 'their purpose is *to conquer* self and *to regulate* one's life'; 'I call it consolation when an interior movement *is aroused* in the soul'; 'every way of preparing and disposing the soul *to rid itself* of all inordinate affections'; 'it is better that the Creator and Lord *in person … himself* dispose the soul'.[8] The words need to be placed in the context of an experience of growth:

> The *more* the soul is in solitude (the more it co-operates as best it can to dispose itself), the *more* fit it renders itself to approach and be united with its Creator and Lord. The *more* closely it is united with him, the *more* it is disposed to receive … gifts …. (Exx 20)

All growth towards God is, from the beginning, at the same time both passive and active. The Exercises might be described as an art in which the 'giver' is aware that with God anything is possible.

Nadal, faithful to Ignatius' mind, demonstrates the same refusal to close doors that is implicit in the Exercises and that Ignatius trusted to the good sense and discernment of the men he trained to give them:

> We are sure that the privilege given to Fr Ignatius is granted to the whole Company; the same grace of contemplation is meant for all of us and is given along with our vocation. … Superiors and prefects of prayer are to show that good sense that we know to have been native to him and that we say is proper to the Society. When they judge in the Lord that someone is growing in prayer and led by the good Spirit, they are to avoid interfering. They should rather give him heart and confidence, so that he may grow with ease and strength in the Lord [*in Domino suaviter quidem et fortiter*]. (MHSJ MN 5, 163)

---

8 Exx 21, 313, 1, 15.

The Exercises are a point of departure. But towards what destination? We know that at the beginning some found, through making the Exercises, Carthusian or Dominican vocations. Many were led into the new, purely apostolic vocation. It seems evident that even the second generation of Jesuits did not altogether grasp the originality of a life in which everything, including prayer, its kind as well as its measure, was to be determined by the overriding claims of the needs of others. But Nadal was sure that the apostolic vocation, if faithfully lived, would mean a participation, in however modest a degree, in the privilege given to Ignatius. He describes it as a contemplative gift: 'To *contemplate* and to *savour affectively* the things of the spirit and God present in all things, in all activities and relationships'.[9]

We know that Ignatius' own prayer was Eucharistic and Trinitarian. But that of itself would not indicate any difference from the tradition of monastic prayer. The account we have of his prayer in the diary fragment of 1544-1545 reveals the highest mystical graces.[10] It is not a prayer that abstracts from the world of creatures. It is absorbed in God and focused on the concrete and the particular. We find sense, sensibility, imagination, will and intelligence, the whole person concerned with a practical decision, with finding what God wants in the matter of poverty in the new order. It is a kind of sensibility of the intelligence.

The great bulk of the Western writings on mysticism belongs to the tradition that goes back from John of the Cross, through the Rhenish mystics, to Denys the Areopagite. It does not follow that most of those raised by God to close contemplative intimacy were of that tradition; we simply do not know. But so great is the authority of the tradition that some writers, including Jesuit writers on apostolic prayer, assume that 'mysticism' is of one kind.

Such an assumption has practical consequences. A spiritual director may take it that everyone who is drawn to prayer must follow

---

9 MHSJ MN 5, 651: *in omnibus rebus, actionibus, colloquiis. … Dei praesentiam rerumque spiritualium affectum sentiret atque contemplaretur.*

10 de Guibert, *The Jesuits*, 44: 'We are in the company of a soul that is being led by God in ways of infused contemplation to the same degree, though not in the same manner, as a St Francis of Assisi or a St John of the Cross'.

more or less the same road. And those who want to pray may similarly assume that the contemplative path described by John of the Cross is the only one, or the only 'real' one. If they are also called to consecrated apostolic life, they may become bewildered and lose their way, or give up and turn to 'activism'. Or they may become 'Carthusians in action' or 'Carmelites in action'. But this may not be what God was drawing them to, to the possible detriment of apostolic effectiveness.

Michael Wadding of Waterford—the only Irish Jesuit who has given a small classic to the literature of spiritual theology—in his *Practica de la theologia mistica* (1681), used a terminology that goes back to Denys to distinguish different kinds of contemplative gifts: the 'seraphic' and the 'cherubic'. Auguste Saudreau added a third kind, the 'angelic'. De Guibert accepts the rough categories and finds from his analysis of Ignatius' letters, from the autobiography, and from a close examination of the diary, that Ignatius belongs, like St Paul, to the third kind.[11]

The terms conveniently describe different ways in which men are led by God's infused gifts, 'three main currents of catholic mysticism'. St Francis of Assisi is an instance of the first: in him affective love is dominant; the direct effect of grace falls chiefly on the will. St John of the Cross is an example of the second: grace chiefly affects the intelligence. In the third kind the infused gifts more directly affect the memory and imagination, the faculties that look to the concrete and to action. In Ignatius, says de Guibert:

> We do not find any trace of ideas or words influenced by pseudo-Denis. The part played by imagination, by the sensibility, by tears, as much as the direction of his mysticism, not to contemplative union seen as centre and summit, but towards the service of God, placed him outside the current of intellectual and 'speculative' contemplation .... Service of God is not, of course, lacking in either the cherubic or the seraphic kind of mystic. But in Ignatius service is not simply the sequel or consequence of the infused light. It is the very

---

[11] For what follows, see de Guibert, 'Mystique ignatienne', 135-137.

object towards which all his infused gifts tend and upon which they centre.

The Holy Spirit is not confined by human categories, no matter how rough or how refined. They serve, however, sufficiently to point out the differentiations that may be made between the contemplative ways in which the Lord guides men in the monastic and apostolic callings towards the perfection of charity. No adequate study, to my knowledge, has yet been made of the common ground, and the important differences, between monastic, mixed and apostolic contemplation. It is misleading simply to equate John of the Cross' *nada* with Ignatian 'indifference'. It can be unhelpful to assume that Carmelite prayer is the way for all. What is inescapable in any way is an experience of purification and illumination, whether the image of night or darkness be used or not. Maurice Giuliani is convincing in finding the apostle's purification and illumination in the radical contemplative abnegation of faith-full obedience.[12] The frustrations of apostolic life are a part of that obedience.

Which brings us back at last to the curious fact of Borja's reserve towards Cordeses, of Mercurian's towards Alvarez, of Vitelleschi's towards Lallemant.[13] It was not, as has sometimes been suggested, a simple alignment of ascetics against mystics. (There was a time when writers on spirituality tended, like some journalists, to dramatize differences of emphasis into confrontations of schools. We would hope to avoid doing that.) In a sense both sides were right and both were wrong. The Generals were right in seeing that not all that the mystics were saying was according to Ignatius' mind. The 'mystics' were right in seeing that Jesuit spirituality is not a pure asceticism. But Cordeses and Alvarez, like all the Spaniards of that time who took prayer seriously, and Lallemant later, were influenced by Herp. When Ignatius' good friends the Carthusians of Cologne dedicated an edition of Herp to him, his reply was a classic of courteous

---

[12] Maurice Giuliani, 'Nuit et lumière de l'obéissance', *Christus*, 2 (1955), 349-368; ET in *Finding God in All Things*, edited and translated by William J. Young (Chicago: Henry Regnery, 1958).
[13] Vitelleschi, the successor of Acquaviva, wrote on 5 April 1629 that he was disquieted to hear that Lallemant, whom he had recently appointed instructor of tertians, was *totus mysticus*. See Michel de Certeau: 'Crise sociale et réformisme spirituel au debut du XVIIᵉ siècle: une "nouvelle spiritualité" chez les jésuites français', in *Revue d'ascétique et de mystique*, 41 (1965), 339-341.

embarrassment.[14] There was something in Herp, whose work dominated sixteenth-century Spanish spirituality, as there was in Tauler,
that Ignatius found unacceptable. But he had found himself
immediately at home in the tradition he discovered in Ludolph and
Cisneros.

These are not just battles of long ago that have nothing to do with
us. The only way to dissolve false traditions is by trying, as best we
can, to get at the real ones. We are now in a position to discard a false
impression, common at one time, that writers like de la Puente and la
Paz were marginal and out of step, that the ascetic tradition was the
central and authentic one in Jesuit spirituality. We can see, too, that
we have somewhat less to learn from the French mystical writers of
the seventeenth century than we have from Gregory the Great,
Bernard, Aquinas, Bonaventure, and the great Carthusians and Cist-
ercians. The words Ignatius received from them and transposed,
especially key words like *sentir y gustar, affectus, devotio*, begin to be
understood as soon as they are seen in the tradition of monastic
theology and contemplation.[15]

Besides, there are present trends in spirituality and Christian
living that we need to look at. There is the possibility of a new
illuminism in the charismatic movement. There is the constant
danger of subjectivism in theology. Ignatius left us in his art of
discernment, if we can use it, a way of avoiding the pitfalls of
subjectivism and objectivism. In the tenth part of the *Constitutions* he
has also left us his balanced sense of the relationship between the
human and the divine. We need that if we are to avoid the extremes
of neglecting the human and neglecting the divine. There is a new
devout humanism in the air, less elegant than the seventeenth-
century kind, that can be so concerned with the development of
human potentialities as to soften the gospel's point and pain. We
must hope, too, that we are not in for a new version of the mutual
incomprehension of the 'mystics' and the 'ascetics', with the

---

[14] Ignatius to Leonhard Kessel, 18 December 1555, MHSJ EI 10, 348-351.
[15] Jean Leclercq, 'Theologie et prière', in *Chances de la spiritualité occidentale* (Paris: Cerf, 1966), 209.

possibility of an *ascéticisme*[16] coming from the world of psychology. A new Pelagianism might tend, as Tomás Pedroche did, to say of the fifteenth Annotation, 'There is no such experience'. In the work of the Exercises we need all the help we can get, since 'human means ought to be sought with diligence … and the art of dealing and conversing with men'. But it is 'the love which will descend from the Divine Goodness', 'the interior gifts', that alone will make the 'exterior means effective'. [17]

It would be failure indeed to fail to help those whose vocation it is to labour in the world to find a way towards a contemplation that goes with work and transforms it, so that eventually by God's gift the world of work and the world of prayer compenetrate. Karl Rahner once committed himself to saying: 'I dare to think that Ignatius belongs to the future, not to the age now coming to an end'. But he added the observation: 'It remains to be seen whether those who historically call themselves his disciples and pupils will be the ones who really represent this spirit in the future'.[18]

[16] Henri Bremond's barbed neologism for a spirituality centred wholly on *ascèse*, on human discipline.

[17] X. 3 [814 ]; VII. 1. 8 [671 ]; X. 3 [813].

[18] Karl Rahner, 'Ignatian Spirituality and Devotion to the Heart of Jesus' (1955), in *Mission and Grace*, volume 3, translated by Cecily Hastings (London: Sheed and Ward, 1966), 176-210, here 185-186.

# Part 4

# *St Ignatius and Contemporary Ministry*

# Introduction

M OST OF JOE VEALE'S published work focused on Ignatian texts,
on retreat giving, and on how the tradition had developed. But
he always wrote with an acute sense of how Ignatian wisdom could
enrich the contemporary mission of the Society of Jesus and of the
Church at large. This final section of *Manifold Gifts* presents six essays
in which this concern comes to the forefront.

The first piece is one of Joe's earliest. In 1975, the 32nd Jesuit
General Congregation published a wide-ranging and controversial
document, its so-called Decree 4, entitled 'Our Mission Today'. Its
tone was challenging: 'The mission of the Society of Jesus today is the
service of faith, of which the promotion of justice is an absolute requirement' (GC 32, d. 4, n. 2). Joe Veale was asked to write a commentary
on the decree's implications for the ministry of the Exercises. His
intuitions about the links between contemplation and justice ministry
were unusually perceptive at the time, and they foreshadow the
passionate calls which we find at the end of this section.

We then move forward to 1989, to a presentation which Joe gave
at a seminar held at the Milltown Institute in Dublin. The theme was
that of devotion to the Sacred Heart, and Joe brought a characteristic
freshness to a theme that had already been treated magisterially by
such figures as Karl and Hugo Rahner: the connections between the
devotion and the Society of Jesus. Around the same time, he was also
asked to talk to the European Jesuit Provincials gathered in Flanders
for what was then their biennial assembly abut the issues involved in
Jesuit renewal. The result was the acute and stimulating 'Renewing
Jesuit Life in the Spirit', here published for the first time.

The final three pieces move decisively beyond simply Jesuit concerns. In the late 1980s, Sr Elizabeth Smyth, a Cenacle sister, was one
of a number of people who founded the Ignatian Spirituality Course in
London. Over a three year period, it offers training in Ignatian spiritual
direction to a wide range of people from across the different Churches.
After Elizabeth's tragically early death from cancer, Joe was invited
to give the first Elizabeth Smyth Memorial Lecture in 1996. He took
the opportunity to undertake some research in Anglican and Puritan
spiritual writing, and the result is a magnificent reflection on the

presence of the Spirit in all the churches, and on how a ministry of the Exercises might enrich not only ecumenism among Christians, but also the evangelization of secular culture.

In the last years of Joe's life, Irish Catholicism was challenged grievously by the uncovering of sexual abuse perpetrated by a number of priests and religious. The event touched a nerve in Joe, and he wrote a passionate piece that was published only in a short-ened and expurgated form. For *Manifold Gifts* we have attempted to edit it in full: a raw typescript has been cleaned and ordered, but nothing of substance has been omitted. At one level, the piece is a plea for the crisis to be addressed with theological and spiritual seriousness. Abuse represents a problem in the whole Church, not just in particular individuals, and it points up the need for the whole Church to experience the graces of the Ignatian First Week. But the event also prompted Joe to express a powerful anger about the human impover-ishment of what had passed for spiritual culture in his youth. Once one has read this piece, everything else Joe wrote appears in a new light.

The final piece, 'The Silence', was originally written for the Irish Jesuits' internal magazine *Interfuse*, and was first published in 2002, some months before Joe's death. Joe suggested that contemporary Jesuits had become silent about God, that they had put their trust too much in human means, such as the promotion of just economic relations, or strategic plans. What was needed was a willingness to talk openly and honestly about how we experience God. Perhaps this was Joe's valedictory message; given that as a young man he had written an important article on education called 'Men Speechless', it is striking that his penultimate sentence is 'we shall stand there, disarmed, unmanned, speechless'.

On reading the original version, Philip Endean as editor of *The Way* invited Joe to reformulate his message for a wider readership. Joe's death intervened, but, after some reflection and consultation, it was decided that *The Way*'s staff would attempt the editorial task themselves. The result was an article that provoked more reaction than any other piece published by *The Way* in recent years. This passionate, pained, prophetic essay was the last of the manifold gifts with which Joe enriched us. May he now rest in peace.

# 10

# 'OUR MISSION TODAY' AND THE SPIRITUAL EXERCISES

THE IGNATIAN VOCATION AND GRACE is contemplative action in the service of others for the greater praise, reverence and service of the Divine Majesty. The Jesuit seeks God the better to do God's will, and he contemplates human needs so as the better to find God.

When, therefore, the 32nd General Congregation began its attempt at a modern account of Jesuit mission by focusing first on the needs of people today, it was being entirely Ignatian. It might have chosen to attend first, as previous Congregations did, to spiritual renewal and then to the demands of the apostolate. But to separate interior life and exterior action does not work for Jesuits. The Congregation insists on the need for conversion: we too share in the blindness and injustice of these times; we ourselves have need to be evangelized; we also need to learn how to find Christ as he works in our world and our time through the power of his Spirit (GC 32, d.4, n.23). But the Congregation is wholly faithful to St Ignatius in insisting on the single end of service and on the indivisibility of action and contemplation (GC 32, d.2, n.11). Similarly, the decree on mission insists on the indivisibility of the service of faith and work for justice, just as it insists that they are not to be confused or identified. The Christian message requires conversion to the demands of justice; there can be no promotion of justice unless we also preach Jesus Christ (GC 32, d.4, nn. 28, 27, 30). The spirit of the Exercises should pervade every other ministry of the word that we undertake; equally, experiment and study are needed to ensure that the Exercises are in touch with the real world now (GC 32, d. 4, n. 58). Concern for justice is to be a dimension of all our work; we are encouraged to search for a renewed understanding of the Exercises in function of our times (GC 32, d.4, nn. 7, 47, 51, 58).

For some years before the Congregation, men engaged in work for justice were critical of the way in which, it seemed to them, the

Exercises were being given. Some of the criticisms were wild and angry and betrayed a misunderstanding of the Exercises and of what they are for. But most were illuminating and helpful. In particular, a seminar in the United States consisting of men engaged in both works published its papers and tentative conclusions.[1] The result of the exchange was a better understanding of the limits of what the Exercises may be asked to do and of the demands now being made on spirituality by the world and by the Church.

Towards the end of the 1960s and the beginning of the 1970s, as interest in work for justice seemed to be declining, interest in retreats and prayer increased. Some talented young priests were turning from work for justice to work in spirituality and the Spiritual Exercises. The critique of the renewed retreat movement made such points as the following. Energy was being diverted from social action and devoted instead to the less frustrating and less demanding work of prayer and spiritual direction. Retreats for laymen had, over the years, been tranquillisers for the social conscience and had not had any marked impact on social or political life. It was possible to fall into a trap of interiority and to emerge from many days of prayer suffering from 'autistic spiritual narcissism'. Religious who had made the Exercises often showed no sensitivity to the demands of justice. Religious congregations formed by the Exercises made decisions and policies unaffected by concern for justice, unaware that decisions were influenced by their unconscious political and social biases. The Exercises, in short, may have been converting individuals, but they were leaving them innocent of any sense of the world's injustice and the Church's demand for action to bring about change.

It is a long-standing charge against the Exercises that they are individualistic. It is an accusation that can equally be made against all Christian spirituality of the last five hundred years. The western European consciousness has been individualist and Christian prayer has tended to be so too. It is only relatively recently that theology has taken account once more of community. Even more recently theology has begun to reflect on how faith and revelation cast light on

---

[1] *Soundings*, 'A Task Force on Social Consciousness and Ignatian Spirituality', (1973). *Soundings* was an occasional publication of the Jesuits' Center of Concern in Washington DC.

political and social experience. 'Social theology has not been integrated into the catechesis and spirituality of the Church.'[2] The men concerned for justice have drawn attention again to the danger that individuals can use prayer to escape from painful human tasks. They go further and warn that groups may become trapped in an interiority of religious experience, while the exterior relationships of life are controlled and structured by the values of the prevailing culture rather than by those of the gospel. We have some way to go before the spirituality of many will have assimilated a sense that 'action on behalf of justice and participation in the transformation of the world' is now 'a constitutive dimension of the preaching of the gospel'.[3]

All Christian spirituality is thus confronted with the task of re-thinking theory and practice. It is highlighted in the giving of the Ignatian Exercises. The solution, at first glance, seems simple. Those who give the Exercises should simply, for example, enlarge their consideration of sin to include the developed mind of the Church on social, economic and political sin. And so on. But that could well remain at the level of tinkering with words and ideas, and fail to tackle the deeper problems involved.

The Spiritual Exercises can legitimately mean a great variety of adaptations on the lines suggested by the text itself, in the eighteenth and nineteenth Annotations. Traditionally there has always been a continuum of Ignatian ways of bringing people closer to God, depending on where they are and on their dispositions and aptitudes, ranging from parish missions and weekend retreats, based mainly on the first week, through various adaptations in eight-day retreats, through what are called directed retreats, to the full Exercises given intensively only to those who have the necessary disposition of wanting to give themselves completely to the discovery of the divine will.

The further we move on the continuum from the Exercises in their pure form, the more suitable it is to give theological or moral instruction. The closer we move on the continuum towards the strict

---

[2] 'A Task Force', 3.
[3] 'Justice in the World', document of the 1971 Synod of Bishops, n. 6.

Exercises, the more difficult it becomes to justify inserting instructions, even on matters about which every Christian has an obligation to inform himself. When the one making the Exercises genuinely and generously wants to find God in finding his particular and concrete will for him, the 'director' is warned by St Ignatius to be 'as a balance at equilibrium' concerning the outcome of the exercitant's prayer; his presentation of the matter for prayer is to be cursory; he is to avoid interfering, lest he prevent the Creator and Lord from Himself moving the soul directly.[4] That does not seem to be the time to begin instructing a person in essential Christian teaching. The Exercises must not be asked to do everything, much less to do everything at the same time.

Yet Ignatius' guidelines for thinking and feeling with the Church are an integral part of the Exercises; the believing community is an essential norm for discerning God's will. It is part of the task of the director to ensure that the exercitant is attentive to the whole gospel. An individualistic or privatised prayer is not Catholic. There can be no question, then, as to the need to assimilate the Church's mind on justice into the work of the Exercises. The only question is how to do it without distorting the Exercises in the process. What we are considering here is the full Exercises. St Ignatius allowed no one to begin them until he was satisfied that he had the needed maturity and dispositions. Ignatius often spent a long time preparing a man, by means of instruction, spiritual direction and prayer. Fr Bernard Bush, among others, has suggested that people unaware of the Church's teaching on justice may be equated with those whom the eighteenth Annotation refers to as 'of little natural ability' and 'from whom little fruit is to be expected'.[5] In some places those who ask to make the full Exercises are prepared over a fairly long period by means of pre-Exercises: 'some spiritual exercises' that combine prayer and direction with education in the demands of justice.

---

[4] Compare Vincent O'Flaherty, in 'A Task Force', 19: the director's function 'is not to proselytize the retreatant concerning a cause, however worthy, even the reforming of unjust structures and the serving of the needs of the poor'.

[5] Exx 18; Bernard Bush, in 'A Task Force', 21.

'We call spiritual exercises every means of preparing and disposing the soul to rid itself of all ill-ordered attachments, and, after their removal, of seeking and finding the will of God.' (Exx 1) Today it is clear that among such ill-ordered attachments are deeply ingrained prejudices and attitudes that blind us to our own close involvement in injustice and to what God may want us to do about it. Most of us, directors and exercitants, are prisoners of our culture, ideological captives. We may know much but we do not see. We may know a lot about injustice in distant places, we may have a clear conceptual grasp of the teaching of the recent encyclicals and of the 1971 Synod of Bishops. But little is changed. We are unaware how much our unacknowledged assumptions and conditioned feelings inhibit our freedom and prevent effective action or radical choices.

It takes more than one or two instructions about justice to expand the imagination of an exercitant who has no experience of the effects of oppression. Information, instruction, exhortation and education can do something to open us to what the Church has been calling us to. But more is needed. We need 'some exercises' to awaken us to our own experience of being oppressed. Such exercises have been called a raising of awareness, or, to use the technical term from which cultivated English-speakers shy away like startled thoroughbreds, 'conscientisation'. It is a means of raising the awareness of a community, in an experience of action, to the realities of their social, economic and political situation, by attending to the unacknowledged determinants of their choices and to their power to change the situation; it moves from action to reflection, to appropriation of experience, and leads again to action. Even such a borrowed description must strike a note of recognition and familiarity in anyone who knows of St Ignatius' ways of forming his apostolic companions.

'Every way of preparing and disposing the soul to rid itself of all ill-ordered attachments.' Is it we who liberate ourselves from the oppression of ill-ordered attachments? Or is it the power of the Spirit that liberates us? For St Ignatius, of course, in the Exercises, we begin to dispose ourselves because God enables us to do so, and then God disposes and composes and frees us. We cannot be freed from our more deeply ingrained attitudes except by an experience of God in prayer. We are not free, as a rule, to hear what the Church is saying until the Spirit has opened us to change. It is such an experience, too, that relativises all ideologies and gives us 'indifferences to all created things', that critical distance we need from all idols and ideologies (GC 32, d.4, n.58). Conscientisation may liberate men from one ideological prison only to make them captive in another. It is,

> ... the Spirit of the Lord who continually breaks down the horizons within which man's understanding likes to find security, who breaks through the limits to which his activity would gladly restrict itself. There dwells within him a power which urges him to go beyond every system and every ideology.[6]

It is significant that the mission decree does not speak of conscientisation. It urges us to discover the means to *evangelica conscientisatio* (GC 32, d.4, nn.60, 73). Part of the problem of combining the giving of the Exercises with the promotion of justice is that contemporary techniques of raising political awareness would have little to teach St Ignatius. He formed men in the process of an experience of action by helping them to reflect on their experience and to pray through it, to find God in it and to find his will, and then led them forward into another experience of action. The Exercises radicalise; they lead to a radical appropriation of the gospel, which, God knows, is subversive of all the powers of this world. They could certainly be used, as a mere technique, to produce a high degree of political consciousness. But that would no longer be the Ignatian Exercises.

There are further inconveniences that might arise from a hasty or ill-considered or superficial insertion of concern for justice into the various kinds of adaptation that are popularly called the Spiritual Exercises. As Thomas E. Clarke has pointed out, all people,

> ... are called to share in the struggle for peace and justice, but not all in equal measure or in the same way.... God calls us according to our ability to respond at any given moment.[7]

---

[6] *Octogesima adveniens*, n.37.
[7] Thomas E. Clarke, 'Holiness and Justice in Tension', *The Way*, 13 (1973), 184-190, here 185.

Just as it is possible to be so preoccupied with one's private faults that one is blinded to social evil, it is equally possible to be so attentive to political evil that one is blind to one's own anger or falseness or resentment, or to one's personal responsibility. It would be all too easy, besides, to preach justice in such a way that some would experience only a feeling of impotence in the face of unjust structures, would experience merely an increased weight of unmanageable guilt and be pushed into a further degree of alienation. Only God can reveal to each of us that his wrongdoing is sin. 'Any knowledge of societal sin which takes place outside of God's self-revelation … leads only to despair and death.'[8] The mission decree tells us to look to the personal evil that is the deeper root of both structured injustice and atheism (compare GC 32, d.4, nn.27, 29, 32, 33). Action for justice can do only harm if it is motivated by unredeemed feelings of anger or outrage or hatred. 'Premature social action based only on restlessness, anger or guilt feelings perpetuates the evil.'[9] The source needs to be purified by the Spirit.

So far we have been considering the work of giving the Exercises to those who are not yet sufficiently aware of the demands of justice. The important questions that arise in regard to the Exercises for those who are already engaged in political or social action have been well treated elsewhere.[10] It is time to turn to some consideration of the life and renewal of those who are called to the consecrated apostolic life and who, it is assumed, have already experienced the full Exercises.

When one has previously made the Exercises, a subsequent retreat may be understood as a 'repetition' of the Exercises or of some parts of them.[11] Such repetitions can well be combined with the insights that the mission decree elicits from the original Formula of the Institute, from the practice of Ignatius and his companions and, pervading every part of the decree, from a more accurate and authentic understanding of Ignatian spirituality than many Jesuits

---

[8]  Bush, in 'A Task Force', 16.

[9]  Bush, in 'A Task Force', 16.

[10] Dominic Maruca, in 'A Task Force', 25-27.

[11] Exx 62, 118. Compare Brian O'Leary, 'Repetition and Review', in *The Way Supplement*, 27 (Spring 1976), 48.

have been given. The decree presupposes that the reader is familiar with the meaning and experience of Ignatian discernment, of Ignatian contemplation that 'finds God' in all his experience, of a growing compenetration of action and contemplation, of the subtleties of the conflict in our deeper selves between the Spirit of the Kingdom and the spirit hostile to the Father, of the centrality of 'real poverty' in the Exercises (Exx 98, 116, 135, 147, 157, 167). It presupposes the wider and deeper understanding of Ignatian prayer and 'immense labours' that comes from the way the Ignatian *Constitutions*, the experience of the first companions in the *schola affectus*, and the Exercises illuminate each other. For the early companions, the *schola affectus* (the education of the heart) was the experience of working in the slums and hospitals of Venice together with days of intense prayer, rather than the more monasticized tertianship of later times. It is this integration that gives to the decree its inner logic and unity. Without a lived sense of that background and cogency its coherence can be missed.

From God's loving gaze upon the world springs the mission of Jesus. From the mission of Jesus is born the mission of all Christians, members of the Church sent to show what salvation means, and to labour that men may have more abundant life. Ignatius and his first companions wanted (in that same perspective of the Three Persons) to observe attentively the world of their time in order to discern its needs. They contemplated at length 'the three divine Persons looking down on the face of the earth' and deciding 'that the Second Person should become a man to save the human race'. With God they lingered over the contemplation of the men of their day (*Deum in sua contemplatione imitati*), one group after another, with their 'great variety of dress and customs, some white, others black; some at peace, others at war; some weeping, others laughing; some healthy, others sick; some being born, others dying. And so on.' They searched how they might labour, in response to the call of Christ, to build his Kingdom (GC 32, d. 4, nn. 13, 14).

The Three Persons are contemplated as themselves missionary in the sending of the Word and the Spirit. We are called, in the continuing Ignatian experience, to contemplate the world in its present detail and concrete reality, not just to take it as read, nor merely to analyze it or reflect upon it or plan for it. It is God who casts light on his work in the world, not we who in some Promethean way wrest plans from it. Only in that contemplation of apostolic projects will our action be contemplative and safe from the waste, the fever and the fret that defeat our best human contrivances.[12] It is only in this light that the decree's prescriptions and argument and its command to harness all our efforts towards helping to free the oppressed for the sake of the *diakonia fidei* are coherent and obvious.

The decree's shorthand for that wider and deeper sense of Ignatian spirituality is 'the spirit of the Exercises' (GC 32, d. 4, n. 58). We cannot safely embark on what we are now told to do without a renewed and authentic experience of both the *Constitutions* and the *Spiritual Exercises*. This is particularly true of the mine-field of social and political involvement (GC 32, d. 4, n. 80). That the field is mined is all the more reason for entering it boldly. But the hazards should come as no surprise to any Jesuit who is at all familiar with the ambiguous results of the well-meant efforts of some of his predecessors, who too easily identified political action with the Kingdom.

The decree tells us that we are to labour to find 'a new language and a new set of symbols that will enable us to find the true God, beyond the idols we will have destroyed'. The idols are 'false images of God that serve to support and justify oppressive structures and that can no longer be tolerated; and even more ambiguous images of God that relieve men of their personal responsibilities'. 'It is the living memory of Jesus Christ that calls us to that creative fidelity.' (GC 32, d. 4, n. 26) That creative effort of faith is an 'immense labour' that will require all the combined resources of theologians, of experts in the human sciences and of men in close contact with the experience of the disenchanted believer, of the groping unbeliever, of the oppressed and of the oppressor, who is himself the prisoner of his oppression. The enterprise is foolhardy (if not absurd pride) and fated to fail, apart from the contemplation that is 'the spirit of the Exercises'.

---

[12] Compare Maruca, in 'A Task Force', on the form of desolation experienced by those who work for justice.

An integration of the tasks of faith and justice is something that we do not yet have; we are challenged to discover it. Before we can articulate it, we need first to integrate contemplation and justice in our own experience. Spirituality has had its deficiencies. But the trap of interiority is mirrored in the trap of empiricism. I have no doubt that it is possible to 'find God', in the full Ignatian sense, in statistics. But I wonder how. Ignatius was no stranger to the pitfalls of a close engagement with the powers and processes of this world, nor was he afraid of it. He knew, however, what it costs to keep in harmony and union the things we always try to divorce or to invert: contemplation and action, the divine power and human means, the end that slips insensibly from view and the human devices that quickly usurp the proper place of the end.

When we become immersed in the practical and the empirical, it can come to seem, as all our own experience tells us, that contemplation cuts no ice, that prayer butters no bread. The decree tells us that,

> ... we must 'contemplate' our world as Ignatius did his, that we may hear anew the call of Christ dying and rising in the anguish and aspirations of men and women (GC 32, d. 4, n. 26).

Such language can be felt to be mere rhetoric or poetry and not very pertinent to the pain of the oppressed. When we spend many hours of every day in an empiricism that prescinds from faith and revelation, faith itself may end in becoming marginalised (GC 32, d. 4, n. 5).

I have heard a Jesuit expert on the promotion of justice make two observations. Having visited many social institutes all over the world, he said he was struck by their lack of originality. He also said that a preliminary condition of any effective work for justice is a deep experience of God. The two things may not be unconnected. The contemplation of the apostle is a mode of decision and a mode of insight; one might say, a mode of creative imagination.[13] What characterized such experiments as the Paraguay Reductions was a

---

[13] 'We must use spiritual discernment to acquire a deeper knowledge of the movements, hopes and conflicts of our contemporaries, of all that shakes the human heart.' (GC 32, d. 4, n. 10)

daring of imagination. I believe that this was one of the fruits of the Exercises in the early days. Perhaps it is one of the fruits of the prophetic freedom which the Exercises dispose us to receive.

It is the living God who relativises everything that is not God, even our concern for justice, even the Spiritual Exercises. We are always liable to allow our techniques to take the place of God. He relativises every ideology, even the Jesuit ideology. Without Ignatian indifference we are in danger of allowing an 'absolute requirement' like the promotion of justice (GC 32, d. 4., n. 2), or an absolute require-ment like the promotion of prayer, to supplant the end, which is God's will in the concrete for both justice and prayer.

The whole purport of the mission decree is that neither sociology nor spirituality is enough; nor theology, nor metaphysics, nor the interdisciplinary work that is indispensable (GC 32, d. 4, nn. 35, 60). The primacy is given to the cost of indifference and apostolic freedom and to prayer (GC 32, d. 4, n. 72). What is said of the promotion of justice has wider application. We cannot rest satisfied with merely re-casting our work for justice. We need to examine ourselves and ask whether we have the competence to communicate the reality that gives work for justice its meaning. Are we competent to help people in the light of the gospel to find Christ at the heart of all their experience? (GC 32, d. 4, n. 52) For it is that which is the goal, both of Ignatian spirituality and of apostolic mission.

# 11

# IGNATIAN SPIRITUALITY AND DEVOTION TO THE SACRED HEART

I SHALL TRY HERE TO SHOW THE WAYS in which there is an affinity between devotion to the Sacred Heart and Ignatian spirituality. There are differences too, and the one does not simply derive from the other. But we can find in Ignatian spirituality elements which make it understandable how, historically, it was Jesuits who were among the strongest defenders, promoters and preachers of the devotion in its Paray-le-Monial form.

No spirituality is complete or free from human defects. The same can be said of every devotion as it is experienced and practised. A spirituality, in emphasizing one or other aspect of the immense Christian mystery, can become lopsided or narrow, can detach itself, as it were, from the complete context of revelation and can come insensibly to imply that those who follow another path are in some way lacking in fervour or defective in their grasp of the gospel. The same occurs with devotions.

Bringing together devotion to the Sacred Heart and Ignatian spirituality will enable to see one in the light of the other. The comparison itself may be a useful way of helping us correct the distortions of both. Their very affinity, I think, invites us to look at the differences, and thereby to situate both in what we know of the whole Christian mystery.

## How St Ignatius Regarded Devotions

Let me begin by reading from that integral part of the Spiritual Exercises called 'Rules for Thinking with the Church':

> To praise sacramental confession, the yearly reception of the Most Blessed Sacrament and praise more highly monthly reception and still more weekly communion ...

> To praise the frequent hearing of Mass, the singing of hymns, psalmody and long prayers whether in church or outside; likewise the hours arranged at fixed times for the whole divine office, for every kind of prayer ...

> To praise veneration for the relics of the saints and praying to the saints, visits to the station churches, pilgrimages, indulgences, jubilees, crusade indults and the lighting of candles in churches. (Exx 352, 355, 358)

Quite apart from the Lutheranizing influences at work in the Church of his time, we know that St Ignatius' sense of the whole Church in its concreteness made him react strongly against those who disdained popular devotional practices as being insufficiently interior and as fostering only an external and material practice of piety.

He clearly does not place pilgrimages, indulgences, jubilees and the lighting of candles in churches on the same plane as the Mass, the Divine Office, confession and communion. To praise is not the same as to practise something oneself. There is no evidence that St Ignatius practised devotions. To praise is not to impose practices, to insist on them as required by sound Christian living. St Ignatius would merely have us show our esteem for popular devotions.

**Devotions**

What are popular devotions? They are extra-liturgical practices, whether privately performed or publicly celebrated, which nourish the personal faith of Catholics. One thinks of particular devotions to the saints, to St Jude, to St Anthony, to St Francis Xavier in the Novena of Grace, devotion to the Infant Jesus of Prague, to the miraculous medal, to a particular icon of Our Lady. One can hardly in the same sense speak of the practices promoted by the charismatic movement, which has brought such blessings to so many since Vatican II, as a set of devotions; they would more properly be called a spirituality.

Devotions are of great help to many of the faithful. Devotions introduce people to God and to prayer, often through simple prayer of petition for favours or for defence against calamity. They have for many been a threshold to holiness.

They can, though not necessarily, be mingled with some element of superstition and become external and narrow. They can be accompanied by an un-Christian anxiety to assure salvation. When they are multiplied and given something of an absolute value, they can induce anxiety and scrupulosity in their performance. They can be partial and partly blinding when they float free from the whole context of revelation, when they are out of touch with the Church's liturgy and when they do not lead beyond themselves into the entire mystery of Christ and to the Father.

But in individual cases, such concerns need not be considered too gravely. 'It makes little difference through which window the full sunlight enters a room.'[1] When devotions help an individual to come closer to God, then we can be confident that in the end God will not require a certificate of doctrinal accuracy.

## Devotions and Liturgy

Vatican II in its decree on liturgy insisted, in its only reference to popular devotions, that 'these devotions should be so drawn up that they harmonize with the liturgical seasons, accord with the sacred liturgy and are in some fashion derived from it and lead people to it, since the liturgy by its very nature far surpasses any of them'.[2] One of the effects of Vatican II was to remove clutter in the personal living of the faith. To many it brought a life-giving simplification of their piety and a door into the spacious freedom of the children of God.

But in many lives it created a kind of vacuum. 'Devotions' seemed to fade into some obscure and forgotten corner of Christian living. At the least they became less prominent. Karl Rahner complained of writers who 'whored after relevance', jettisoned precious elements in the Church's tradition, replaced them with

---

[1] Josef A. Jungmann, *The Good News Yesterday and Today*, translated by William A. Huesman (New York: W. H. Sadlier, 1962), 133.

[2] *Sacrosanctum concilium*, nn. 13, 17.

nothing; and thereby created an un-Christian vacuum in many lives. He said, 'Beware Christians with no devotions'.[3]

It seems evident that in Ireland the hopes placed in the new liturgy as a nourisher of Christian piety and as the natural means of instruction in the faith have not been realised. The liturgy of itself, without a preliminary and accompanying life of prayer, can remain distant and mystifying. The liturgy is not enough. Whether this is due to poor pastoral pedagogy or to unprayerful celebration of the liturgy is not clear. It may be attributable to the austerity of liturgy and to the inaccessibility at first hearing of many of the scripture readings. The evident decline of faith and practice, and the indifference of many young people to the Mass, are to some extent signs of that. Many of the faithful need also, as a simple introduction to an interior life of piety, the colour and warmth, the engagement of the emotions and senses, that go with the practice of devotions.

### The Devotion to the Sacred Heart

The devotion to the Sacred Heart is not, in the mind of the Church, simply on a par with other devotions. Pius XI and Pius XII called it the epitome of Christian piety, *summa religionis*. Cardinal Ratzinger identifies it with the whole Easter mystery.[4] It has, then, a status which is not just the same as that of devotions to particular saints or to a particular icon.

Devotion to the Sacred Heart as we knew it when we were young derives both in its content and in its style from St Margaret Mary. We may speak of the devotion's Paray-le-Monial form. For most people, this is what the devotion amounts to, despite the labours of Pius XII in *Haurietis aquas* to root the devotion in Scripture, in the Fathers and in a deeper theology, and despite the frequent work along the same lines of the two Rahners and many others.

The devotion was, of course, practised by individuals in the Church long before St Margaret Mary. It had for a long time been a

---

[3] Harvey D. Egan, in his foreword to Annice Callahan, *Karl Rahner's Spirituality of the Pierced Heart* (Lanham, Md: UP of America, 1985), vi.

[4] Josef Ratzinger, *Behold the Pierced One: An Approach to a Spiritual Christology*, translated by Graham Harrison (San Francisco: Ignatius Press, 1986), 47-48.

private devotion of some mystics and saints, of some cloistered religious and of some friar preachers. It found expression in devotion to the five wounds, and in the prayer *Anima Christi*. The devotion predates, then, both St Margaret Mary and St Ignatius.

It may be recalled too that St John Eudes preceded St Margaret Mary with his preaching and writing on the devotion. It was in 1647, when St Margaret Mary was born, that the authorities in her diocese authorised St John Eudes to celebrate publicly a Mass in honour of the Heart of Mary. Karl Rahner has observed that there is almost no element in her private revelations that cannot be found in the writings of her congregation or in the books she read.[5]

The Church was slow to encourage or to give recognition to the Paray devotion. It was strongly opposed at the centre, in Rome, both by theologians of the centre ground and by those who were of the Jansenist party. It was not until 1765, almost a century after the private revelations of Paray, that Clement XIII granted a special Mass and office of the Heart of Jesus. It was only in 1856 that Pius IX extended the feast to the whole Church. The story is a striking example of how in Church history a movement from the people and from particular dioceses is first strongly resisted, is purified in the process, and is eventually blessed and strongly promoted by papal authority. The liturgical and ecumenical movements are instances in our own day.

The devotion spread rapidly even in the eighteenth century but more amazingly throughout the whole Church in the nineteenth. It is no accident that it arose in the seventeenth century, when liturgy had long grown remote, and when spirituality had long lost touch with theology, to the impoverishment of both. One can make a similar observation of the nineteenth century and indeed of the twentieth up till about 1965. In this situation, the devotion filled a vacuum and met a need in people's piety.

---

[5] Karl Rahner, *Visions and Prophecies*, translated by Charles Henkey and Richard Strachan (London: Burns and Oates, 1963 [1958]), 63.

*The Style and the Substance*

We cannot but praise and show esteem for a mode of piety that so engaged the hearts of so many and led many to profound faith, piety and holiness. Theologians such as Karl Rahner, aware of so much distaste for the forms of the devotion, have laboured to disengage its pure theological essence from the style. But there is something unsatisfactory in that enterprise. In the popular reception of the Paray devotion it is impossible to separate the substance from the style. The style itself was intrinsic to the message, and part of its enormous appeal. Rahner's great number of writings in praise of the devotion extract the substance from its clothing, and leave us with a beautiful and elevated theology. But it is hard to be persuaded that it is a theology that is accessible to most of us or that it could easily be popularly preached.

Three characteristics of the Paray devotion are singled out by Rahner as central to it. He names 'inwardness', 'belief in the presence of the love of God' and 'reparation'.[6] We might add the focus on the Eucharist in the devotional practice of the holy hour and in a communion of reparation on first Fridays. One might ask to what extent the appeal of the devotion was also due to the promises given to St Margaret Mary. The devotion arose in a time of widespread anxiety about salvation among the devout and spread widely in the nineteenth century when the same anxiety remained.

## Jansenism and the Enlightenment

We are familiar with the fact that the Paray devotion arose in a France excited by Jansenism. It was also a time when a scoffing spirit accompanied a growing deism and rationalism, the beginning of what we have come to term secularisation. The devotion, with its emphasis on the human love and mercy of God, engaged powerfully the senses and the affections in the ordinary piety of the faithful. It was a protest against and an antidote to coldness of heart, to the

---

[6] Karl Rahner, 'Some Theses for a Theology of Devotion to the Sacred Heart', in *Theological Investigations*, volume 3, translated by Karl-H. Kruger (London: Darton, Longman and Todd, 1967 [1956]), 331-352, here 340.

withering effect on the religious sensibility of a stern Jansenism and of
a chilly rationalism.

It was marked from its beginnings with some of the
characteristics of the spirituality of its time in France. Though it was
publicly celebrated, it took on the colouring of a spirituality that was
not only inward but also private and individualistic. It would be
anachronistic to demand of it that it should have included our
contemporary sense of solidarity with those who suffer, our solidarity
with others in both sin and grace, our present sense that God wants to
be served by us in going out to others whether in direct apostolate or
in simple help.

The devotion was clearly in opposition with Jansenism and the
hatred of Jansenists for it was soon made plain. If Jansenism, as a
religious climate rather than as an identifiable party, may more
properly be termed neo-Augustinian pessimism, then it has to be said
that the Paray devotion was not entirely free from the infection to
which it was an antidote. Both shared the same religious climate. It
arose at a time of what Rahner calls an anti-Christian pessimism
about the possibility of salvation, a cold Calvinist wind. Much of the
preaching and practice of the devotion up to our own time has never
entirely shaken free of that.

In Ireland from quite early in the nineteenth century until
recently, the devotion was immensely popular and salutary. It is not
simply that it was forcefully preached; it was welcomed by the people
as supplying something needed and fruitful in their piety. It could be
claimed, perhaps with some reason, that the spirituality of many of
the Irish faithful consisted in the rosary and in devotion to the Sacred
Heart, materially represented by the rosary beads hanging on a nail
in the kitchen ready to be used in family prayer in the evening, and by
the red lamp before the picture of the Sacred Heart.

For many generations the devotion brought warmth and colour
into lives that were very harsh. If we can make any judgment on the
basis of the evidence in *The Sacred Heart Messenger* of thanks for favours
received, the devotion was associated with (though not simply
identical with) a trust in the Sacred Heart as a recourse in the face of
those things that threatened the happiness and stability of the family:
sudden grave illness, economic ruin, the burden of debt, the

drunkenness of a husband or son, the arbitrary decrees of official-dom, the health of livestock on which a homestead depended. Many were brought to learn to pray through such simple prayer of petition and thanksgiving. The spirituality the devotion encouraged could be simply stated in the prayer 'O Sacred Heart of Jesus, I place all my trust in thee'.

One of the practices of the devotion, however, was the Apostle-ship of Prayer. From the mid-nineteenth century, when it began to become widespread, the Apostleship introduced an apostolic and outward-looking element to the devotion, as a counter to any tend-ency in the spirituality inherited from seventeenth century France to introspectiveness or self-preoccupation. It enlarged the horizon of many lives to incorporate in their prayer a concern for the worldwide Church and for matters outside a religiously and nationally insular world.

In its essence the Paray version of the devotion was a powerful reminder of the mercy and the tenderness of God, a way into a deep spiritual appropriation in faith of the human heart of Christ who loves us with the love of the Three Persons. Its emphasis on reparation brought home the redemptive value of the ordinary chores and work, of the family responsibilities of every day, of the pains and joys of living. It was a prayerful way into a meditative encounter with Jesus in his passion. Its flesh and blood reality was a corrective to a too spiritualised spirituality, whether Jansenist or rationalist. The devotion was centred firmly in the concrete realism of the Incarnation.

The prominence given to reparation in the Paray version of the devotion was in its time a reminder of the evil of sin and the need that reparation be made. What arouses now our theological scruples is that reparation was to be made to the heart of Christ, not in and with Christ to the Father. We would have difficulty, too, in explaining how our prayer or penance now could have consoled Jesus in his passion. We tend rather now to be aware that it is suffering women and men who need his compassion and ours. But the devotion did bring home that what we do and suffer matters to God, that we are invited by the divine courtesy to unite our pains and struggles with Christ's, and that they have redemptive value.

## The Spirituality of Mystics

There is a problem with taking the profound experiences of a mystic like St Margaret Mary and simply preaching as helpful for all her acute and agonized sense of Christ. She, like all the saints, was led by the Holy Spirit in her particular way. Such great graces presuppose a long and careful ascetical and spiritual preparation and normally also a robust psyche. One may wonder with Jungmann at,

> … many prayers of atonement and many invocations [that] seem to push one headlong into the innermost sanctuary of all piety. The fiery furnace of love encompasses the one praying, if he has been able psychically to follow the steep ascent of the words of the prayer. In many instances little attention has been paid to preparatory steps and preliminary conditions.[7]

Something the same can be said of a great saint's acute sense of sin. We know that the holier a soul becomes the more the evil of sin is vivid to it. But a healthy sense of sin will be free from an oppressive and un-Christian guilt that hides the face of the living God and that constrains the Christian spirit with a fear alien to the gospel. This is not something that can be aroused in large numbers of people simply by preaching unqualified the privileged experience of a mystic. It requires a more delicate pastoral pedagogy.

## St Ignatius and the Manifold Gifts of the Spirit

St Ignatius was accustomed to blame directors and teachers of others who measure everything according to themselves and who want to impose the same manner of life and way of prayer that has proved useful for themselves. The manifold gifts of the Spirit are given and shown in a great variety of ways. It is brought home to us in giving the Spiritual Exercises how variously individual persons are led to respond to God's love made visible in Christ Jesus our Lord, with what hesitations, returns and approximations they enter into the way in which God discloses Himself to them. Some will, following the tradition of St Margaret Mary's 'reparation', experience the personal

---

[7] Jungmann, *The Good News*, 146.

and intimate love of Christ in the bitter and driven passion confronting the stark experience of their sinfulness and of the world's sin.[8] But it is not for anyone to judge unfavourably or to interfere with the free action of the Spirit if a person is drawn to respond to the passion with glad gratitude and confidence in Christ victor over evil.

Another concern of St Ignatius in matters of the spirit was to be clear on the difference between the means and the end. For him, particular modes of prayer or particular images or symbols, or particular practices such as devotions, were means. If the work of God in the soul dispenses with or bypasses the human means, then the human means are not needed. One has known persons who have a deep personal affective relationship with Christ, the love of God made visible, who relate with him familiarly and directly, but in whose prayer the icon of the heart does not feature. They have the substance of devotion to the Sacred Heart in the sense in which the Church's documents call it the *summa religionis*. They have the substance but not the form or the imagery. What is helpful and salutary for some as a means of entry into the human love of God is not their way to the same end. It is not for anyone to prescribe or insist on the means.

*Spiritualities of the Cross*

There are many ways of coming in faith to know Christ in his passion. Some are more in harmony with the New Testament gospel than others. Some lead to a more vigorous and life-filled engagement with one's human responsibilities and a more hope-filled support for a life of Christlike service of those in need. One might derive from St Ignatius' Rules for Discerning the Spirits some criteria for discerning what is more and what is less in harmony with the *sensus Christi*.

There can be a spirituality of the cross and also of devotion to the Sacred Heart where something else comes in: an attitude to pain that is not Christlike; something of a dampening sense of martyrdom; a fatalism towards what oppresses or diminishes our humanity; a passivity in the face of evil and an excuse to evade our human responsibility; an attitude that gives an opening to gloom and

---

[8] See Edouard Glotin, 'Réparation', in *Dictionnaire de spiritualité*, 13.369.

despondency (which are not the same as sadness or sorrow); even sometimes an illusion that we are different from others in their human struggling and sin. All meditative considerations of the cross must begin from the truth that all human pain is displeasing to the Father, including the suffering of his Son.

How might the work of the Holy Spirit be discerned? Even amid sadness or darkness or pain of whatever kind there will be the presence of some note of faith and hope. At some level of the spirit, however deep, there will be a note of peace and joy. *Passio Christi, conforta me* (Passion of Christ, strengthen me) from the *Anima Christi* is a touchstone. The person's focus of attention will move increasingly away from self-preoccupation towards the person of Christ. Consequently, the heart will be turned outward, away from the self, towards Christ disclosed in the needs of others. The heart will grow to share more in the movement of forgiveness and compassion revealed by Jesus in the heart of the Father.

### Affinities and Differences

I have tried to say something about the devotion to the Sacred Heart, both in its finest expression and as it has sometimes in fact been expressed, in the light of some of the things I have learned from St Ignatius. There remains the question of the affinities and differences of the devotion and Ignatian spirituality.

I have to confess that when I turn from the seventeenth-century world of French spiritual writers to the beginning of the sixteenth century and to the late medieval world, I experience a sense of relief and release. It is like coming out of a drawing room where the windows have long been closed into the fresh and spacious outdoors.

Historically the Paray devotion appeared at a time when Jesuit spirituality had to some extent lost touch with its Ignatian source. There has been a form of Jesuit spirituality that was wary of the heart, that tended, in spite of the plain meaning of St Ignatius, to be indiscriminately suspicious of feeling. It was inclined to be anti-mystical, voluntarist and rationalist, and had lost a sense of the tenderness and companionship with Jesus encouraged by the Exercises. If we may, with the Church, give the Church's credence to the private revelations of St Margaret Mary, then the commission given to Jesuits to promote the devotion was and is a reminder to them to return to the heart.

St Ignatius' sense of the goodness of the world and of the world as sacramental of God went together with a realistic sense of sin, of the evil in the world, and above all of the ways in which the human heart can be misled and its best efforts betrayed by the deceits of the bad spirit.

As he walked towards Rome in 1537, he had been praying to our Lady that he might be 'placed with her Son'. At La Storta he was given a sense of the presence of the Father and of the Son carrying his cross. Diego Laínez recounts the incident as follows:

> The Eternal Father ... said to Christ: I want you to take this man for your servant. And so, Jesus actually received him and said: I want you to serve us. And because of this, getting great devotion to this most holy name, he wished to name us the Company of Jesus. (MHSJ FN 2, 133)

The Christ of St Ignatius is the one who continues to carry his cross in the world and continues his work of redemption in us and through us by inviting us to share in his labours, poverty, humility and suffering. From the Third and Fourth Weeks of the Exercises, we learn that the Christ carrying his cross is also the Risen Christ who delights to console his friends.

'Reparation', then, for St Ignatius, is to welcome gladly the suffering that is entailed in being with Christ in his continuing work, in healing and repairing the God-forsaking world. Jerónimo Nadal, the theologian trusted by St Ignatius to convey his mind to the fledgling Company, instinctively turned to St Paul to interpret the meaning of La Storta:

> For this we must realise that, while Christ who rose from the dead dies no more, he still continues to suffer and bear his cross in his members. It is to this therefore that God the Father calls us, so that in this company we may follow Jesus, each one carrying his cross, suffering for Christ; and we ought to find courage and comfort in this .... We follow Jesus ... even now carrying his cross in his Mystical Body which is the Church; and so we are to fill up what is wanting to the passion of Christ .... And so with a large heart, great faith, great

liveliness and joy of spirit, let us follow in the humility of our hearts.[9]

For St Ignatius, the pains and stresses, the frustrations and failures of the missionary task are as unitive (given certain costly conditions of ascetical freedom) as is prayer (given certain costly conditions of ascetical freedom).

## What Can We Learn?

What help can the devotion give us as we seek to be pastors in Ireland during changing and confusing times. Pius XII's encyclical, *Haurietis aquas* was a statement that the devotion in its Paray form was not as widely helpful to the faithful as it had been. Is the devotion dying or dead? It could be that it has accomplished its task in the Church. If God wants some other way for the faithful to centre their piety in the love of God made visible in Christ Jesus (which is the essence of the devotion), then it is not for us artificially to keep it alive. It is plain that a great number of the faithful need devotions to enliven and enrich their faith. It may be that there are other forms in which they can be helped to enter into the love of God made visible in Christ Jesus our Lord.

The wide circulation of *The Sacred Heart Messenger* is an indication that the devotion is still helpful to many in Ireland. May it long continue to nourish them with the bread of the human love of God. But the more pressing pastoral task is with the many, especially in our cities, whose faith has been confused or eroded or simply taken from them. Rahner has given it as his opinion that the devotion is only for those whose faith is already firm.[10] The confused and the alienated are more likely to be brought to know the love of God by encountering Jesus in the gospel: the one who reveals the father of the

---

[9] MHSJ MN 5, 52. For further references, see Herbert Alphonso, '"La Storta": Its Foundational Significance for Jesuit Spirituality', *CIS*, 19/1 (Spring 1988), 72-86.

[10] 'In our times many people are searching for God and are not sure of his existence or presence in their lives. Devotion to the Sacred Heart is not relevant to those who have not answered basic questions of faith.' From a private interview, 25 February 1982; see Callahan, *Karl Rahner's Spirituality of the Pierced Heart*, 106.

prodigal and who calls us to repent and believe because we are already invited to allow ourselves to be forgiven.

There is a middle group, those who continue faithfully to go to Mass, but whose lives of piety are no longer nourished by devotions. They are confused, lost, at sea. They protest that the preaching Church no longer speaks to them with a bold and clear voice. They often show a hunger to be taught how to pray better. It is from among them that one hears the complaint that they no longer hear clearly about sin, or about what actions are sins. Someone experienced in pastoral work has said of them, 'they are desperately trying to feel as guilty as they think the Church is telling them they ought to. But they have little sense of their sinfulness.'

They need to know the goodness and the love of God. But they are not hearing the full gospel if a bland preaching merely conveys an image of a harmless God, an image as faulty as the remote and demanding God of a former time. It would seem that the two images may exist uneasily together. The devotion to the Sacred Heart is wholesome and evangelical in that it is both exigent and consoling. It is not bland.

Perhaps the most difficult task for the Church is to get sin right. Fear is so clearly an obstacle to God's work in souls that reinforcing guilt or increasing irrational guilt is not the way to bring people to know God's love. God is not mocked and all evil is abhorrent to him. But a true sense of sin presupposes a living faith. A living faith in the love of God made visible is what devotion to the Sacred Heart is about. It may be that in God's providence for his people in Ireland it may remain a way in which many of the faithful may learn again how demanding love is. And that after such a gift, God will not refuse anything that He can give.

# 12

# RENEWING JESUIT LIFE IN THE SPIRIT

It is not through human means that the Society can be pre-
served and developed, but through the omnipotent hand of
Christ …. Therefore in Him alone must be placed the hope ….
(X. 1 [812])

SPEAKING AS I AM TO PROVINCIALS, maybe I am like a fool at a
medieval court. The licensed fool was allowed to say things that
wiser and more balanced personages could not say for fear of giving
offence or because they had a reputation to lose. The fool was
allowed to ask awkward questions and was expected to say rude
things. And sometimes a nugget of insight might come through, or a
different and fresh way of seeing what was familiar.

In any exchange of this kind we should bring with us the hope
that comes from looking at what God has done for us Jesuits in recent
years. It is no good preparation for discernment to spend time
wringing our hands and being intimidated by difficulties.

Secondly, we should keep a sense of perspective. It was never all
perfect. Ignatius thought that only some of the early Jesuits had really
appreciated the Society's spirit. A historian told me once that when
thirty men entered the early Society, it was expected that ten would
die, that ten would fall sick and be ineffective workers and that ten
would be effective in the mission.

But let me take our lead from that observation, and divide the
membership of the Society into thirds. (There's the story of the Jesuit
sociologist who said once in a fit of absence of mind that the Society,
like every group, consisted of men, women and children.)

In my own province, there have been many resources given for
spiritual growth and conversion. But it seems to me that the different
opportunities were repeatedly availed of by the same men, by
roughly one third of the province.

What of the other two thirds? It is impossible to label them without being offensive. But it has to be said that one part (perhaps 10%) includes the following: those who are alienated from the Society; those who feel they don't belong; those whose life of faith has been eroded, perhaps grown dead; those who are apparently obdurate, who seem unreachable; those who are simply hostile to Vatican II, to our General Congregations, to all that Fr Arrupe stood for; those who live in a kind of constant desolation; those who are imprisoned in *idées fixes*; those whose sense of themselves is so damaged that they can no longer hope for personal change or growth or more life; those who still belong juridically to the body of the Society, but who have long since ceased to be living members of it, *emigrés* who remain within.

There is then a middle third, who work hard, perhaps far too hard. They are dutiful at their prayers and are often very holy. But they are not joiners. Many of them obscurely feel that they don't belong, that they don't count. They feel left out. They think little of themselves. They cannot imagine themselves being part of an active team that would be eager to discern the mission together. They include those who are fearful of directed retreats; their annual retreat is always private. The *magis* does not fire them; it is a concept that does not feature in their thinking. They are puzzled by anything they happen to hear about the re-discovered meaning of the Exercises. The 'new' language, as it seems to them, is a foreign language, and those who speak it are strangers. It can trigger surprising bursts of anger and resentment in good men. They find repeated exhortations to discernment bewildering and oppressive. They often write it off as jargon. They are obedient men. They would go to Timbuktu if they were told to. But they cannot be told to change their minds. Many have never been inculturated into the Ignatian way of seeing things.

Among them are thousands of 'ordinary' men who faithfully carry the donkey-work of the Society. For all we know it could be they who are keeping the body of the Society in spiritual well-being. How can more of these be enticed to risk using the means that might enable them to be changed and fired by the Spirit?

**Learning to Discern Together**

It seems to me that many in the middle third could be enticed out of their fears. In a sense they may be sitting on the fence, waiting to see which way the wind is blowing and waiting to see whom they can safely trust.

GC 32 speaks of how a profound conversion to God and to a life in the Spirit comes to Jesuits from an urgent sense of the needs of God's people. It hoped that a creative reflection on ministry would enable Jesuits to discover God, to experience their impotence, to come up against their unfreedoms, to be challenged to desire to be given 'a thoroughly right and pure intention'. Somehow they would begin to learn that work, however efficient, professional and exhausting, is unfruitful without the unction and the power of the Spirit. The method was to be 'a constant interplay between experience, reflection, decision and action'. The result was to be effective apostolic decisions. The *aim* was 'to ensure a change in our habitual patterns of thought' (GC 32, d. 4, n. 73). Our 'way of proceeding' itself contains the means of continuing conversion and renewal.

Have we been assuming in practice that first attitudes must change and that then behaviour will follow? Suppose we were to change that around? Could it be that when forms of behaviour change, then attitudes will change. As a wise Irish Jesuit has said: 'More would be done if we were firmer in requiring minimum changes of behaviour and letting attitudes catch up with the reality of our life'.

**Overwork and Zeal**

As for the 'converted' third, we are entitled to draw some consolation from the spiritual growth of the body in recent years, but that should not stop us from giving a hard critical look at the quality of the process. How has our life in the Spirit nourished apostolic renewal? It seems to me that the interplay has been rather poor. We should not be complacent about the fact that more Jesuits are praying or that more Jesuits are praying more. What of the quality of their prayer? And what of the connection of their prayer with their zeal? The Ignatian criterion is never a question of quantity of prayer. It is a question of how prayer is affecting the mission of building the Kingdom.

I see plenty of evidence of over-work. I do not see the same evidence of zeal. Our zeal is often listless, measured, balanced, prudent, staid, sedate and unimpassioned. We lack the passion of the first few generations of the companions. When I was a scholastic, the old men, the parish missioners and preachers and *operarii* had what we might now see as an impoverished or distorted grasp of the Exercises. But there was an edge or fire to their zeal that I don't see now. It is as though a particular perception of the theology of Vatican II had stolen the fire from our bellies.

The renewed individual practice of the Exercises has not enabled us to face up to and to pray through and work through a certain apostolic loss of nerve in the presence of a widespread decline in people's faith. We lack boldness and clarity. But we are good at maintenance. We are unsure in reaching *ad extra* to the lost and bewildered and unbelieving. It is easier to focus on justice. Our zeal is flabby and our words sound faltering and give an uncertain note. We do not share this sense together. We keep it to ourselves and fail to use the means to be freed from that continuing mild desolation.

Perhaps the problem is that we are so polite to each other. We do not confront, and we are afraid to challenge. Peace is more comfortable. There is some missing factor in our practice of the individually directed retreat. The Exercises made by Jesuits do not produce the fruit they should. I recall a comment made by a young layman: 'I've read about the Exercises. I look around at you and I wonder. I see the intensity. But where is the joy?'

**When the Exercises Work.**

St Ignatius had a remarkable insight when he joined the Exercises with experiences or experiments. The Exercises 'work', they bear something of their full fruit, when some experience of life has led to a kind of interior dislocation. When a man has had his leg broken and sees the end of his career as a courtier, then God has made him open to God, he begins to see his need of being changed by God and he begins to see the need to make some hard decisions about his life and about God. (The experience of dislocation need not be dramatic. Nor is it to be confused with a prolonged desolation.) The ideal occasion for a profound conversion would be something like this: an experience that somehow shakes the foundations, followed by the making of the Exercises, followed by an unfamiliar experience, for example, of exposure to people in an entirely fresh environment. And throughout the process, the person should be helped to reflect through and pray through what God is saying about His world

### Integration of Prayer and Experience.

We worry about our failure to integrate justice into our spirituality and pastoral work. It is right that we should. But that is only part of a larger question, our failure truly to grasp and live all that is entailed in the seeking and finding God in all things. Many of us as yet have no adequate grasp of the Ignatian integration of faith and living, of prayer and work. We may speak the language. But the reality is another thing.

*How* can we help older and many younger men to a better understanding of what is involved in the dynamic of seeking and finding God in all things? Or, to use a terminology that St Ignatius deliberately, as I believe, avoided, in the sense of how action is intrinsic to contemplation and contemplation to action? The dynamic intrinsic to the Ignatian 'seeking and finding God in all things' itself contains the means to continuing conversion and deepening in the Spirit.

Yes, but *how*? Jesuits are unlikely to find this understanding from reading articles in *The Way* or by new books on the *Constitutions* or by a piling on of more lectures and exhortations. They are weary of those. They have enough of theory. What we need are personal testimonies to how Jesuits find the experience in their lives and mission.

The concrete way into a rediscovery of the renewing effect of seeking and finding God is an enlivening practice of the examination of consciousness. I believe some—or one?—Latin American provinces have succeeded in making the Examen an instrument of province-wide conversion and apostolic spiritual fruit.

## Catalysts and Prophets

It is in the first of my thirds, the converted third, that Provincials will find their catalysts and prophets. Both are useful. We are all converted by persons more than by paper. Catalysts are those who have, besides the unction of the Spirit, some God-given gift of stirring up others, of encouraging them, of attracting them, of drawing them into something that is seen to be life-giving. The sluggish, the tardy and the fearful can be drawn by what is patently attractive. Catalysts are probably seen to be men of joy. A Provincial can identify such men and use them.

Prophets are another matter. They embody and exemplify something that others can hope to emulate. They infuriate some. They may be a thorn in a Provincial's side. They sometimes serve as models to be admired and imitated. In my own role as director of tertians, it is impossible to say what I owed to the 'model' of a tertian master presented by Fr Paul Kennedy much more than to any written instruction. We all need models, human, fallible, tangible, visible, that we can imitate. Prophets, and perhaps catalysts too, are probably more effective if they are not seen to be favoured by a Provincial or seen to be part of the establishment.

Nevertheless, true though it is that Jesuits are changed by people more than by print, it does not follow that print is pointless. It is good serenely to face the fact that most busy Jesuits do not read long letters. But many ordinary busy Jesuits do read brief ones. Other things being equal, the shorter the communication the better. Besides, a constant beating of the same drum can induce ennui, and bring diminishing returns.

## Bringing the Horse to the Water

I believe that Provincials must continue to provide a variety of opportunities for spiritual renewal and growth. But a Provincial must often reflect that you can bring a horse to the water but you can't make him drink. The how question comes up at once: How to you encourage the horse to want to drink?

Most Jesuits feel unimportant and small. A Provincial can twist an individual's arm to get him to partake of some of the fare on offer.

He can urge and encourage him. But it is probably more helpful if he can convey that he believes in him, that he is important, that he is important to the province's mission, that he has hopes of him, that he would find happiness and freedom in risking taking part. There is power in the personal invitation that conveys, 'We want you ... We need your contribution'. A Provincial's effort in that direction is likely to fail if it is not seen to be genuine. But many a Jesuit responds to a Provincial's concern for him. And we all feel the better for being consulted. It is only in such a relationship that fence-sitting Jesuits will be able to be cajoled or enticed out of their self-depreciation and fears.

## Local Superiors

For most older Jesuits a man's Provincial has a spiritual and moral authority that a Provincial might be tempted to underestimate. But Provincials cannot be all-the-year-round holders of individual Jesuits' hands. They cannot be spiritual directors to each of their subjects. In this process of a *collective* conversion of the body of the Society, it may well be that local superiors, superiors of particular houses, are more important than the General or the Provincials.

People are changed by people. Local superiors are one key, perhaps the crucial one, in the process of helping a greater part of the body of the Society to be converted and of bringing communities to collective spiritual renewal. They work at the coal-face of the Society, in the day to day encounter with concrete situations, and with Jesuits at a variety of stages of being conjoined with God. Their mission is often intractable and crucifying. Many of them probably feel that it is for most of the time impossible.

I believe that a local superior needs to identify those of his men who are in desolation and to help them to be moved into consolation. To do that he needs to be helped to learn how to use flexibly a variety of Ignatian means ('now using one means, now another'). He needs to be able, gently, like a good director of the Exercises, to disclose a man's deeper desires, to reveal his deeper good to him, good that lies hidden maybe under loads of debris, years of conviction of moral failure and guilt and hopelessness in himself or in God. He needs to be a diagnostician of the different causes of desolation, of the devices of the bad spirit. Or, in other words, to be an expert in the Two Standards. That expertise is not learned from theory. It can only be learned by plunging in, and by being helped to learn the art in the course of experience.

Recently I got two hints of what younger Jesuits think and expect. One said, 'My rector is great. But if only he believed in his grace of state, he'd be bolder in giving a lead and deciding that certain things shall be done'. The other said, 'I'm tired of superiors who only want you to feel good'.

The important word in that statement is 'only'. To say that people are changed by people is the same as saying that people are changed in relationships. Jesuits who are fearful of being changed can be helped to emerge from their privacy and fears in a relationship with a superior that is open, genuine and spiritual. To build a relationship that opens the possibility of spiritual change may take a long time and much wasting of time on trivialities. It is good to make a Jesuit feel good—provided it does not stop there. Jesuits who are apostolically listless or who have lost their apostolic nerve or who are underemployed, who have given up on prayer or whose prayer has stopped growing, all these in some degree probably think too little of themselves (even if they are also trapped in self-preoccupation). They have given up hope that they might change or grow or become happy. No one can be confronted with the negative things in him that need changing until some degree of proper self-esteem has been confirmed or restored and the hidden goodness in him affirmed. It is only later that a superior can introduce the surgeon's knife.

We need people who do not rely on words, but who are rather steeped in the sources, at home in the use of the Ignatian language and way of seeing things, and who therefore see the need to share and exemplify rather than just to exhort.

### Sabbaticals

If we sometimes wonder at the slow pace of change or of our growth in the Spirit, we might evaluate the cost effectiveness of sabbaticals. Or, in Ignatius' language, 'What is the spiritual fruit?'

People are changed not by ideas but by being plunged into a new experience. But not by just any kind of experience. It could be argued that Jesuits will be converted by exposure to the people of God, and by the faith of simple people. As an Indian Jesuit once said: 'After four years of theology we send them out into the villages so that the people may give them back their faith'.

How many Jesuits are insulated from the people? The insulation, of course, may be physical or psychological. One can work in close contact with many people and be protected against real contact with their joys and pains. 'You Jesuits will work for us, slave for us. But you won't relate with us. You are interested in our problems. But you are not interested in us'.

Has anyone found a good way to monitor sabbaticals, to make sure that they are prepared for, tailored to a man's needs and subsequently evaluated? Would it be helpful to see a sabbatical in terms of the Ignatian experiments? A new experience of itself effects little change. The experiments that achieve something of what St Ignatius wanted are those that are linked in some organic way with the previous experience of the Exercises. They are a kind of extension of the Exercises, further 'spiritual exercises'. They have to be adapted to an individual's capacity and need. They deepen, confirm, and sometimes question the consolations and the graces of the long retreat. The experience is likely to be unfruitful if it is not prayed through and reflected on with a director. That dialogue is needed to make explicit and to confirm what God is saying through the encounter with the poor or the handicapped or the spiritually impoverished.

Can it be put strongly to Jesuits embarking on sabbaticals that they should make a good retreat, preferably a renewed experience of the full Exercises? One of my contemporaries said that his chief complaint against the Society was that it has never given him the Exercises.

Fr Tony de Mello's retreats attracted Jesuits from beyond the frontiers of the converted third. I think I remember him saying that he had given up giving directed retreats to Jesuits because he had found too many Jesuits who did not have the dispositions required. Nevertheless, the exercises which he devised freed many Jesuits from a weight of unnecessary guilt and imprisoning self-reproach. He had the gift of restoring their confidence that they could pray and provided them with a great variety of ways of prayer that they could manage and that many of them continue to find life-giving. His exercises were a kind of pre-Exercises. Perhaps his methods still need to be explored.

**Indicators from the *Constitutions***

But in the end, all depends on prayer. In Christ alone must be placed the hope 'that He will preserve and carry forward what He deigned to begin ... the first and best proportioned means will be prayers and Masses ...' (X. 1 [812]).

I remember the three thousand Masses that St Ignatius promised when the confirmation of the Society was in jeopardy. The General is not the only Jesuit who needs to pray, 'that from God, the fountain of all good' we,

> ... may the better obtain for the whole body of the Society a large share of His gifts and graces and also great power and efficacy for all the means which will be used for the help of souls' (IX. 2. 1 [723]).

Ultimately, the gift comes from the Spirit. All I have been doing is 'opening the way by some suggestions' which may 'dispose one for the effect, which must be produced by divine grace' (IV. 8. 8 [414]).

# 13

# THE SPIRITUAL
# EXERCISES IN
# ECUMENICAL CONTEXT

WE MIGHT BEST HONOUR Sr Elizabeth Smyth, and her many gifts shared with you, by pausing contemplatively to make a tentative discernment of what your experience together has taught you. Or, more properly, we should ask what God has taught us all through you. Over the last thirty years, two of the most significant movements that we have experienced have been the ecumenical movement and the ministry of the Exercises. In you they both meet. What is God trying to get us to see in that conjunction brought about by His Providence, through the boldness and energy of Sr Elizabeth?

I shall speak today mainly of the ministry of the Exercises, since that is where I can move most confidently. But I hope that I may be allowed to use St Ignatius' idiom and to suggest that the movement towards union of our different Churches has entered a phase that a giver of the Exercises would diagnose as 'desolation'. An experienced director of the Exercises knows that one should not palliate the desolation, deny it, cover it, evade it, or offer false consolation in its stead. The way to the genuine consolation of the Spirit is to pray through and work through the desolation.

The signs of desolation, whether in an individual or, by analogy, in a group or in a web of relationships, might be named as:

- a marking of time;

- a nervousness or dread before decision;

- a lethargy that descends when hope wanes;

- an escape into words and self-deceiving argument;

- a turning in on the self rather than a light-hearted turning to the power of the Spirit;

- a disappointment with oneself that progress has been slow;

- a fear of risk;

- a fear of the costs of decision;

- a weakening, simply, of faith.

In the same period of thirty years there has been an enormous growth in our experience of the Exercises and of St Ignatius himself, so much so that some have claimed it to be not a development so much as a radical turning on its head of our previous understanding. That is an exaggeration. Radical revolutions are rare. Historical changes are never in entire discontinuity with what went before. The Reformation itself was not separate from the earlier long clamour for reform and popular demands for a more interior and living faith. But the claim with regard to Ignatius and the Exercises is only just an exaggeration.

**Learning from History**

In two other areas there has been a shift in our knowledge and understanding. One has been in our comprehension of the history of spirituality; the other in the historiography of that period in the history of our shared Christianity that we would be wiser not to label but simply to date from 1500 to 1600. In our understanding of the history of spirituality, especially of the growth of contemplation (a word to be preferred to 'mysticism'), much learned ink has flowed under the bridge since Gordon Wakefield's important study 'Mysticism and its Puritan Types' in 1966.[1] In the historiography of the religious changes in the 1500s, historians like John W. O'Malley have drawn attention to the distortions of understanding caused by the label 'Counter Reformation'. Neither are they happy with Hubert Jedin's proposal that there were two simultaneous but distinct movements: 'Catholic Reform and Counter Reformation'. A view that commands growing agreement holds that the religious changes from

---

[1] Gordon S. Wakefield, 'Mysticism and its Puritan Types', *London Quarterly and Holborn Review*, 191 (1966), 34-45.

1517 into the seventeenth century are more accurately seen as two streams (or several streams) of the same widespread desire for a deeper and purer life of faith. This was accompanied by a desire for reform that was rooted in the gospel, in a contemplative presence to the Word, in a more authentic interior living of the life of Jesus and in a truer desire to seek and to find God.[2]

Throughout the centuries before the Reformation, many different schools of piety responded to the voiced needs of ordinary people. In those less rigid days the frontiers were open. One writer or school borrowed freely from another. There was no scrupulous guilt about plagiarism or any pressing need to acknowledge dependence. Teachers of prayer were not all that touchy about copyright. There was a relaxed family borrowing of one another's clothes. For example, it is obvious that Ignatius' ways of apprenticing beginners to prayer are simply a borrowing and an adaptation of the teaching on meditation widespread among contemporary Christian people. He picked up what was commonplace from Ludolf the Carthusian, from Ludolf's own Franciscan sources, from the *devotio moderna* and so on. I believe that his simple way of entering contemplatively into the experience of Jesus in the gospel mysteries is best seen as a development (not necessarily an improvement) of the monastic *lectio divina*.

## A Digression

At this point I wish to indulge in a short digression. In the vast literature on the Ignatian Exercises one can sense a distinct gulf between three kinds of exposition. There is the material that comes from a study of the text, or in other words, from book knowledge. Then there is that which rings truer, since it comes from the experience of making the Exercises. But what rings truer still is the material that comes from a long experience of accompanying others in the Exercises. It is this last that marries a reverence for the text with a suppleness in seeing its infinite variations and what St Ignatius

---

[2] See John W. O'Malley, 'Was Ignatius Loyola a Church Reformer? How to Look at Early Modern Catholicism', *The Catholic Historical Review*, 57 (1991), 177-193.

called 'the manifold gifts of the Spirit'. The action of the Holy Spirit is various and lithesome. Our grasp of the dynamic of the Exercises has grown from the interplay that arises from bringing our experience of the Exercises to cast light on the text, and our bringing of the text to cast light on our contemplative experience of all things and of the gospel.

So it is only proper here to confess my awareness that (to garble a well-said truth), 'to speak Lutheran one has to have lived Lutheran'. It must be the same with the Elizabethan divines and their Puritan critics in whose works I have been immersing myself as preparation for this lecture. I can only enter into a restricted understanding of someone like the great idiosyncratic Puritan Richard Baxter (1615-1691), however much I have come to admire him from a lifetime's experience of trying to be a Jesuit Puritan.

The advances in learning of these last few decades have cured us of the compulsion to impute originality or uniqueness to any one spiritual teacher or writer or school of 'godly living'. It is with a certain Christian glee that I have been discovering once again the continuity in the practice of piety in England in the last half of the 1500s and into the 1600s, a continuity specifically with the late medieval writers on contemplation. And I have experienced a sober but godly pleasure in the discovery of the extent to which Puritan and non-Puritan members of the English Church eagerly sought spiritual nourishment in translations of early Jesuit books on prayer inspired by the Exercises.

## A Common Tradition

We know how many of the great religious thinkers in the Elizabethan Church and later went back to the Fathers for spiritual food and for a theology that was expressly aimed at piety or godly living. We might say that their learning aimed at the love of God, at a savouring or tasting of the Mystery, at contemplation.[3] As we know, St Bernard was greatly favoured. A great book on prayer like Bishop Joseph

---

[3] See Jean Leclercq, *The Love of Learning and the Desire for God: A Study of Monastic Culture*, translated by Catherine Misrahi (New York: Fordham UP, 1982 [1957]).

Hall's *The Art of Divine Meditation* (1606) was happy to acknowledge its sources in the *Rosetum* (1494) of Jan Mombaer. This in turn had drawn on the work of Wessel Gansfort (*c.* 1419-1489). Hall names Origen, Augustine, Bernard, Hugh of St Victor, Bonaventure and Gerson.[4] Both Hall and Baxter cite Gerson's *On the Mountain of Contemplation*; more universally, Gerson 'exerted a germinal influence upon all the most important meditative and mystical treatises of the sixteenth and seventeenth centuries'.[5]

Richard Rogers (1551-1618), Puritan curate of Wethersfield in Essex, published in 1603 his *Seven Treatises, Containing Such Direction As Is Gathered out of the Holy Scriptures, Leading and Guiding to True Happiness, … and May Be Called the Practice of Christianity*. Its prefatory remarks by Stephen Egerton make clear that the work was intended to be a response, or 'counter-poison' to such popish 'enchantments' as 'the Resolutions of the Jesuitical Father Parsons or meditations of Friar Granatensis [Luis de Granada]' which had ensnared the minds of simple Christians. Robert Persons the Jesuit had, characteristically, been unable to contain an ill-tempered taunt: 'Where or when have any of (your) religion set forth (of themselves) any treatise dealing with devotion, piety, and contemplation?' Persons was riled by the pirating of his *A Christian Directory* by the Puritan Edmund Bunny, although he must have been pleased by its extraordinary popularity among Protestants. Richard Rogers 'referred specifically to two works, Persons' *Christian Directory* and Gaspar Loarte's *Exercise of a Christian Life*, but directed most of his wrath against Persons'.[6] Persons had a way of eliciting ill-temper.

---

[4] Louis L. Martz, *The Poetry of Meditation* (New Haven: Yale UP, 1954), 113.

[5] Bishop Hall's theology was Calvinist. It is no wonder that 'some Calvinist theologians from the low countries have castigated the Puritans as "the English mystics" and deprecated their spirituality as "the cultivation of a soft-life of feeling" in contrast to Calvinist rigour': Gordon S. Wakefield, 'English Spirituality', in *A Dictionary of Christian Spirituality*, edited by himself (London: SCM Press, 1983), 131-133, here 132. See, too, Martz's comment in *The Poetry of Meditation*, 168: 'Baxter deliberately sets out to recover for the Puritans some of these devotional practices which had fallen away as a result of Calvinist thinking. This is perfectly clear from his constant marginal references to St Bernard, Gerson, Nicholas of Cusa, the Jesuit Nieremberg, and, with special frequency, to Bishop Hall—who was himself engaged in this kind of devotional recovery.'

[6] Elizabeth K. Hudson, 'The Catholic Challenge to Puritan Piety', *The Catholic Historical Review*, 57 (1991), 1-20.

## Controversy or Godly Living?

The irony is that Persons and many of the recusant exiles in Leuven were at one with many Puritans in deploring the busy industry in controversial writing. It at last came home to Puritans that too much of their intellectual talent, energy and time had been given to controversy, although such controversy had been aimed at purifying the Elizabethan Church of remnants of popish superstition and idolatry. A purer Church would surely lead to worship in spirit and in truth. A Church nearer to the purity of the gospel would lead to universal godly living.

Meanwhile the Catholic exiles were conscious that their flock in England, deprived of the personal instruction and direction of priests, was eager to supply this lack with a flood of books to help them to lead godly lives. The books that flowed from Persons' illegal press in east London, and from the printers at Antwerp, Leuven, Rouen, Paris, Douai and Reims, were indeed concerned with apologetic and polemic. But the exiled recusants were well aware that the books of greater value were those that treated of the ways and means of seeking and finding God. These were smuggled into England with great expense and danger, and were avidly borrowed and read with godly fruit by godly Protestants. For example, Richard Baxter describes in his autobiography how, as a stripling, he was converted root and branch to a godly life by reading a tattered book given him by an artisan in his father's village. The book was Robert Persons' *Christian Directory*, and Baxter acknowledges both its author and its Jesuitical provenance.

Robert Persons himself, never shy of a fight, was nevertheless convinced that works of controversy, however necessary, actually hindered devotion. Devotion required 'a quiet and peaceable state of soul'.[7] Thomas Harding, Wykehamist and once a fellow of New College, writing from exile in Leuven, was of one mind with Persons in deploring the effect of controversial writings which, though

---

[7] Robert Persons, quoted in Hudson, 'The Catholic Challenge', 4. The quotation is from Persons' original 1582 edition called *First Book of the Christian Exercises, Appertaining to Resolution.*

necessary, were 'not profitable to devotion'.[8] Richard Hopkins, in his *Of Prayer and Meditation*, acknowledged Harding's persuasion:

> It is now about fourteen years ago, since the time that Master Doctor Harding (a man for his great virtue, learning, wisdom, zeal, and sincerity in writing against heresies, of very godly and famous memory) persuaded me earnestly to translate some of those Spanish books into our English tongue, affirming, that more spiritual profit would undoubtedly ensue thereby to the gaining of Christian souls in our country from Schism, and Heresy, and from all sin, and iniquity, than by books that treat of controversies in Religion: which (as experience hath now plainly tried) do nothing so well dispose the common people's minds to the fear, love, and service of almighty God, as Books treating of devotion, and how to lead a virtuous life do. The due consideration whereof hath so provoked or rather pricked me in conscience .... [9]

The Yorkshire Puritan minister Edmund Bunny, who borrowed and expurgated Persons' revised and expanded 1585 edition of *A Christian Directory Guiding Men to Their Salvation*, was motivated by two concerns. Firstly, he saw that Persons' book helped readers to a godly life. Secondly,

> ... the most interesting justification offered by Bunny was the argument that a favourable response to such Catholic works as could be accepted by Protestants might moderate the bitterness between the two groups, demonstrate their common beliefs, and win some to the national Church.[10]

Richard Baxter, so sickened by religious faction and wanting to find ways of union and peace, brought Bacon to his case:

> ... and as Sir Francis Bacon saith (in his *Essay of Peace*), that it's one great benefit of church-peace and concord that writing

---

[8] A.C. Southern, *Elizabethan Recusant Prose 1559-1582* (London: Sands, 1950), 181.

[9] Southern, *Elizabethan Recusant Prose*, 181

[10] Hudson, 'The Catholic Challenge', 5. Bunny appended a 'Treatise Tending to Pacification' to his edition of Persons.

controversies is turned into books of practical devotion for increase of piety and virtue.[11]

Bunny was well aware of the barrenness of controversial writings, and could write in his preface: 'let us put aside all hatred, malice and wrathful contention ... praying for one another'.[12]

Catholic recusants, non-Puritan writers and Puritans all desired the same end: to be open to the intimate action of God in the relationship we call faith. The purpose of all ways and means, including forms of church government and of doctrine, was that the believing community might allow the Word, already present within, to convert people to a personal hearing of the word of the gospel. Richard Baxter, more than anyone, saw the barrenness of contention, and how contentiousness hindered godly life. He came to prefer 'books of practical devotion for increase of piety and virtue'.[13] He was not afraid of the word 'contemplation':

> Sirs, if you never tried this Art, nor lived this life of heavenly contemplation, I never wonder that you walk uncomfortably, that you are all complaining, and live in sorrows, and know not what the Joy of the Saints means.[14]

Even though Baxter's theology led him to reject monasticism, he believed that Puritans went too far, and could exclaim: 'We are fled so far from the solitude of superstition that we have cast off the solitude of contemplative devotion'.[15]

I find a close affinity between Richard Baxter and St Ignatius. Baxter expresses, better than St Ignatius could, the principle governing the dynamic of the Exercises: '... the love of the end is the poise and spring which setteth every wheel a-going, and must put us on to all the means ....'[16] Like St Ignatius, he saw the potency of the senses and the imagination. Keeble writes that for Baxter,

---

[11] *The Autobiography of Richard Baxter*, edited by N. H. Keeble (London: Dent, 1974), 106-107.

[12] Edmund Bunny, 'Preface to the Reader', in *A Book of Christian Exercise* (1584), sig. *6ᵛ.

[13] Baxter, *Autobiography*, 107.

[14] Baxter, *The Saints Everlasting Rest* (1650), cited in Martz, *The Poetry of Meditation*, 153.

[15] Cited in N. H. Keeble, 'Baxter, Richard', in *A Dictionary of Christian Spirituality*, edited by Gordon S. Wakefield, 38-39, here 38.

[16] Baxter, *Autobiography*, 113.

The senses too are a divine gift, which may be used in God's service. Baxter shows himself sensitive to natural beauty, music, poetry, and encouraged his readers to use their imaginations in meditation quite as strongly as the Roman Catholic treatises of the Counter Reformation.[17]

## The Contemplative Life

Protestant distancing from 'mysticism' is not, I believe, a distancing from the contemplative tradition of entering into an intimate relationship in faith with Jesus in the gospel.[18] It seems to me more of a reaction to the intermittent Catholic fallacy of identifying the contemplative life with the cloistered life, and of assuming that all 'mysticism' is identical with the neo-Platonising tendencies of the northern schools of contemplative prayer. For example, Luther's growing coldness in later life towards Tauler parallels Ignatius' own later coolness towards the northern schools of mysticism as a whole. For Luther the mystical ascent is a false way to God, in the end because Christ, divine and human, is the only way to the Father. And in St Ignatius' mystical prayer, the Incarnation, the humanity of Jesus is central.

Richard Baxter, we have seen, came to desire a return to the older Catholic tradition of contemplation and grew tired and disenchanted with controversy. In his great review of his life, sins and views he saw how in his youth, 'I did not sufficiently discern then how much in most of our controversies is verbal and upon mutual mistakes'.[19] Contention for him was the bellows that fans the fire of hatred. Therefore he came to want to see religious union come about

[17] N. H. Keeble, 'Introduction', in Baxter, *Autobiography*, xix.

[18] 'Puritan spirituality was supremely of the word .... In terms of spirituality, this means that meditation was central to Puritan prayer .... Contemplation, seen as a stage beyond meditation, was suspect. Mystical states were not encouraged, as tending to a kind of Purgatory in devotion. Irrationalism was dreaded; the mind was a gateway to God. Yet there were transports and ecstasies, and, if a word so ethereal and imprecise is allowed, it is appropriate to speak of a Puritan mysticism': Gordon S. Wakefield, 'The Puritans', in *The Study of Spirituality*, edited by Cheslyn Jones, Geoffrey Wainwright and Edward Yarnold (London: SPCK, 1986), 443.

[19] Baxter, *Autobiography*, 105.

by 'mere Christianity'.[20] When he was accused of promoting Baxterianism, he protested, 'It is simple catholic Christianity which I plead for'.[21] 'The Creed, the Lord's Prayer and the Commandments are … acceptable and plentiful matter for all my meditations.'[22] Baxter's hopes for 'mere Christianity' and the underlying longing for a ground on which to find reconciliation, longings that run through the devotional writings of so many English divines, Puritan and non-Puritan, were subsumed in a search for common doctrine. On one level, as we might say today, theological agreement was primary in their eyes. But underlying and permeating much of their writing was a far more profound level of affinity that reaches deeper than doctrine or theology.

## The Contemporary Scene

I believe that such is also the situation today. It is here that reflection on your experience of sharing the process of the Exercises within many traditions of Christian faith may refute or confirm my conviction. The work of theology has been well done. My conviction is that the desire for a radical conversion to a life surrendered to God, *beyond theology*, is at that deeper level where unity in Christ will eventually begin to be realised. The Exercises are one way of opening the person to the liberating action of the Spirit; in the prayer of the Two Standards and the Three Classes we seek to be given the light and the courage to move beyond the fears that blind and paralyze us. Patriarch Athenagoras, coming from a different Christian tradition, has nevertheless identified the symptoms of 'desolation' that one faces in the meditation of the Two Standards:

> We are afraid. We want to keep things that are out-of-date because we are used to them … we hide a spirit of pride and power beneath conventional expressions of humility …. What

---

[20] The term was gratefully taken over and popularised by C. S. Lewis.

[21] 'These are my fixed resolutions and desires; even to be Catholic in my Estimation and respect to all, Loving all Christians of what sort soever, that may be truly called Christians … and … with this Catholic Charity to have the Conversation of such as the world hath long called Puritans; and in this state I desire to die ….': *The Grotian Religion Discovered* [1658], cited by N. H. Keeble, 'Introduction', in Baxter, *Autobiography*, xiii.

[22] Baxter, *Autobiography*, 107.

Churchmen most lack is the spirit of Christ, humility, the
dispossession of self ....[23]

An experienced giver of the Exercises recognises at once in these
words the manifest signs of desolation, and the operation of what
Ignatius calls 'the bad spirit' or 'the Enemy'. It is a function of the
Exercises to uncover the sources of desolation and to give heart and
courage to be open to the gift of God. This alone frees the person (or
the community) to face risk and the possibility of failure, the cost of
embracing the cross. Patriarch Athenagoras is calling us to conversion and to contemplation. His words have nothing to do with the
conversion of the bad. He is addressing the question of the
conversion of the good. Ignatius would say that surrender of self and
identification with the experience of Jesus are alone what free the
person from fear and shame. This too is a shield against the blindness
attendant upon ecclesiastical pride and power.

Coming as I do from more than half a century of immersion in
the world of the Exercises, I have found delight in so much of the
spirituality of the Puritans, just as for so long I found myself at home
in the world of George Herbert, Henry Vaughan, Thomas Traherne
and T. S. Eliot. I find no compulsion to ascribe dependence or
influence from one school of writers to another. It is enough to
recognise the affinity that needs no literary parentage but only the
operation of the Holy Spirit leading the whole-hearted Christian to
find God, and particularly to find the Father in Christ, in the
humanity of Jesus, and in all things. Ulrich Zwingli said: 'True piety
is the same everywhere and in all men, having its source in one and
the self-same Spirit'.[24]

St Ignatius' principle and practice were to prefer the simple and
positive assertion of Christian truth to polemics or refutation. In his
eyes, and in the feeling of the first Jesuits, it was a conversion of
people to God that would lead to Christian unity as they understood
it. Ignatius would heartily agree with the older Baxter that there is

---

[23] Cited by Alan D. Falconer in 'Turning Again to the Common Centre', *Doctrine and Life*, 45
(1995), 621.
[24] Ulrich Zwingli, 'An Exposition of the Faith', in *Zwingli and Bullinger*, edited by G. W. Bromiley
(London: SCM, 1953), 247.

small fruit in contention. It only makes people cling more obstinately and more rigidly to their original positions. Controversy is the bellows that fans the fire of hatred, division and opposition.

## 'Mere Christianity'

What I now propose is that we allow ourselves to press Baxter's 'mere Christianity' to mean something that he did not quite say, but would surely agree with. Since I must not presume to interpret your experience, may I put what I want to say into the form of a series of questions, exploring what your experience of these past years has shown?

Does reflection on making and giving the Exercises together not bring home to us (whatever our tradition, our religious culture, the form of our worship and faith) that what is crucial is the radical conversion worked in the human spirit by the operation of the Holy Spirit within and between us? Such a conversion entails an entire surrender to God and to a daily living of the gospel in an affective relationship with Jesus who is our way to the Father. That, and only that, is what the Exercises are about.

Furthermore, have we not seen that it is the experience of consolation, entirely *de arriba*, as Ignatius would say, the experience of the gratuity of God's gift of faith and the growth of faith, that alone can move us beyond the lethargies and timidities of marking time?

Can we even say that our seeking together of that depth of the spirit, prescinding from particular doctrines or formulations of doctrine, is what Ignatius called consolation? Is not this shared consolation precisely what will carry us beyond the postponements and rationalisations of a collective ecumenical desolation? In Ignatius' language such consolation is something 'that neither was nor could be from himself but came purely from God'.[25] Hence it is what we are forced to call, nebulously, the mystical, but what the older tradition called simply contemplative.

---

[25] Pedro de Ribadeneira, cited in O'Malley, *The First Jesuits*, 18.

## Where the Spiritual Exercises Are Going

What has experience taught us about the ministry of the Exercises after thirty years of enterprise, experiment and reflection on experience? One way in which we can come to understand St Ignatius is by pointing to his grasp of the value of experience. His way of forming others was to encourage them to trust their experience, to pray reflectively on it, to learn where God was to be found in it, and to prefer such praxis to book-learning.[26] It follows that a text like the *Spiritual Exercises*, handed down to us from the past, must indeed be reverenced as a classic, but not in such a way that we are paralyzed by it. A rigid or literal clinging to its prescriptions kills them. What Ignatius liked to term the unction of the Holy Spirit will always be imparting the gift of flexibility of spirit, and opening the imagination.

In the *Constitutions* Ignatius uses the term *discreta caritas* (a discerning wisdom that is the fruit of love) for the gift of the Spirit that enables us creatively to adapt the wisdom of tradition to an infinite variety of changing concrete situations in the present. The Spirit's gift of wisdom is supple and open-ended. The freedom of the Spirit, what Ignatius calls indifference, liberates the imagination to go beyond the timid self-serving of rational prudence.

This flexibility or freedom is a necessary quality in the one who gives the Exercises; only so will that person be able to listen to where the retreatants find themselves on the road to God. The director's suggestions of particular 'exercises' are adapted to the person (Exx 17). A basic virtue of the Exercises (and so of all Ignatian approaches to 'helping souls') is accommodation. You take people where they are. The Exercises disclose to the person their desires, indeed their core desire. They uncover what the person is capable of, what will best open their spirit to the action of the Holy Spirit already operative within them. They will bring to light how far a person is being called and enabled by grace to go beyond their native limits in seeking God, and where the Spirit is calling them now to be contemplatively identified with the experience of Jesus in the gospel.

---

[26] Nevertheless Ignatius revered learning and the intelligence. His 'Rules to follow in view of the true attitude of mind that we ought to maintain [as members] within the Church militant' (Exx 352-370) make it clear that he was no subjectivist, and that he held dogma in honour.

This freedom in the director is a fruit of contemplation of God's sovereign freedom and, if we may be allowed to say so, a participation in God's own reverence for the person's freedom. Nothing is to be imposed. No psychological manipulation or force may be used. No ideological hobby-horse is to be given a gallop. No theological schools or preferences are to be pressed. The art of the director is in listening for the signs of the only true force there is: the power of grace inviting or calling the person to be moved by love, so as to be taken out of self and placed with Christ. The dynamic of the Exercises is simply a particular way of entering into the normal dynamic of faith and grace. It encounters a person in whom the Spirit has already been active and in whom the Word is already silently present.

**Learning as Directors**

Long reflection on the great variety of ways in which individuals are drawn into that dynamic of grace gives a director a sense of the scope and range and length and breadth of the journey to God. John O'Malley, in *The First Jesuits*, shows how all Jesuit 'help of souls' was formed by the experience of the Exercises. The people they served included the struggling sinner irresolutely longing to be set free from inveterate habit; the lukewarm, affrighted by the demands of the commitment of faith, wanting only to be left undisturbed in a happy irreligion; the pious wallowing in unconscious self-deception; and the one who 'desires to make as much progress as possible' (Exx 20), generously struggling toward self-abandonment to God, but nevertheless hesitant or confused or even terrified. The first Jesuits were profoundly realistic about the range of human response to the desire of God to give Himself to humanity.[27] They were inclusive in their

---

[27] Exx 370. The final words in the text of the Exercises exhibit this realism: 'Given that the motive of pure love in the constant service of God our Lord is to be valued above all, yet we ought also greatly to praise fear of the Divine Majesty. The reason is not only that filial fear is a good and holy thing, but also that where someone is not capable of attaining anything better or more useful, even servile fear can be a great help to escape from mortal sin, and once free a person can easily reach filial fear, which is wholly acceptable and pleasing to God Our Lord, as it is all one with divine love.'

welcoming of all and sundry, the spiritual 'riff-raff' and the marathon heroes. They had a sense of gradation in the work of 'helping souls'.

Reflection on the experience of being present to those 'manifold gifts' of the Spirit and on the infinite variety of His ways with the individual spirit gives the pastoral minister a sense of the whole terrain. The operation of grace is seen and sensed as a process, as a path of growth. The art of guiding anyone at any point in that process of growth is the art of discerning where they are coming from, where they are at this moment, how authentic and far-reaching is their desire to be changed, and where the Spirit of Jesus might now be encouraging them to move forward. The Church of Christ is a home for the sinner, and for the saint who is a sinner. God's own freedom does not force, or else exclude, the ones who could not care less about religion, who are turned off by it, who do not particularly want to be expected to lead 'a godly life'. If God's freedom is patient with them, then who are we to be unwelcoming? So: how do we keep the door open and the challenge fresh to enter more into the consolation of God?

In the sixteenth century there was widespread anxiety about salvation and a strong sense of sin. But even then not all church-goers wanted to be harried into a devout way of living. Nowadays, in our secularised world, experience poses us questions about our boldness in proclaiming the gospel and our ability to help or to embrace the fitfully believing, the selective believer, the wholly contented atheist, the religiously tone-deaf or colour-blind, the person immersed in doubts and hesitations, the good woman or man who has decided simply to shelve all ultimate questions and to get on with living and doing what good may come their way to do. Our experience of the extraordinary range and variety of ways in which the Spirit leads people through the instrument of the Exercises should make us chary of generalisations or simple formulas.

## A Ministry of Consolation

Yet we must attend with respect to Karl Rahner's conviction that he puts into the mouth of Ignatius speaking to Jesuits in the 1970s:

> I was convinced that … I had a direct experience of God. This was the experience I longed to communicate to others

.... This very simple and yet in reality stupendous conviction … seems to me to be the core of what you today usually term my spirituality. [28]

O'Malley, in *The First Jesuits,* finds that the historical evidence shows the same conviction in Ignatius' early followers:

> They sought to be mediators of an immediate experience of God. With varying degrees of clarity, that purpose shines through all they wrote and said as the ultimate goal they had in mind when they spoke of helping souls.

They saw every ministry as a ministry of consolation. They 'wanted to live according to such consolation themselves and to help others to do the same'.[29] They worked out of an unshakeable conviction of the abundance of God's grace. Our reflection on where the ministry of the Exercises stands now in a publicly godless culture (a phrase that says nothing about the deeper longings of individuals) demands that we take very seriously Karl Rahner's assertion that the Christian of the future will be a mystic or will be nothing.

Anyone experienced in giving the Exercises will well know that spiritual consolation has nothing to do with feeling good. Even in its gentlest manifestations, spiritual consolation is profound. It can be present in suffering. It is experienced as *de arriba,* from above. It is a deep experience of gratuity, of the paramount initiative of God and of the free endowment of faith. The challenge to the ministry of the Exercises in the West now is how to make that experience available, how to make it attractive to the sceptical and the indifferent. This ministry accustoms us to diagnosing the great variety of forms of desolation and consolation. The Exercises open the way to sensing in another the leading of the Holy Spirit, the presence of the *sensus Christi*, the Pauline 'mind of Christ'.

They open the way, too, to noticing the signs of the operation of the bad spirit, of the blindness and delusion that distort and mislead the good in seeking the good. The history of religious polemic and the

---

[28] Karl Rahner, 'Ignatius of Loyola Speaks to a Modern Jesuit', in Karl Rahner and Paul Imhof, Ignatius of Loyola (London: Collins, 1979), translated by Rosaleen Ockenden 11-38, at 11, 13.

[29] John W. O'Malley, *The First Jesuits* (Harvard UP, 1993), 19, 83.

misconceptions of the positions of adversaries are a powerful demon-
stration of the ways in which good and prayerful people can be
blinded and led into un-Christlike words and ways. Many of my more
pugnacious Jesuit forbears were past masters in that school of self-
deception. But, apart from such historical examples, the experience
of giving the Exercises constantly makes one aware of the rationalisations and fears that make a person mark time, postpone decision,
evade the Spirit-prompted risk. It is an experience that may tell us
more than a little about that sense of stagnation or torpor or timidity
that many today feel on the path to the unity of believers in Christ.

### Apprenticeship to Discernment

The Exercises, then, are an apprenticeship to discernment, to living a
discerning life. A Puritan word for it was 'watchfulness'. The freedom
that is the gift of the Spirit (however precariously it may be felt to be
held) and the fruit of the Exercises would, in Ignatius' aspiration, lead
to 'walking in the Spirit', to a living and moving and breathing and
deciding and acting, at all times, by the interior leading of the Holy
Spirit. Puritan books on the godly life are full of that trust in the
indwelling Spirit. So one who led a godly life, whose life was
possessed by an evangelical desire, could be described (in Ignatian
terms) as a supple instrument in the hand of our Creator and Lord. It
is only women and men so surrendered and free, so aware of their
own vulnerability to the illusions of the Enemy, who can imagine
creatively where God is leading His Church, and who can suffer the
consequences of the risk that such a challenge entails. What I am
trying to say is that the Exercises cannot well be given, or Christ
incarnated again in changing situations and cultures, without a
constant free praying of the prayer of the Two Standards and without
the desire to be one with Jesus in all his experience. Without that
grace one is imprisoned by fear and open to self-delusion.

In the absence of that real desire, the giving of the Exercises,
indeed all spiritual direction, slips into a comforting therapy with a
cosmetic top-dressing of religion. The gospel is full both of consolation and of uncomfortable challenge. We must not let ourselves be
pedlars of an unvarying diet of the love of God that effectively
preaches a harmless God and domesticates the terrifying, purifying

fire, or the dread before the transcendently Holy. Directors of the Exercises have to be at home with this apparent contradiction. They must listen sensitively to where the person is, to their history of grace or of unbelief, to the pace at which the Spirit is leading them gently beyond their contracted boundaries. But at the same time directors betray the gospel if they are not able at the right moment to disclose the wholehearted radicality of the Exercises, a radicality which is simply the radicality of the gospel.

If the Exercises today sometimes seem to us to lack the explosive, dynamic force which they had in the hands of Ignatius and his immediate followers, it may well be because directors are not themselves committed to the radical graces of the triple colloquy of the Two Standards, and to the experience of the Third and Fourth Weeks of the Exercises. The Exercises *are* dynamite—and if they are to be handled with care, it is because of their explosive power. But we can easily be careful in a bad way, unconsciously wrapping them in tissue-paper and confining them within an inoffensive cardboard box. What Patriarch Athenagoras boldly challenges us to do is to face up to the deceits that attend pride. The illusions insinuated by the Enemy in men and women dedicated to religious ideals are there present in the meditation on Two Standards; all the subtle falsenesses of self. The only way to move from lie to truth, from the way of the Enemy to the way of Jesus, is the way of the gospel.

Making and giving the Exercises together are a way, *the way*, I suggest, towards going forward boldly into the uncharted and dangerous territory of Christian unity. Does such a proposal resonate within you? Where may your own experience together in these recent years have led you? What have you learnt together? What may all of us now dare to include in our vision? Theology has brought us far indeed, but only so far. In a secularised culture in which official religion is written off, what may we as individuals and as Churches hope for together?

## Towards the Future

There are some simple and obvious things that are not new to you; but for completeness may I quickly rehearse them? We need to bring the Exercises out of retreat houses and back into the streets and into those places where people live. It is not acceptable that the Exercises should largely be available only to those who have money. If the Exercises are to excite and console a great spectrum of lay people, they must be made financially affordable or open to the moneyless. The movement of guided weeks of prayer in parishes or wherever has been the most exciting and fruitful enterprise in the last twenty years.

The dynamic of the Exercises finds its spring in the deepest true longing of a person. If we could pray together and hope together, we might discover how the dynamic we have come to know with our fingertips might help us to disclose to unbelieving individuals what in fact their deepest longing is, what it may mean, and how they can move within that longing to an interior freedom that will deepen the springs of desire and the natural yearning of the human heart for goodness and relationship. Even the agnostic or atheist cannot *not* want to be more free, and to live in harmony with their authentic longing. We believe (even if we may not always proclaim it) that that longing is the gift and work of the Holy Spirit. Therefore we may allow ourselves quietly to hope where that freedom may lead. This unexplored territory, unknown and so furnished with cartographic monsters, is something boldly claimed by Carlo Maria Martini in his book entitled *Letting God Free Us*:

> [St Ignatius] says, 'Help all without exception, liberate them, free them' .... [Jesus says] that we are to teach them that true liberty of heart which all need—the baptized and the non-baptized, the practising and the non-practising, Jews, Muslims, Buddhists as well as atheists, agnostics, progressives, conservatives and the indifferent. Because all are called to enter into the liberty of Christ .... They want to be freed of their anguish, they want to find peace.[30]

But Martini does not tell us how. The further and more challenging discernment before us is a bold discovery of how the Sermon on the Mount might bring many who are by honest conviction not Christian to a freedom, within their own religious or non-religious culture, to know in consolation where they are, and who

---

[30] Carlo M. Martini, *Letting God Free Us: Meditations on Ignatian Spiritual Exercises*, translated by Richard Arnandez (Slough: St Paul, 1993 [1992]), 112, 113.

they are, and where their desire is leading them. The enterprise before us all, if we can enter contemplatively into it together, is to deepen the radical effectiveness of the Exercises in such a way that more and more people, of all religions or of none, may enter into an unambiguous surrender to God and daily 'walk in the Spirit'.

# 14

# MEDITATING ON ABUSE

*'Lord, if it is your will, you can make me clean.' Jesus answered: 'It is my will, may you be clean'.*[1]

MANY VOICES ARE INSISTING THAT THE CHURCH ought to ask for forgiveness. We need a symbolic public act of repentance. But what does this mean? A quick fix? Something we need to do before we get on with living? And who is this Church? The hierarchy? The priests? The religious orders in the person of their Provincials? Or the Church as the whole people of God? Will the people of God be consulted, asked if they want the top people to confess the people's sins for them? Or is this an apology from the abusers to the abused within the Church? (Some writers take it for granted that the ones who are asked to forgive are outside the Church.)

And to ask for forgiveness for what? Are we sure what constitutes the abusing? Who has been abused? Who has done the abusing? The angry wing of the media writes as though we all know who are the criminals and who are the victims, as though it is clear in black and white.

We have had a rush to public confessions of guilt. There is something that doesn't quite ring true about this breast-beating by the Pope and others. We apologize to the indigenous people of Latin America for our treatment of them in the sixteenth century. Tony Blair apologizes for the Great Irish Famine. What exactly is the meaning of this? What is the reality of it? My guilt for my sins is a different kind of reality from my acknowledgement that in the 1940s and 1950s 'society' (including me) and the state were guilty of ill-treatment of young people. The word 'guilt' in the two cases is not univocal. The same word does not mean the same thing.

---

[1] Antiphon from Morning Prayer, Sunday of Week 6 of the Year, *The Divine Office*.

What is the reality of my doing public penance for something I did not decide to do and for something which I was impotent to change? Do I really want my bishops or my top politicians to say for me what I can't say for myself?

## Truth and Its Cost

I think my problem is with the question of truth. What is it about these papal or prime ministerial breast-beatings that feels phoney? Jesus said something about not standing on street corners doing penance. He was addressing the Pharisees. By all means let people do penance privately for their own sins, providing they mean it. But Irish Catholics are wary of what they sense to be Pharisaism in the official Church. And a public act (of what? Of reconciliation? Of confession? Of guilt?) runs the risk of being false. It can be facile to beat one's breast for other people's sins. Words come cheap. They used to say that corporations don't have a bottom that you can kick. It is equally true that institutions don't have a heart that can grieve.

A shared public act of repentance must not be cheap. Private repentance is hard enough. It does not happen by saying it or thinking it. Anyone who has been engaged in the Spiritual Exercises, or in any Christian process of conversion, knows how long a person may have to pray and strive and yearn before the grace of compunction is given. Even personal contrition can be costly and sometimes the fruit of long waiting. Collective repentance is likely to take longer and to need strenuous collective preparation.

Any symbolic act or statement or repentance needs to be costly. The Church and the religious orders could set aside millions in reparations, as they are doing now, and people could yawn. It is not finance that is costly.

There are other conditions. When a person is very deeply hurt or outraged, they need to hear some expression of sorrow; but they also need the offender to go even a step further. When the apologizer says, 'I am sorry, but ...', when there are qualifications, the sorrow is not heard and the wound is made more painful. The asking for forgiveness has to be unconditional, simple.

To devise words that ring true is not a slick public-relations exercise. It takes longer and needs more prayer. And at least two things need to be present.

The first is an acknowledgement that we are all capable of doing what the abusers have done. This is a healthy requirement of any Spirit-led reflection on abuse and on anything that we might say or do by way of public penance. Secondly, we have to face how we feel in the presence of abuse and when faced with the attitudes of the press. It may be that individuals have privately done that. But if the community of faith is to emerge from trauma, from a loss of nerve, from denial, some collective attempt to voice our feelings, to acknowledge what we actually feel, may be needed.

The whole people of God in Ireland, the whole body, has been wounded. The injuries have not been simply on the surface. They have not just harmed a few reputations. They are deeper, probably deeper than we yet realise. Just as individuals do not really know their sin as it is until after they have repented and been forgiven, so we will not know how deep our collective spiritual hurt has been until we have been together through some process of recognition, acknowledgement and sorrow.

Before we make apologies, we need to *grieve*. Grief is a slower business than being seen and heard to repent. It is also more important and more necessary.

## Grief

What would be entailed were the Church and Irish society as a whole to enter on a collective First Week?

The Church is in shock. Many are in denial. (Denial is the first stage of grief, and the denial of anything to be ashamed about is often a phase in private repentance.) The disclosures of sexual abuse and cruelty came when people were already long since disenchanted with the Church, with the whole set-up, with religion in general. That goes back a long way. It was masked by a smugness on the part of the official Church and a deference and conformism, masquerading as respect, in the presence of the clergy. Craw-thumping came naturally to many and could go along with secret contempt. It suited many to connive with putting priests on a pedestal, to have plaster statues to keep at a safe distance, to have an authority figure to gripe about. The sinless, not fully human priest was a fiction created by knowing peasants and gullible clerics in collusion. No one really believed it, but it served a purpose to pretend that it was true. The revelations of paedophilia fell into a culture that for decades had seen through clerical screens.

In particular, lay cynicism about celibacy was there long before the press got going on abuse. Now there is a widespread scepticism that any priests are really celibate—a scepticism that is almost universal and is shared by the most devout. Dublin suburbs are not all that different from the squinting windows of the country towns. In Ireland it was never easy to get away with much in secret. A lawyer friend assures me that now all priests are felt to be potential paedophiles.

The conversion of many a saint was occasioned by an experience of failure, of the upsetting of a comfortable goodness, of a dislocation that disturbed deep layers of unattended reality. The Irish Catholic Church has been humiliated and interiorly dislocated. It can take refuge in changing this or that. It can maintain a semblance of life, offering comfort to the troubled remnant, while leaving familiar structures untouched. Or it can embark on the 'long and painful path of conversion, a path that will lead us to re-examine the very foundations of the Church'. How is it that the Christian faith has … 'been pressed into service of a different kingdom'.[2]

### Resentment at Repression

It is at least thirty years since I knew idealistic young men who 'left the Church' convinced that the Church in Ireland is the obstacle to the gospel. There is a younger generation now who are simply indifferent to the Church, to religion; the plight of the Church does not impinge on them. Religion is not part of their conscious world. But what is interesting is an older generation, from say fifty upwards, who keep at it, who often grimly cling to something they sense to be of the

---

[2] Eamonn Conway, 'The Service of a Different Kingdom: Child Sexual Abuse and the Response of the Church', now available at http://www.cctv.mic.ul.ie/Child Abuse & Catholic Church.pdf.

greatest value, but who do not quite know why they bother. Some of that generation are committed and devout; many have taken the trouble to learn why they are. It is worth asking why these devout people are not speaking out to praise the Christian Brothers, the Sisters of Mercy, the Oblates. That is a strange silence.

Perhaps I am wrong, but I believe that the average devout Catholic today feels a deep, perhaps unconscious resentment at what they perceive to have been the Church's repressive sexual restrictions. Whether they are married or not, their sexual lives, the central energy of their humanity, have been mucked up by Catholicism. They feel that they have been sexually abused by the Church. And accusations about purity and sexual abuse touch off that resentment as though the two are connected by an electric current.

If the Church wants to protest its sorrow, it needs to spend first a long time looking unblinkingly at its use of power. The issues here are far-reaching, going well beyond the disclosures about sex abuse and brutality. Indeed, talk of sexual abuse distracts attention from this wider reality. The experience is already within each of us. The raw material of conversion is not far to seek.

**The Roots of Powerlessness**

We imagine that the Church's collective life before Vatican II was reasonably happy and sure. But perhaps there was much private bleakness, at least in the clerical world. Perhaps there was much loneliness and isolation. Young men had no human being to relate to. There was a desert in the heart, and a rhetoric of self-denial that twisted into self-abasement. There was self-hatred, a conviction of worthlessness, an unattended guilt, resentments, rage at things being done to us. We had no say in the disposition of our own lives. Authority could be impersonal and demeaning, and there was a culture of comfortable dependency that could suddenly reverse into angry rebellion. And the living environment was spartan in the lack of amenity, the walls denuded of beauty, the 'spiritual' assumptions that dehumanised. Can we imagine the levels of private pain that might have their roots in this complex? The longing for human contact, for touch, for talk, for being listened to, the unavailability of spiritual direction, the ache for a little tenderness or gentleness? The simple clamouring of the body?

People naturally focus on celibacy. Young men were shunted undiscerningly into a sexless life, and left to sink or swim, without instruction or counsel or sympathetic care or the kind of human community that alone makes chastity wholesome. There is an old medieval saying: 'Chastity without charity shall be chained in hell'.

But celibacy was lived in conjunction with poverty and obedience. There was a culture of religious and clerical life so impoverished, and so deeply shaped by a debased rhetoric of obedience and a skewed spirituality, that it could be a feeding ground for delinquency. We all stood by and said nothing. If we sensed that something was wrong, no-one shouted 'Stop'. That whole mode of living was assumed to be holy and *by itself* a road to holiness, because it was taken to be ageless. When Vatican II came not everything changed. It is only now that the costs to people's humanity are coming to light—costs which are great. But disclosure is a blessing.

This whole system was marked by the abuse of power. Hence it is not surprising that there was sexual abuse. Sexual abuse flourishes amid systems that systematically abuse power.

When children were neglected and rejected, the State (which means society, which means us) was exploiting religious congregations; and the superiors of religious congregations were exploiting their subjects; and those subjects were abusing their charges. It is easy and natural to scapegoat, and the trauma of recent years has led to convulsions of mutual scapegoating. From every side you get the whiff of self-righteousness. But the reality is that cruelty is handed down. That there was also much love and caring present was nothing short of a miracle of God's graciousness.

We also need to face issues about sexuality, about the Church's pathological nervousness in the presence of eros. Official reiteration of impeccable theological principles about the beauty of connubiality does not deceive anyone. For quite another message is given by the uneasiness with their own sexuality that the celibate males of the system generally convey.

We need to recognise, too, that there was collusion—not on the part of those sexually abused, to be sure, but on the part of society at large. The way the media in general speak, it is as though 'the Church' was a clinically free agent standing above the helpless people it tyrannized. But the official Church consists of males formed by a particular culture, by Irish mothers and fathers and sisters and brothers, by a society that is urban and suburban and rural. The official male Church is the product of a society emerging painfully from the famine, from destitution, from British deprivation. We are now on a crash course teaching us how to emerge from the mentality of the colonised.

The loveless clerical culture of the past was formed already by attitudes and feelings and fears and prejudices. These were absorbed by osmosis, not by rationality. Nor was there any softening influence from poetry or literature or art. The great fear was softness. A cattle dealer said to me once that young Irish boys come from small cottages schooled in courtesy by their mothers, enter the seminary, and six years later emerge un-gentle. The clerical world (diocesan and religious) was aggressively masculine, philistine and assured of its superiority to women.

**The Cullen Church**

The Cardinal Cullen Church was built on a collusion between clerics and people, on a gentleman's agreement that a few would get on with running the show, and leave the rest in a blissful ecclesiastical passivity. The Irish chapel congregation recognised in their clergy their own fears and phobias and hang-ups, their own panic at personal freedom, their relieved handing over of responsibility for the loftier things to an authority that knew best what was good for them. The people of God had, no doubt, their own ways of applying common sense to harsh laws, of knowing how to cut comers. They also knew how to welcome strict laws and admonition and censure when they needed ankle-shackles to give them inner security and the assurance of the prodigal son's elder brother.

Irish clerics could indulge in a Chaucerian verbal bawdy quite as much as their flocks. But maybe there was an agreement to keep that side of the Irish character in separate compartments and at separate tables. The exercise of book censorship in the new Irish state was not just the imposition of clerics. It was the work of zealot lay people, encouraged by some frightened clergy. The more widely read clergy were silent. There were strains of pessimism and repressiveness in the Irish Church that were not simply the imposition of Maynooth or of the clergy. There was already something in the Irish that welcomed it. Of course there were other things besides. Modern Irish Catholicism was a remarkable achievement, the bearer of great good, and unique in Church history. But there was something in it that had to die, and which would have died even had there been no clerical scandals. An educated laity would not have been content to be present inert at Mass and to let the clergy run things.

There are other things besides cruelty and sexual sins that the Church needs to confront within itself. There are other things about which the Church must pray for the grace of repentance. The bullying that keeps the truth under wraps and the cagey economizing with truth 'so that the simple faithful may not be upset' are part of the surviving features of clericalism. The clerical Church is thought to react defensively to any shadow cast on the institution and to protect the institution at any cost to the gospel values of compassion, tenderness, kindness, goodness and truth. That the conviction may be exaggerated does not detract from its strength. The system appears dominated by 'those who want to make a good showing in the flesh ... only that they may not be persecuted for the cross of Christ' (Galatians 6:12).

### Clericalism

Clericalism is characterized by a faintly condescending air towards non-clerics, an air of being a separate and maybe superior caste. If lay men were patronised, women were given tongue-in-cheek respect, and trebly condescended to. The truth was passed down from above. The institution knew what was good for people. The weight of responsibility, ambiguously accepted, led to the clerical world functioning as an over-protective, anxious parent. There was an eagerness to make people's moral judgments for them, something which many of the people wanted and were encouraged to want. But we know what happens later to well-behaved, over-shielded children. The result is an infantilism that has patently shown up in the failure of a generation of politicians and business people to internalise principles of moral integrity.

Above all there was need for control. Freedom is dangerous. You cannot trust it. And, as Dostoyevsky's Grand Inquisitor knew, the people want to be relieved of its burden. If legislation does not buttress moral behaviour, goodness knows what moral debauchery might happen. The desire of most human beings to lead a decent life is not trusted. Fear insists on being in control.

## Repentance

And so, back to repentance. What does the Church need to repent of?

We should not speak of scandals or of forgiveness until we have, as individuals, first scrutinised our own feelings about 'sex abuse'. What do the allegations make me feel? What, in my most secret self, has been my response? What is my personal cocktail of emotions? Perhaps I have worked through a whole process: from anger, from anger at exaggerated charges, at fabrications fuelled by greed, to rage at the motives of TV presenters. What have been my fears? What exactly have I been afraid of? What different kinds of fear? What different kinds of hatred?

Perhaps there are some special questions for us who are clerics. Do I feel shame at being part of a caste derided and hated? Of being part of a celibate class when celibacy is the object of sardonic disbelief? Do I judge celibates among us whose sexuality broke out in cruel or self-deluding ways, or do I have some feeling for them? Perhaps they themselves were the victims of a particular culture that bullied them or exploited them in the name of obedience, that reinforced a native sense of worthlessness, that was harsh and loveless, and lonelier than necessary, that failed them by its failure to show them how to welcome their sexuality? Perhaps they need our compassion for what we did to them?

How do I experience the decline from belonging to a revered class to which once men always doffed their hats? Feelings of simple incredulity—'it's just not true'? Denial? Anger or despair that the Church is being destroyed? Anxiety about what it will be like? Depression at being seen to be part of a discredited Church? Shame at being associated with a debased religion? We need to hear the prayer of the Psalms:

> I am the scorn of all my adversaries, a horror to my neigh-
> bours, an object of dread to my acquaintances; those who see
> me in the street flee from me (Psalm 30: 11).

If we balk at using words like those and reject them, we are not able to put words on the feelings that are actually there. What is my *experience* of being a victim, or of being an offender? How have I contributed to the abusive behaviour, and to the twisted thinking that favoured sexual abuse? Questions like these are not answered in an hour or a day. And when they are answered, it will normally take longer than days for us to be given the grace of compunction.

Until I have dealt with my feelings, I cannot move towards participating in repentance. And until we share those feelings openly, we cannot move towards an authentic collective repentance. For the individual, it can be a long road to repentance. For a group of people it is an even longer road to being able to ask for forgiveness. And then reconciliation is not there until the injured one says 'I forgive'. The injurer has to wait upon the freedom of the other, to wait in patience and without manipulation or making emotional demands until the one harmed is ready to forgive.

Each of us needs to explore also our own experience of being abused. If we do not do that, we cannot know what the accusers of the Church are feeling. If we protest that we have no memory of being abused, we cannot enter into the feelings of those who have been abused.

We celibates need to examine our personal histories for the symbiosis of violence and celibacy. Violence breeds violence. Each of us has experienced it in our own way. And this violence is symbolic. Perhaps the brutal discipline of some of the school abusers—who knows?—may have been the helpless handing on of violence experienced. Hurt spreads in that way. Harsh punishment is the child of fear, the fear of losing control. It is not an accident that some lay observers (often sympathetic) have seen a direct line between such violent fear and the deeper fear of not being in control that could go with a celibate way of life.

### The Loss of Holiness?

Then perhaps, we can ask wider questions. Has the Church been grieving for its loss of power when in fact we should be grieving for the loss of holiness?

The loss of power will turn out to be a blessing, provided certain conditions are met. We will need to stop clinging, to let go of power—and to do so in generosity, in freedom, and because the abandonment of power is closer to the mind of Christ. The Church needs publicly to give up power. Like Paul writing to the Corinthians, it should not seek to proclaim the mystery of God in 'lofty words or wisdom', but only through the knowledge of 'Jesus Christ, and him crucified ... so that your faith might rest not on human wisdom but on the power of God' (1 Corinthians 2: 1-5).

All this may sound strange, when the public perception is that the Church in Ireland has already been stripped of its power. But what is being said here is about the Church's own needs, needs that go deeper than any public act of repentance.

Firstly, as members of this Church, we need to forgive ourselves. The body needs to acknowledge its own feelings of guilt, its sense of being soiled and shamed by what has been done by some of its members. When one member is in pain, the whole body suffers. When one of the members sins, the whole body is ill. When one of the members sins, it is because we have been sinful.

Secondly, we need to face the fact that the reality of abuse is a shared one, a collective one. Individual repentance is important and necessary to be sure. But we do not fulfil all justice when we repent as individuals. And what has happened in the Church in Ireland is a God-given opportunity to experience a thoroughly Catholic insight that has become dim in our awareness. We do not sin alone; we do not suffer alone; we do not welcome grace alone. For 800 years the Church has hammered home an individualist morality. No doubt truths have been conveyed. No doubt this teaching has been useful up to a point. But it has weakened our sense of belonging to each other.

We should not scapegoat any sinner who belongs to us. We should know in our bones that we are in no position to throw the first stone. Each of us knows that. What has preserved us from public shame has simply been that our capacity to do the same things, our complicity, our solidarity in weakness have not been broadcast. We need to rely on Christ's solidarity with us in our weakness, and on our solidarity in the whole Christ.

We need first to be reconciled with ourselves, which is insep-arable from being reconciled with each other. We need to confess our sins to one another. Then, perhaps, quietly, without a parade of street-corner tears, an authentic humility may become possible. And perhaps then there will be some chance that our public pleas for the forgiveness of those brutalised by sexual abuse will have some ring of truth.

# 15

# THE SILENCE

WE KEEP LOOKING IN THE WRONG DIRECTION. We keep asking sociologists, cultural analysts, pundits, to tell us about what is out there in the world that we are meant to be evangelizing. In one way or another, liberal-minded people in the Church have been doing this for the last thirty years. We have been over and over that ground so often. And we come back a few years later to much the same discourse from a different expert. We listen or read politely; we pay attention; we are stimulated by one or two new insights; we allow two or three familiar questions to surface. The answers are familiar too. Sometimes we have a lively discussion. We are good at that. But then we leave the meeting or put the book down and get back to whatever it is, our jobs, our capsule of responsibility. There is no follow-up. Has anything changed? Are we changed?

Fairly rarely, someone speaks or writes from a deeper level of experience. They may be listened to respectfully. But sooner or later, the wider body turns to safer ground. The person is rarely responded to. The next contribution is often a conceptual statement that cuts across the possibility of a follow-up and knocks the tennis ball far outside the court. More or less consciously, the unacceptable has been sidelined. We continue, privately, to carry a dull feeling of unease and unsatisfactoriness, and a wan dismay in the face of indifference and irreligion.

There is a place for description and analysis. It is indispensable. But it cuts no ice until some other level of experience is stirred and attended to. Then the subsequent analysis can bear fruit.

## Jadedness and Second-Hand Language

There is a deadness in Western Europe, and it is there also in the Church and in the Ignatian family.

The institutional Church in Western Europe is, by and large, written off, even by the devout. Its language is no longer being heard. The Church institution (and religion in general) invites yawns or condescension or indifference or contempt. As soon as you open your mouth about God you have the handicap of being associated with a discredited Church. (There—I am falling into the trap of rehearsing most of those cultural analyses we have been reading for years.) But the very familiarity here can mask a pain we can all too easily deny, the pain of wondering how to speak of God from within the crumbling walls of a discredited institution.

The problem is that the language has gone stale. The only language that has any chance of getting through is first-hand language. The trouble with most attempts at religious communication is that they are couched in a language that is tired, in tired images, in a churchy idiom that is remote from life and has grown repulsive. (Do we not ourselves, honestly, find much religious talk repulsive? I do.) Many of our words about God are second-hand, third-hand, reach-me-down, ready-made.

First-hand words are those that come from a level of experience that is sensed to be in touch with God. Never mind how fragile, how filled with doubt or dread, how inadequate. People only hear words that are freshly minted, that come from intimacy and contact.

If a speaker has been given the gift (a kind of poetic gift) of discovering fresh images, that is good. But few have it. Even older words, older idioms, strike home when the speaker speaks from some core, where God is a familiar presence. Otherwise our words fall dead. It is no great matter—it is almost certainly better—if the contact with God is a wrestling and contention with God, a cry from a disbelieving ache, a groan of the spirit out of darkness. It can be heard because it is real. That God is real.

Against such thoughts we protect ourselves. All too easily we say: 'Yes, yes, of course. We should all be more prayerful. (And stop making me feel more guilty about it.)' But we know that. We've been told it. It serves as a conversation stopper. It allows us to turn to more manageable levels of discourse that we find easier. Nothing happens. The talk turns to the palpable, to what our education has made us good at, to more words, to the intellectual analysis of a culture or a situation.

But the focus needs to be elsewhere, on our own unbelief. If we were able (not just once, but continually) to come clean, to share the anxieties and denials of our fogged sense of belief, of our unbelief, we might begin also to grasp what is ill in the private and public life of the West. Immersed as we Christians are in our culture, we ourselves may be the best laboratory specimens for examination. It is easy to make general statements. General statements are not wholly useless, God knows. But what cuts the ice are the particularities, the differences, of our personal experience. If we can explore these, perhaps together we might begin to get in touch with what is happening in Europe.

Are we ready yet to begin to answer the questions put to Europe by the events of 11 September 2001? The clear question about the spiritual contamination that Islam experiences from the West? One of the strengths of Islam is its unselfconscious ability to say the simplest things about God in the simplest way. The average devout Muslim is not lumbered with a baggage of theological debris. What they have is a daily, familiar, taken-for-granted relationship with God, an easiness (rare among equally devout Catholics that I know) with spontaneous words to speak of God.

## Desolation

Another way of perceiving our present apostolic experience is to see it as desolation. To rehearse the obvious: desolation is a movement of the spirit in a direction away from God. Or shuttered from God. Desolation moves inward. It gets trapped in the self. It likes privacy. ('Don't tell anyone'—Exx 326.) Desolation is confused, in the dark, in twilight, in avoidance. It is dispersed; its single focus has been lost. It wriggles so that it can escape facing reality. The mechanisms of avoidance include escape, escape into words, into semantic parsing and analysis. Impeccable reason is its stoutest ally. Avoidance will do anything so as not to make a decision. It marks time. It postpones the pain of giving up, of giving in. It clings to the dull discomfort of its condition, rather than facing the sharp pain that may liberate it into peace. Its fruit is lassitude. It feels there is no point to doing anything. It is good at masking torpor with an energetic semblance of vitality, with business. It is busy about good works. Good works are an effective cushion between the spirit and God. Desolation thrives on faction and division.

The individually directed retreat over the last thirty years has (we hope, but we do not know) helped many individuals to a deeper conversion. But that has failed to flow over into a revitalised and shared sense of mission.

A British Jesuit admonished me some years ago, and told me I should not be so hard on the people closest to me. There were plenty of good reasons why they could not be more active. The Irish Church itself was in trauma. Vocations, at least in the conventional sense, had dried up. He may have been right. If he was, the desolation he picked up in me will remain so long as it is not attended to, not acknowledged. But at the same time, those external realities could be experienced in consolation. What has to change for that to come about?

## Dispersed Focus

Church institutions keep trying to plan. We come up again and again with more or less the same priorities. They are diverse; there is no cohesion. There is no one focus that would alert or excite or unite us. There is nothing there to fire the belly, nothing that would send us to the barricades. We lack passion. Diffusion and confusion are signs of desolation.

In the 1970s, many were inspired by liberation theology to strive for the promotion of justice. They hoped that the Church might become excited, united around one objective. All that certainly had positive fruits: there was a shift towards the poor, the oppressed, the demeaned. But we need to assess the deficits too. Talk of justice was also divisive. More recent shifts in emphasis surely indicate some unease with how it all worked out in practice.

Vatican II was, in fact, quite preoccupied with atheism, and Paul VI gave the Jesuits a formal mission to address it. I do not think we have looked plainly at our response to Paul VI's mission. We walked away from it. We did not know what to do with it. Perhaps that avoidance was a silent or submerged acknowledgement of an unbelief in ourselves? If so, then the concern with justice in the 1970s was perhaps itself an avoidance mechanism, a makeshift? We could pretend that this was the *real* response to atheism. We could turn in relief from the discomforts of not knowing what to do about the unbelieving world, the West. (Where the East and the South are not yet contaminated, God is there. Palpably.) Justice was mercifully concrete, manageable; it promised visible results; you could *do* something about it.

None of these reflections are offered in a dogmatic spirit. But the question is there to be looked at. Have we ever seriously faced it? It may be the wrong question. Even so, to stay with it might throw up insights that we are not seeing.

Since 1970 the clerical Church in Europe has been crumbling. There is nothing new in that, goodness knows. It has been shedding credibility. For thirty years there has been a visible haemorrhaging of faith. Meanwhile many believers have been investing a great deal of their energy and talent in justice—not an enriched justice that is seen to be rooted in a personal faith, but rather an impoverished concept of economic justice. The faithful listen, take in the message, assent to it, but are ultimately unimpressed.

Good has come of the commitment to justice. But the field has now long since been won. Many who count in the Church are long since converted. Equally, committed people outside the Church have no need of Christians to alert them to concern for the poor. But during all those thirty years and more we have been doing nothing about the haemorrhaging of faith.

### Mission and Maintenance

Over the last thirty years I have met many well-intentioned people doing ministry in a variety of countries. Most of them have been and are competent, more than competent, at maintenance. Within that rubric they are active and creative. But not in mission. We have been good at what we are good at, and are comfortable with the ministry to the believer. But there have been no new, creative risks, no bold assertions of God. God for the committed Christians I know became what God was rapidly becoming in European culture more generally: the loony relative always kept in the kitchen and never mentioned to the guests.

And perhaps that provokes a wider question. Where was the effort to look together, unblinkingly, at the areas of fading faith? At the growing numbers for whom contemporary Western religion was becoming incredible, unworthy of trust, an intolerable burden on the spirit, ringing false? We had articulated the ideals all right in the 1970s.

The Jesuits, for example, were 'by a creative effort of faith ... to find a new language, a new set of symbols ... and that for our own sake just as much as for the sake of our contemporaries' (GC 32, d.4, n.26). But we had missed the urgency. Might we attempt now to wonder together how that was so, how we were so uncreative in addressing waning faith? So unaware, really, of that question at all? Might that cast some light on how our own faith has dimmed?

**Speaking of God**

John O'Malley has shown that the early Jesuits saw all their pastoral work as a ministry of consolation. They 'wanted to live according to such consolation themselves and to help others to do the same'. It was the dominant conviction governing their whole 'way of proceeding'.

> They sought to be mediators of an immediate experience of God that would lead to an inner change of heart or a deepening of religious sensibilities already present. With varying degrees of clarity, that purpose shines through all they wrote and said as the ultimate goal they had in mind when they spoke of helping souls.[1]

The first Jesuits had a focus. Whatever they were doing they had a clear desire and the same objective. Karl Rahner has St Ignatius say that the Exercises were not for an elite:

> I certainly didn't think that the grace of Manresa ... was a special privilege for a chosen, elite individual. That was why I gave exercises whenever this kind of offer of spiritual help looked as if it might be accepted. I even gave exercises before I'd studied your theology and had managed with some effort (I laugh) a masters degree from Paris. And also before I had received priestly and sacramental power from the Church. And why not? The director of the Exercises is ... just giving (when they can) support from a distance, very circumspectly, so that God and humanity can really meet immediately .... God is able and willing to deal immediately with His creature; the fact that this occurs is something that human beings can

---

[1] John W. O'Malley, *The First Jesuits* (Cambridge, Ma: Harvard UP, 1993), quotations from 82, 83, 19; see also 370-375.

experience happening; they can apprehend the sovereign disposing of God's freedom over their lives ...[2]

For Rahner, what the Exercises are all about is the disclosure of God's sovereign freedom as the unifying focus of all our scattered enterprises, of all our scattered selves:

> ... your pastoral care must have this goal in sight always, at every step, remorselessly ... the awakening of such divine experience is not in fact indoctrination with something previously not present in the human person, but rather a more explicit self-appropriation, the free acceptance of a reality of the human constitution that is always there, normally buried and repressed, but nevertheless there inescapably ... . This realisation I wanted to pass on to others through the Exercises that I gave ... . Do you understand me now when I say that the central task for you Jesuits, around which everything else is centred, has to be the giving of the Exercises? Of course this doesn't mean beginning with official and organized ecclesiastical courses, given to many people at once—still less is that the main point. Rather it means *mystagogical* help, so that others don't repress God's immediacy but come to experience it clearly and accept it.

'The central task for you Jesuits, around which everything else is centred, has to be the giving of the Exercises.' Neither Rahner nor, in his ventriloquist's voice, Ignatius, is saying that 'the giving of the Exercises' means 'retreat houses'. All these voices, rather, are pointing us towards a streetwise ease in using our bread-and-butter familiarity with the experience of the Exercises to create a pedagogy of freedom. When love is liberated at a profound level, then God is found to have been there all along. You don't have to 'give retreats' to engage in that ministry. It is what the Exercises are about.

There is thus no question here of our abandoning the other good things which the Church does. As Rahner's Ignatius puts it:

> I'm also not devaluing all the other pastoral, academic and political enterprises that you've thought you needed to try in the course of your history. But all this other stuff should really

---

[2]  Rahner, 'Ignatius of Loyola', 13-15.

be understood as a preparation for, or as a consequence of, the ultimate task, a task which must remain yours in the future: helping people towards the immediate experience of God, the experience where it dawns on a human being that the mystery all grasp that we call God is near, can be spoken to, and enfolds us with blessing precisely when we don't try to make it something under our control, but hand ourselves over to it unconditionally. Everything you do you should be constantly testing to see if it serves this goal. If it does, then a biologist among you can also investigate the mental life of cockroaches.[3]

To subsume all our energetic and efficient apostolic enterprises under that overarching aim would focus our mission and harness our diverse employments.

But what the Ignatian tradition challenges us to do really is embarrassing. You have to talk about God. You cannot enter with your partner in conversation (Muslim or Jew or recovering Catholic or agnostic or whatever) at that level, unless your own experience of God is alive. Nothing else will do. Your experience is alive if it is in pain, in aridity or darkness or despair. And of course it can be alive if it is freed from that agonizing or dismay. But it is not alive if it is in desolation.

### The Silence

None of this has anything to do with political or ethical questions. It touches all of us who are believing Christians today, wherever our integrity asks us to stand, on the left or on the right, as a traditionalist or as a progressive. These are no more than labels which the media have conditioned us to use as a way of seeing our own reality.

We need to help each other, wherever we stand. We need to emerge from a strange blanket of silence. We need to wonder about the great silence of these last thirty years. To speak simply about God. We are good at talking *about* faith. We are not good at *expressing* faith. We may, rightly or wrongly, feel that the word 'God' cannot be used

[3]  Rahner, 'Ignatius of Loyola', 15, 16. At the end, Rahner is referring ironically to the work of his colleague, Adolf Haas, a notable biologist and also a significant Ignatian scholar.

any more, because it has been so cheapened by its pious users. We may feel the same about most of the language of our religious ghetto. That vocabulary may carry with it so black a cloud of attendant woes, and remind recovering Catholics of so much intolerable guilt or religious boredom, that we cannot stomach it ourselves. Do we listen, ever, to contemporary religious talk and recognise how boring it is?

Yet the word 'God' is not a dead word. We have all heard it luminous and alive when the simplest believer (who may be Muslim or Jewish or whatever) speaks limpidly of a person, of persons, of a familiar presence, and in speaking has no designs on the hearer but is just voicing the reality that cannot be contained. It is not the vocabulary (primarily) that is faulty. It is the people who use it. It would serve the Kingdom of God if religious people would simply place an embargo on themselves and refuse to say words they do not mean, to voice sentiments they do not believe.

Nevertheless, there remain questions about our public utterances. Can we ask why we try so hard to be inoffensive? Is it that we are trying to keep our voices down in the presence of our betters? Do we secretly feel that the secularisers know better, that they are more intelligent than we are? Do we feel we're not up to them? Browbeaten? Do we baulk at being labelled by the media as belonging with the extremes of right or left? Is it time to speak out? To be heard again? To help, with many others, to discover a fresh gospel language that attracts? A language that rings true?

## To Be Met with Silence?

And suppose no one pays the slightest attention? Just a shrug and an amused turning away? Suppose we emerged from silence and encountered another great silence? Our words not even heard? Does it matter? Is effectiveness always a measure of God's will? There are times—and perhaps our time is one of them—when it is enough to say the truth. The truth may or may not strike home. But at least God would have been let out of the kitchen and shown to the guests. The effect is not our business. The Exercises and our mission call us to be free from the need to see results. You do what God wants you to do and stand free from the need to be effective. The results are God's business.

Never mind the words. They may be freshly minted, or they may be old and tired. If they come from a God who is a familiar, experienced reality, they will be first-hand, new enough to disclose in those among whom we are thrown an affinity that is already there before we open our mouths, a presence of the Word already operative in whomever we encounter.

These days Church people often talk about the gap between faith and culture. We wonder about our faith and about the resistance of so many to the words we use. But is it perhaps unjust to think in terms of us who have it, as opposed to those out there who do not have it? Us and them? It is clear that there is no us and them. We are in it together with them. The gap is not between dumbfounded Ignatian disciples and clever infidels. Or between those who have made the Exercises and the switched-off devout. The gap is within ourselves. The gap is between the spiritual famine and our own incapacity to speak to the hunger.

We stand there disarmed, unmanned, speechless. All that is needed is something very simple.

# Joseph Veale 1921-2002

## A Select Bibliography

*What follows is an attempt to list Joe's most significant publications from the latter part of his life, notably the sources from which the present selection has been taken. During his time as a schoolmaster, he also published a number of pieces on literature and education, as well as some popular books on religious topics.*

'Ignatian Prayer and Jesuit Spirituality', *The Way Supplement*, 27 (Spring 1976), 3-14.

'Ignatian Contemplation', *The Furrow*, 28 (1977), 72-78.

'The Spiritual Exercises and Decree 4', *The Way Supplement*, 29/30 (Spring 1977), 134-141.

'Ignatian Spirituality', *Religious Life Review*, 21 (1982), 181-182.

'The First Week: Practical Questions', *The Way Supplement*, 48 (Autumn 1983), 15-27.

'The Dynamic of the Spiritual Exercises', *The Way Supplement*, 52 (Spring 1985), 3-18.

'Ignatian Criteria for Choice of Ministries,' *The Way Supplement*, 55 (Spring 1986), 77-88.

'How the *Constitutions* Work', *The Way Supplement*, 61 (Spring 1988), 3-20.

'Ignatian Spirituality and Devotion to the Sacred Heart', *Milltown Studies*, 24 (Autumn 1989), 66-82.

'Dominant Orthodoxies', *Milltown Studies*, 30 (Autumn 1992), 43-65.

'The Unique Elements of Ignatian Spirituality', *Milltown Studies*, 30 (Autumn 1992), 97-101.

Review article on John W. O'Malley, *The First Jesuits* (London: Harvard UP, 1993), *Studies*, 82 (Winter 1993), 499-506.

'From Exercises to Constitutions: A Spirit in Search of a Body', in *Constitutions of the Society of Jesus: Incorporation of a Spirit* (Rome: Secretariat for Ignatian Spirituality, 1993), 3-24.

'Manifold Gifts', *The Way Supplement*, 82 (1995), 44-53.

'Saint Ignatius Speaks about "Ignatian Prayer"', *Studies in the Spirituality of Jesuits*, 28/2 (March 1996).

'Saint Ignatius Asks "Are You Sure You Know Who I Am?"', *Studies in the Spirituality of Jesuits*, 33/4 (September 2001).

'The Silence', *Interfuse* 111, (Easter 2002), 4-15, adapted in *The Way*, 42/4 (October 2003), 106-117.

'Meditating on Abuse—and Repenting', *Doctrine and Life*, 50 (2000), 296-303.

'Ignatian Spirituality', in *The Search for Spirituality: Seven Paths within the Catholic Tradition*, edited by Stephen J. Costello (Dublin: Liffey, 2002), 191-212.

*'Ignatian Prayer and Jesuit Spirituality', and 'The First Week: Practical Questions' have both been republished earlier in* The Way of Ignatius Loyola: Contemporary Approaches to the Spiritual Exercises, *edited by Philip Sheldrake (London: SPCK, 1991). The pieces in this volume entitled 'Renewing Jesuit Life in the Spirit' and 'The Spiritual Exercises in Ecumenical Context' are being published for the first time in this collection.*